ON THIS DAY SHE

ON THIS DAY SHE

PUTTING WOMEN BACK INTO HISTORY ONE DAY AT A TIME

ROWMAN & LITTLEFIELD
Lanham · Boulder · New York · London

JO BELL

TANIA HERSHMAN

AILSA HOLLAND

Published by Rowman & Littlefield
An imprint of The Rowman & Littlefield Publishing Group, Inc.
4501 Forbes Boulevard, Suite 200, Lanham, Maryland 20706
www.rowman.com

86-90 Paul Street, London EC2A 4NE, United Kingdom

British Library Cataloguing in Publication Information Available

Library of Congress Cataloging-in-Publication Data Available
ISBN 9781538164563 (cloth) | ISBN 9781538164570 (electronic)

*To all the women whose lives
are unrecorded in history*

How to leave women out of history

after Joanna Russ*

- She wasn't there
- She was there but she didn't do anything
- She was there and she did something, but she was only the wife/mistress/courtesan/girlfriend/muse so she doesn't count
- She was there, and did something, but it wasn't her idea, she was just his assistant, so he should get all the credit and win the prizes
- She was there and she did it and it was her idea and no one else helped, but it was at home so really it was a hobby/craft so it wasn't important
- She was there and she did it but only because she was very masculine – she insisted on wearing trousers for goodness' sake, so she was pretty much a man anyway
- She was there and she did it but we didn't write it down in the

important books these things must always be written in, so later we decided a man must have done it first

- She did it but she was hysterical so we thought it was best to put her away somewhere to calm her down and then we forgot about her and celebrated some man who did it after her
- She did it, but the business was in her husband's name so she had no idea how it all worked until the moment he died when she instantly knew how to run everything and did so efficiently and successfully for many years
- She did it but she only did it for people who looked like/came from the same background as her, unlike the important people in history who did things for themselves and for other important people they knew and are therefore more important
- She did it but she wasn't perfect/made some bad decisions/ murdered people and therefore we should forget her and remember instead the imperfect, evil and fascinating men who screwed up royally and murdered millions of people because that's frankly more impressive
- She did it but then became a mother so that was clearly her true calling all along, not being a painter/composer/teacher/ writer and so she can't be called those things because she can't be both and anyway, that's what she would want because don't all women want to put their children first, and if not what kind of a bitch was she?

*author of science fiction and the brilliant *How to Suppress Women's Writing* (1983)

She did it

This project began when Ailsa Holland was given an "On This Day" calendar of historical events – and became infuriated that women were barely mentioned. When she vented her rage to her friends Jo Bell and Tania Hershman, they shared her anger and decided something had to be done.

Twitter seemed a natural place to start, and so, in January 2018, we sent out our first @OnThisDayShe daily tweet, about a woman who did something and who needs to be remembered. More than three years later, we still tweet every day, featuring women from across the world, all time periods and all fields of endeavor. We try to find a day which was important to each woman rather than the day she was born or died: when she registered a patent, won an election, scooped a gold medal, was convicted of a heinous crime. "Why haven't I heard of her?!" is the response we receive on Twitter again and again. And again. And: "Someone needs to write a book/play/film about her!"

We have been overwhelmed by how many fascinating women we had never heard of; women who have done amazing things, overcoming obstacles of sexism, racism and poverty. Some women we had heard of but thought they were the exception, an anomaly (Marie Curie, Ada Lovelace). Or we had heard of them but weren't aware of the breadth of their achievements – that they had also done something not "typically feminine": Florence Nightingale was not only a nurse, the "Lady of the Lamp," but also a statistician; Nina Simone was a civil rights activist as well as a singer. Even when the achievement of a woman from history is "discovered" (usually by a female historian) it is promptly forgotten again, and so it has to be re-discovered, and re-re-discovered.

How and why are men's achievements remembered? First, we learn about them in school, and then awareness of these men is constantly enforced and reiterated – by statues in our streets, by the names of those streets, by the names of universities and institutes. We watch films about men; historical documentaries tell us about their accomplishments; our galleries are filled with paintings of women, but not by women.

This is not a women's history book. It is a history book. It was incredibly difficult for us to choose the 366 women or groups of women you will find in these pages. Another set of editors would have made entirely different choices. There are so many women who have made our world better – and, sometimes, worse – in so many ways. Here is our selection.

Ailsa Holland, Jo Bell and Tania Hershman

JANUARY

"Something impelled
this wanderlust. I would
not be detained."
– Aloha Wanderwell

The Language of History

Every history is a story of the past. Historians are products of their time, and each word is informed by the writer's own experience and background. In researching this book, we noticed how language used by historians sometimes excludes women entirely. When they *are* included, or even celebrated, the words often belittle them. The classic example is the use of "man" to describe all humans. Lazy writers say, "this is generic"; thoughtful writers acknowledge that this isn't good enough. Reading, "When early man came to the Peak District, he settled the valley areas," we simply don't see women. If you doubt this, try it the other way around: "When early woman came to the Peak District, she settled the valley areas."

Here's another example. Many articles tell us that Catherine of Aragon, Henry VIII's first wife, "failed to provide him with a male heir." A monarch in the 1530s would certainly want a son to secure the future of the dynasty. However, that sentence doesn't just state a fact, it embodies a point of view. The queen should have *provided* a son. In not doing so, she *failed*. These tiny accumulations build up in every history, like scale inside a kettle. The historians who wrote that phrase – and students who unquestioningly absorbed and repeated it, including myself – were using the language of their time. Let's rephrase it: "Catherine and Henry *had no surviving sons*." It's still accurate, but the balance is changed. Other areas of language need to evolve too. We are learning to write of "enslaved people" rather than "slaves," which forces us to confront enslavement as an action.

Language lets us down in other ways too. A woman is often "alleged" or "widely believed" to have done something, when a contemporary man (with no better evidence) simply "did" it. If she belongs to the classical period like Hypatia, the woman "may be mythical." A late classical writer like Egeria, or a medieval one like Margery Kempe, is "reputed" to be the author of her eponymous works. Where a woman is the relative of a well-known man, like composer Clara Schumann, her works are attributed to him. A signed self-portrait by Catharina van Hemessen was attributed to her father for many years. Socrates said that the unexamined life is not worth living; perhaps the unexamined sentence is not worth writing. What we try to do in this book is not correct an old prejudice by applying a new one, but to correct some of history's imbalances, writing a more equal history.

Enheduanna

(2285–2250 BCE)

The first named writer in world history was a woman.

Enheduanna lived and wrote around 2285–2250 BCE in one of the earliest cities – Ur, in present-day Iraq. Her name is actually her title – "High Priestess of Inanna." Inanna was a goddess who ruled over matters sexual and political.

Enheduanna's best-known poems are the forty-two Sumerian Temple Hymns, which were copied and used in worship for centuries after her death. But she was a political, as well as a spiritual, figurehead; her writings also tell of upheaval and exile. Her poem *The Exaltation of Inanna* tells how she was driven out of Ur and later reinstated. The poem is, as scholar Joseph Janes notes, "seven hundred years older than the Egyptian *Book of the Dead*, more than a thousand years older than the *I Ching* and 1,500 years older than the *Odyssey*, the *Iliad* and the Hebrew Bible." In the *Odyssey*, Penelope is told, "Go to your room; speech is the business of men." A millennium and a half before Homer created that line, Enheduanna had already demonstrated that a woman can speak for herself.

> "My king, something has been created that no one has created before."

Huda Sha'arawi

(1879–1947)

In January 1924, Huda Sha'arawi led an all-women picket at the opening of the Egyptian Parliament and submitted a list of nationalist and feminist demands. Called "Egypt's first feminist," Sha'arawi was a key figure in her nation's fight against British colonialism and a leader of the first women's street demonstration during the Egyptian Revolution of 1919.

Sha'arawi was educated first with her brothers and then in a female-only harem; at the age of thirteen, she was married to her cousin, forty years her senior. As an adult, she resolved to make things different for other girls. She successfully fought for the marriage age for girls to be raised to sixteen and, in 1910, opened a school which taught girls academic rather than domestic subjects. When she later organized lectures for women, it was the first time many had been in a public place.

In March 1923, returning from the International Woman Suffrage Alliance Conference in Rome, Sha'arawi performed the iconic act for which she is best remembered. At Cairo train station, she removed her face veil in public for the first time. Women who had come to meet her were shocked, then broke into applause; some were inspired to remove their veils in turn.

"I intend to vocalise my pain and start a revolution for the silent women who faced centuries of oppression."

3 JANUARY

Annie Royle Taylor

(1855–1922)

On this day in 1893, English missionary Annie Royle Taylor was arrested for entering Tibet – then closed to foreigners on pain of death – in the hope of converting its people to Christianity. No European woman had ever set foot in Tibet before.

Taylor's journey, starting from China, was tremendously difficult. Her small party had only a tent as shelter from sub-zero temperatures, and they sold even this for food. Altitude sickness killed one of her companions. They faced hostility in most areas – although in Golok territory, where bandits rode in armed groups several hundred strong, Taylor secured protection from a woman chieftain.

Like other women of her generation, Taylor found in Christian missionary work a vocation which allowed her to travel, organize and lead, to join international expeditions and experience new cultures, without causing a scandal at home. However, such adventures and achievements often came at the expense of indigenous cultures. The Tibetan authorities resented any foreign intervention, so Taylor was expelled from Tibet and returned to China.

In 1895, Taylor was finally allowed to set up a shop and mission in the Tibetan border town of Yatung. Her mental health seems to have suffered; in 1907 her sister fetched her back to England. Taylor is believed to have ended her life in an institution.

Agnès Varda
(1928–2019)

On this day in 1956, Belgian-born director Agnès Varda's first film, *La Pointe Courte*, was released. The first film of the French New Wave, this was the beginning of a sixty-year career, during which Varda moved between documentary, short and feature-length films, taking inspiration from art, music, literature – and real life. "People were inventing a new way of writing – James Joyce, Hemingway, Faulkner. And I thought we had to find a structure for cinema. I fought for a radical cinema, and I continued all my life."

After studying literature, psychology, art history and photography in Paris, Varda first made strange short films for the French tourist board. *La Pointe Courte*, inspired by a visit to a fishing village, mixed realism and fantasy. The citation for her honorary Oscar in 2017 said that her "compassion and curiosity inform a uniquely personal cinema." Two of her best-known works are *Cleo from 5 to 7* (1962), a film about a woman waiting to hear her cancer diagnosis, and the 2001 documentary *The Gleaners and I*, in which Varda talks to people who "glean," or pick things up from the ground. "I would like to be remembered as a film-maker who enjoyed life, including pain . . . What happens in my days – working, meeting people, listening – convinces me that it's worth being alive."

5 JANUARY

Laura Knight

(1877–1970)

British artist Laura Knight grew up in poverty and was determined to earn well from her art. But it was never just about money: "An ebullient vitality made me want to paint the whole world." This *joie de vivre* bursts out of her vibrant paintings, of theatre folk and of young women on Cornish cliffs, on the border between land and sea. During the Second World War, Knight's subjects were very different: commissions for the War Artists' Advisory Committee. These paintings, which include *Corp Elspeth Henderson and Sgt. Helen Turner 1941* and *Ruby Loftus Screwing a Breech-ring* are exquisite, vital documents of women's war work.

After the war, Knight actively sought another commission: to record the Nuremberg Trials, the military tribunals set up by the Allies to try Nazi leaders for war crimes. On this day in 1946, she flew to Germany; for four months she sat in the courtroom at Nuremberg, making sketches. She also saw first-hand how the city had been destroyed by the war. Knight's artistic response was to create her only surrealist work: *The Dock, Nuremberg* (1946). Most of the painting is realistic: Göring, Hess and Ribbentrop sit in the dock surrounded by translators, military police and prosecutors. But at the top of the canvas the scene flows into an image of urban devastation. On the horizon the ruins are still burning.

6 JANUARY

Maria Montessori

(1870–1952)

On this day in 1907, Italian doctor Maria Montessori opened her first school, the first in what is now a worldwide chain of 20,000 schools bearing her name. Montessori had already overcome institutional prejudice to become Italy's first female doctor. Her theory of education, based on discovery and play, was to spread worldwide.

As a girl, Montessori had hoped to be an engineer and studied at a boys' technical school. Later pursuing medicine, she was denied entry to the University of Rome. She appealed to Pope Leo XIII, who intervened on her behalf, but even when admitted, she met with further discrimination. She was not allowed to dissect a naked human body alongside male students so, undaunted, did it alone after class.

In 1896, she qualified as a doctor. Since a married woman would have been unable to practice medicine, she remain unmarried and had a son out of wedlock.

Montessori developed her teaching methods for autistic or disabled children, then for all children – the children learn at different speeds, working independently or helping each other. Montessori believed that education could help establish a peaceful world. As determined a pacifist as an educator, she was nominated six times for the Nobel Peace Prize.

Aisha bint Abu Bakr

(c.613/614–678 CE)

Today we remember Aisha bint Abu Bakr, known to Sunni Muslims as "Mother of the Believers." The third and youngest wife of the Prophet Muhammad – some say his favorite – she was one of the first scholars of Islam, who spread the message in thousands of "hadiths" – the collected sayings and traditions of the Prophet. These form a major part of Islamic law and moral guidance but were not written down until centuries later.

Learned and knowledgeable, bint Abu Bakr was a popular speaker and teacher on subjects from poetry to medicine. Her hadiths concern Muhammad's life and other topics including inheritance, pilgrimage and issues relating to women.

After a young girl complained that her father was forcing her into an arranged marriage, bint Abu Bakr went to the Prophet, who decreed for the first time that marriage was a woman's choice.

However, there is controversy over bint Abu Bakr's own marriage: she may have been as young as nine when she married Muhammad.

She was also active in politics and military campaigns. After losing in the Battle of the Camel, bint Abu Bakr was captured and sent back to Medina, where she worked for the Muslim community until her death.

Learned and knowledgeable, bint Abu Bakr was a popular speaker and teacher on subjects from poetry to medicine.

Elisabetta Sirani

(1638–1665)

Elisabetta Sirani, Italian Baroque painter and printmaker and the most famous female artist in Bologna, was born on this day in 1638. When gout disabled her artist father, seventeen-year-old Elisabetta took over his studio, supporting her family by selling her paintings.

Sirani often focused on strong female subjects, with works depicting the rape of Europa, and Judith beheading Holofernes. She was known for painting very quickly; when locals assumed someone must be helping her, she arranged an exhibition, inviting European artists and the public to watch her work. Also an enormously popular teacher, Sirani taught her sisters and a dozen other women who became professional painters.

After sudden stomach pains and weight loss, Sirani died at the age of twenty-seven. Her father suspected foul play. When the family physician declared she had been poisoned, Sirani's maid was put on trial, but the charges were later dropped. It seems likely Sirani actually died from a perforated ulcer. She had made over 200 oil paintings and etchings, and was such a beloved figure in Bologna that she was given a lavish public funeral.

9 JANUARY

Septimia Zenobia
(c.240–c.274)

In 267, Septimia Zenobia became Regent of Palmyra (in modern Syria) after her husband, King Odaenathus, was murdered. Palmyra was famous for its architecture and culture – "the pearl of the desert" – but as a client state of the Roman Empire, it had limited power and independence. Zenobia wanted to change that. She had her husband's murderers executed and began to annex huge new territories.

In 269, Zenobia's forces seized Alexandria; by 270 she had control of the whole of Egypt. Her empire was now not only independent from Rome, but a challenge to it. Emperor Lucius Domitius Aurelianus decided that Zenobia had ruled "longer than could be endured from one of the female sex." His troops gradually took back territories, and in 272 they laid siege to Palmyra. Zenobia was not cowed. "You demand my surrender as though you were not aware that Cleopatra preferred to die a queen rather than remain alive."

Palmyra eventually fell to Roman forces. Zenobia's subsequent fate is unclear. Did she commit suicide or was she captured and paraded through Rome in chains? Whatever the truth, she is a Syrian national hero and has been an inspiration for visual artists as well as for writers of opera, novels and poetry from all around the world.

Chien-Shiung Wu

(1912–1997)

In January 1975, Chinese-American physicist Chien-Shiung Wu became the first female president of the American Physical Society. Although she solved "the number-one riddle of atomic and nuclear physics" when she disproved the Parity Law, a theory of symmetry in nature, the 1957 Nobel Prize went to her male colleagues. This is an example of the so-called "Matilda Effect," where a female scientist's contribution is not recognized, or credited to her male colleagues.

Wu's family were unusual in early twentieth-century China in believing in education for girls; they even set up a girls' school. At twenty-four, Wu sailed to the US, where, after receiving her PhD, she became Princeton physics department's first female instructor. During the Second World War, she was recruited to work on enriching uranium as part of the Manhattan Project, which developed the first atomic bomb.

Nicknamed the "First Lady of Physics," Wu was the first Chinese-American elected to the US National Academy of Sciences, the first recipient of the Wolf Prize in Physics and the first living scientist to have an asteroid named after her. She was also an advocate for women in science: "There is only one thing worse than coming home from the lab to a sink full of dirty dishes," she said, "and that is not going to the lab at all!"

Beatrice "Tilly" Shilling

(1909–1990)

Early in 1940, fighter pilots waging the Battle of Britain reported that their planes were stalling when they dived during a dogfight. Sometimes this caused the loss of both plane and crew. Beatrice "Tilly" Shilling was the British engineer who solved this problem. She was also a record-breaking motorcyclist.

Shilling's hobby and her career went hand in hand. As a keen teenage biker, she raced her machines and rebuilt them to improve performance. In the early 1930s, she was one of a very few women to graduate as an electrical and mechanical engineer. In 1934, Shilling won a coveted Gold Star for lapping the Brooklands race circuit at over 100 mph. When she married George Naylor, a fellow engineer, it was on condition that he clocked a 100-mph lap himself.

At the beginning of the Second World War, Shilling was recruited to the Royal Aircraft Establishment, a research center supporting the Air Force. Her solution for the Spitfire engine problems was a simple brass disc or thimble with a small hole in it, restricting fuel supply – air crews soon dubbed it "Miss Shilling's Orifice." It was a small but important contribution to the Allied air victory. Shilling later worked on projects including the Blue Streak missile and was awarded an Order of the British Empire.

When she married George Naylor, a fellow engineer, it was on condition that he clocked a 100-mph lap himself.

12 JANUARY

Wang Zhenyi

(1768–1797)

Wang Zhenyi was an eighteenth-century Chinese astronomer, mathematician and poet. Living in a feudal society of traditions and mysticism, she used practical reasoning and questioned accepted wisdom. Educated at first by her family, she used her grandfather's library to teach herself further, also learning from other female scholars.

Her published works on astronomy were revolutionary, including the results of original research on lunar eclipses and celestial movement, explained in uncomplicated language. Devoted to making learning accessible, at the age of twenty-four she wrote *The Simple Principles of Calculation*, a method for teaching maths more easily. Wang Zhenyi favored the Western calendar because it was based on the sun, not the moon, and therefore more precise: "The only important aspect of a calendar is its usefulness. It doesn't matter whether it's Chinese or not!"

Wang Zhenyi also wrote poems. Some were traditional, describing the landscapes of China she saw when traveling with her father, but she also commented on inequality and injustice, showing compassion for poor women in "Woman Silkworm Breeder" and "Clothes Washing." Some poems were radically critical of sexual inequality: "[People say that] women should only do cooking and sewing, and they should not be bothered writing articles for publication, studying history, composing poetry or doing calligraphy . . . [Men and women] are all people, who have the same reason for studying."

"[Men and women] are all people, who have the same reason for studying."

Marguerite Yourcenar
(1903–1987)

In January 1921, Belgian-French writer Marguerite Yourcenar published her first book, *Le Jardin des Chimères* (The Garden of Illusions). She went on to publish around fifty works, from essays to short stories and novels, including her masterpiece, *Memoirs of Hadrian*, a novel about the Roman Emperor. At the outbreak of the Second World War, Yourcenar moved to the US, where she lived with her life partner, literary scholar Grace Frick.

Yourcenar won many prizes, including the 1977 Grand Prix de l'Académie Française. Established in 1635, the Académie only ever has forty members, known as The Immortals; in 1980, Yourcenar became the first female member. (Out of the 732 Immortals to date, only nine have been women.) In her induction speech, Yourcenar expressed respect for tradition and understanding of the "anxiety caused by changing only one stone of a beautiful building that has been standing for a few centuries." Not only the metaphorical building had to be changed: it's said that the toilet signs were altered to read "Messieurs" and "Marguerite Yourcenar." However, there was one tradition she would not adopt. The livery for Immortals, designed in the eighteenth century, includes a jacket with tails and a sword. Marguerite Yourcenar refused to wear it.

14 JANUARY

Eliza Acton

(1799–1859)

In January 1845, Longmans published Eliza Acton's *Modern Cookery, In All Its Branches* (later *Modern Cookery for Private Families*). It was groundbreaking, establishing the now-familiar recipe format, with ingredients, quantities and cooking times for each dish clearly laid out.

Cookery, the ultimate domestic act, was one of the rare spheres in which women were always acknowledged experts. Acton's book swiftly became a bestseller and was constantly in print until the end of the century. It was a huge influence on domestic cookery in Britain and on food writing across the world. Amongst dishes like Brain Cakes and Super-Excellent Bacon, Acton included many references to the science of nutrition, and a few flashes of wit. Her Publisher's Pudding "can scarcely be made too rich," while the Poor Author's Pudding is altogether humbler.

Some of Acton's recipes were used without credit by Isabella Beeton in her famous cookbook, but cookery writing has a long tradition of more courteous sharing and adaptation. Acton herself followed in the footsteps of Hannah Glasse's *The Art of Cookery Made Plain and Easy* (1747). Later writers who acknowledge Acton's influence, and who themselves inspired a generation of home cooks, include Elizabeth David, Jane Grigson and Delia Smith. David called *Modern Cookery* "the greatest British cookbook of all time."

> It was groundbreaking, establishing the now-familiar recipe format, with ingredients, quantities and cooking times...

15 JANUARY

Rosa Luxemburg

(1871–1919)

On this day in 1919, Rosa Luxemburg was murdered by paramilitaries acting for the German government.

Born in Poland, Luxemburg embraced revolutionary Marxism, organizing a general strike while still in her teens. She moved to Switzerland to gain a doctorate in law, then to Germany, where she wrote polemical texts like *Reform or Revolution*. Luxemburg argued that capitalism would always lead to inequality and empire-building. Women, she said, were not a monolithic group but divided from each other by class: "The dancer in a café, who makes a profit for her employer with her legs, is a productive working woman, while all the toil of proletarian women and mothers within the four walls of the home is considered unproductive work."

Luxemburg co-founded the far-left Spartacus League, which opposed German involvement in the First World War. In January 1919, they and others held street protests to overthrow the government. The demonstrations were crushed; Luxemburg and her fellow agitator Karl Liebknecht were abducted, tortured and shot. During the 1950s and 60s, Luxemburg became a key part of East Germany's founding mythology. Although she had opposed totalitarianism, she was held up as a martyred figurehead of the totalitarian East German state.

Mary "May" Morris

(1862–1938)

As the daughter of designer William and artist Jane Morris, English craft designer Mary "May" Morris was at the heart of the Arts and Crafts movement, which influenced décor in every British home.

In a time of mass production, the Arts and Crafts school looked back to the handmade furnishings of the Middle Ages. May began her career as an embroiderer, and by the age of twenty-three was director of embroidery at her father's company, Morris & Co; her flowing, natural motifs were used in wallpaper, tiles and printed textiles. She also designed jewelry, using simple shapes and semi-precious stones, often in the colors of the suffragette movement.

As a woman, however, May could not enter the Art Workers' Guild – which excluded women until the 1960s. Wanting a forum to network and share expertise, in January 1907, May established the Women's Guild of Arts with Mary Elizabeth Turner.

The guild campaigned to raise the profile and status of members, and attracted some of the best applied artists: painter Evelyn De Morgan, jeweler Georgie Gaskin, bookbinder Katherine Adams and sculptor Mabel White. In 1936, May wrote to the playwright George Bernard Shaw: "I'm a remarkable woman," she said, "always was, though none of you seemed to think so."

17 JANUARY

Lucy Parsons

(c.1851 –1942)

On this day in 1915, Lucy Parsons led 10,000 unemployed and hungry people in the Chicago Hunger March. Over the course of sixty years of militant dissent, Parsons, an African-American anarchist and social reformer, wrote, spoke and campaigned for the disenfranchised and dispossessed. This march was only one of many she helped to organize.

In her twenties, her inter-racial marriage to white anarchist Albert Parsons caused outrage in their home state of Texas. They relocated to Chicago, where she wrote for his paper, *The Alarm*, amongst others, and organized workers' protests. In 1887, Albert was executed for his alleged part in an attack on police.

Lucy continued as a journalist, orator and a leading member of international labor organisations. She agitated on behalf of political prisoners, the unemployed, persecuted African-Americans (like the Scottsboro Boys, framed for rape) and homeless people, as well as women. Her campaigns took her throughout the US and to Europe.

Parsons met with racism even inside the radical movement, and clashed with some early feminists, including Emma Goldman.

For Parsons, the global fight for women's rights was only part of a larger campaign for the working classes. After her death in a house fire, the authorities confiscated over 1,500 radical books: the library of a woman once described by the Chicago police as "more dangerous than a thousand rioters."

For Parsons, the global fight for women's rights was only part of a larger campaign for the working classes.

18 JANUARY

Ida Lupino

(1918–1995)

On this day in 1955, Ida Lupino directed her first TV show, an episode of *Screen Director's Playhouse*, which she had also written. Lupino was a prominent female director and film-maker in an overwhelmingly male industry. The first woman to direct a film noir (*The Hitch-Hiker*, 1953), she also directed TV westerns, sitcoms and gangster stories, and was the only woman to direct an episode of *The Twilight Zone*.

London-born Lupino had been a successful actress but, after being often suspended for turning down roles or suggesting script edits, she became interested in working behind the camera. In the late 1940s, Lupino set up a production company with her husband, Collier Young, and writer Malvin Wald. Their films covered controversial issues: unmarried motherhood, disability, bigamy and sexual assault. *Gunsmoke* producer Norman MacDonnell said, "You used Ida when you had a story about a woman with some dimension, and you wanted it really hard-hitting."

But even whilst blazing a trail for women film-makers, Lupino operated within a stereotype of womanhood. "Keeping a feminine approach is vital; men hate bossy females," she said. "You do not tell a man; you suggest to him. 'Darlings, Mother has a problem. I'd love to do this. Can you do it?' . . . And they do it."

19 JANUARY

Joan Jett

(1958–)

On this day in 1982, Joan Jett and the Blackhearts released rock anthem *I Love Rock 'n Roll*. It spent seven weeks at number one in the US. Rock guitarist Jett is part of a generation of pioneer frontwomen, including Siouxsie Sioux, Debbie Harry, Poly Styrene, Patti Smith and Chrissie Hynde. All of them wrote and performed loud, guitar-heavy songs in which women voiced sexual appetite, rebellion and anger: familiar subjects for male rock 'n' roll artists.

As a performer, entrepreneur and producer, Jett is one of the most influential women in American rock. In 1980, she set up Blackheart Records, the first independent record company owned and controlled by a woman. In a 2018 *New York Times* interview she said, "Get more women in decision-making positions, where the money is. If you're not going to give a woman that kind of power, then what kind of power does she have, really?" Jett was a producer for later bands like Bikini Kill and L7 and a role model for the Riot Grrrl punk feminist movement. She scorns those who frown on her choice of dress, expect her to speak out about her sexuality or require anything else of her, feeling that this is a different kind of pressure to conform:

> "If Mick Jagger can go out there and ride a big penis on stage, and that's fine, how come girls can't – girls want to have sex, girls are sexual. Why can't girls own sex the way boys do? It's not fair."

Wangari Maathai

(1940–2011)

In January 2003, Wangari Maathai, the first woman in eastern Africa with a PhD, became Kenya's Deputy Minister of Environment, Natural Resources and Wildlife. In 1976, Maathai had founded the Green Belt Movement. She had met with women from the countryside and seen the impact of "deforestation, loss of the soil that was gradually destroying that environment and impoverishing them." Ten years later, she founded the Pan African Green Belt Network; since then, over 40 million trees have been planted by women on farms and around schools and churches.

A pro-democracy activist, Maathai angered dictatorial Kenyan president Daniel arap Moi with her campaigns to stop seizure of public land and to release political prisoners. In 1992, she discovered that her name was on a government hit list. She barricaded herself in her home for three days but was arrested. Released two days later, she headed back to a demonstration, where she was knocked unconscious by police.

In December 2002, the Rainbow Coalition defeated the ruling party and Maathai was appointed Deputy Minister. The following year, she founded the Mazingira Green Party; in 2004, she was the first African woman to win the Nobel Peace Prize, "for her contribution to sustainable development, democracy and peace."

21 JANUARY

Seweryna Szmaglewska
(1916–1992)

After her homeland, Poland, was invaded by the German army in 1939, teacher Seweryna Szmaglewska worked as a volunteer nurse before joining a resistance organization. Arrested by the Gestapo for running an underground library of Polish literature, she arrived in Auschwitz-Birkenau concentration camp in October 1942.

Two years later, as the Soviet army approached to liberate the camps, the guards began to evacuate their prisoners, forcing them to march west. Around a quarter of those on these winter "death marches" died en route, but in January 1945, Szmaglewska was able to escape. She immediately began to write about her experience.

Her book, *Smoke Over Birkenau*, was published at the end of 1945, one of the first memoirs of life in Auschwitz. It is a distressing read, detailing Szmaglewska's life in a barracks with other women from the Polish intelligentsia, and the humiliation, torture and brutality they faced every day. She also describes seeing people on their way to the gas chambers.

In 1946, the International Tribunal in Nuremberg included *Smoke Over Birkenau* in the material supporting the charges against the Nazi perpetrators. Szmaglewska was called upon to give testimony, one of the few Poles to do so. *Smoke over Birkenau* has been reprinted frequently and widely translated. It is compulsory reading in Polish schools.

Smoke Over Birkenau was published at the end of 1945, one of the first memoirs of life in Auschwitz.

22 JANUARY

Annie Russell Maunder

(1868–1947)

In 1891, mathematician Annie Russell was appointed as a "lady computer" at the Royal Observatory in Greenwich, England. Her duties included using the Dallmeyer photoheliograph to record and locate sunspots; in her first year, the number of observations in her department was over seven times the average. Her supervisor, Walter Maunder, nominated her for fellowship of the Royal Astronomical Society, but the society did not admit women. Instead, Annie joined the British Astronomical Association, co-founded by Maunder.

Annie and Walter married in 1895. Civil service rules specified that women could not work after marriage, but Annie continued at the observatory as a volunteer. She became an expert in sunspots and went on expeditions to observe them. On this day in 1898, in India, she captured the first photo of a coronal streamer – a huge ray-like structure bursting from the sun – with a camera she had adapted to take photographs during a solar eclipse. The wife-and-husband team worked to popularize astronomy, writing books and newspaper articles. In 1916, Annie finally became a Fellow of the Royal Astronomical Society, after their ban on women was lifted.

In 2018, the Annie Maunder Astrographic Telescope (Amat) was installed at the Royal Observatory, the first new telescope in over sixty years. Designed especially for use with digital cameras, its images and readings will be shared with schools and the public. Annie Russell Maunder would surely have approved.

23 JANUARY

Alice Stoll

(1917–2014)

Alice Stoll's research required her to burn the forearms of sailors, but for a good cause: the development of fire-resistant fibers and fabrics.

With masters degrees in biophysics and physiology, Stoll led the heat laboratory at the US Naval Air Development Center from 1960 to 1964, measuring how humans respond to pain at different temperatures. It was Stoll who categorized a burn that blisters after twenty-four hours as "second-degree." The index named after her, the Stoll Curve, shows the reaction of human tissue to different amounts of heat over time, and is used to figure out how clothing or equipment can prevent pain and burns. Her work led to the development of Nomex, a synthetic polymer used in firefighters' uniforms.

Stoll – who was in the Naval Reserves and worked as a consultant for laboratories including Alaska's Arctic Aerospace Medicine Lab –

also researched the effects of cold at high altitudes and g-force in flight, which can result in blackouts and confusion. Alice Stoll received the Society of Women Engineers' Achievement Award in 1969.

Alice Stoll's research required her to burn the forearms of sailors, but for a good cause: the development of fire-resistant fibers and fabrics.

Dorothy Porter

(1905–1995)

In 1930, Dorothy Porter was appointed Librarian at Howard University in Washington DC. Over the next forty-three years she built up a leading repository for black history and culture: "I appealed to publishers, 'We have no money, but will you give us this book?'" The library grew from 3,000 to 180,000 items.

Observing that students at the historically black university were more concerned with "being like the white person," Porter was instrumental in bringing African scholars to encourage students to take an interest in their African heritage. Porter also built on work begun by four other Howard librarians – Lula Allen, Edith Brown, Lula Conner and Rosa Hershaw – to decolonize the classification system. Under the Dewey Decimal System, as used in "white libraries," every book by a black author had been filed under either 326 for "Slavery" or 325 for "Colonisation." Instead, Porter categorized works by genre, to demonstrate the influence of black authors in all subject areas.

Porter published several books herself, including *North American Negro Poets* (1945), *Negro Protest Pamphlets* (1969), and *Early Negro Writings 1760–1837* (1971). "The only rewarding thing for me is to bring to light information that no one knows. What's the point of rehashing the same old thing?"

25 JANUARY

Aloha Wanderwell

(1906–1996)

Aloha Wanderwell was born Idris Welsh in 1906 in Winnipeg, Canada. She spent her youth in boarding schools in France and Belgium and resisted attempts to make her – a tall, self-described "tomboy" – into a "proper young lady."

In 1922, aged sixteen, Welsh replied to an advertisement in the *Paris Herald*: "Brains, Beauty & Breeches – World Tour Offer For Lucky Young Woman . . . Wanted to join an expedition . . . Asia, Africa . . ." She took the job and became driver, translator and film-maker for an expedition launched by "Captain" Walter Wanderwell (real name Valerian Johannes Pieczynski). It was he who renamed her Aloha Wanderwell. She became the expedition's star – newspapers called her "the Amelia Earhart of the open road." On this day in 1927, after five years, Aloha arrived back in Nice, France, becoming the first woman to drive around the world.

She had traveled 380,000 miles over six continents, making films and giving lectures on the way.

The round-the-world trip was followed by a flight to the Mato Grosso region of the Amazon basin – piloted by Aloha in a German seaplane. Here she made a film, *Flight to the Stone-Age Bororos*, the earliest filmed record of the Bororo tribe, which is now housed in the Smithsonian Institute's Human Studies Archive.

26 JANUARY

Joanna Wilson (unknown);
Lotta Kronlid (unknown);
Andrea Needham (unknown);
Angie Zelter (1951–)

In January 1996, Joanna Wilson, Lotta Kronlid and Andrea Needham, British members of the global Plowshares activist movement, were arrested for causing £1.5m of damage to an RAF Hawk jet aircraft. A fourth woman, Angie Zelter, was charged with conspiracy. In an action called "Seeds of Hope," the four had broken into a hangar at the British Aerospace plant in Lancashire with six other women. They had then used hammers to smash the controls of a plane which was about to be delivered to the Indonesian government for use against civilians in illegally occupied East Timor.

After campaigning unsuccessfully for several years to prevent the sale of the aircraft to Indonesia, the women felt they had no other choice. "The only thing left to do was to disarm [the planes] ourselves." They left a fifteen-minute video in the cockpit to explain what they had done.

During their trial, the women argued that by their actions they were preventing a greater crime, the crime of genocide in East Timor. The jury agreed, and all four were acquitted. This was a landmark moment: of the fifty-six actions by the Plowshares group worldwide, this was the first time activists had been found not guilty.

"The only thing left to do was to disarm [the planes] ourselves."

Leontyne Price
(1927–)

Leontyne Price grew up in a small town in the segregated south of the US. When she was nine, her mother – known for her singing in church – took her on a 100-mile bus journey to hear African-American contralto Marian Anderson. "She came out in a white satin gown, so majestic, and opened her mouth, and I thought, This is it, mama. This is what I'm going to be."

In 1948, Price won a sponsorship to study at New York's Juilliard School. Seven years later, she was the first African-American singer to appear in an opera on television, in the title role of Puccini's *Tosca*. On this day in 1961, Price became the first African-American woman to open a season at the Metropolitan Opera House in New York. Her performance as Leonora in *Il Trovatore* was given a thirty-five-minute ovation, one of the longest in the Met's history.

Price went on to build an international career. On 16 September 1966, she sang Cleopatra in *Antony and Cleopatra*, commissioned for the opening of the new Metropolitan Opera House and written especially for her. Price became an iconic figure in the US and sang at many state occasions; on 30 September 2001 she came out of retirement to perform in a memorial concert at Carnegie Hall for the victims of the 9/11 attacks.

Flora Tristan

(1803–1844)

Flora Tristan moved with her children from Peru to France to escape an abusive marriage. In 1835, she began to campaign for women's rights, seeing herself as "the woman messiah." Petitioning for the legalisation of divorce, she was finally legally separated from her own husband only when he was imprisoned for shooting her. (The bullet was never removed from her body.)

In the 1840s, Tristan's political interest expanded from women's rights to the situation of the working class as a whole. In 1843, she published her pioneering analysis of socialism, *The Workers' Union*, five years before the publication of *The Communist Manifesto* by Marx and Engels.

Tristan's book proposed practical solutions to problems faced by the working class: her "Workers' Union" would collect dues to pay for "workers' palaces," where children could be educated and the old and injured cared for. Tristan was also ahead of Engels in seeing the parallels between class inequality and the inequality of the sexes. Forty years before Engels stated in *The Origin of the Family* (1884) that, "In the family the man is the bourgeois, the woman represents the proletarian," she wrote, "The woman is the proletarian of the proletariat."

Frieda Dalen

(1895–1995)

Norwegian teacher Frieda Dalen was the first woman to address the United Nations at its inaugural General Assembly, held in London on this day in 1946. "When the nation was in danger the women were called upon and they came, did their jobs, sacrificed and suffered." Dalen was not speaking in general terms: when Norway was invaded by Germany in 1940, she herself took on a leading role in civil resistance, not only spearheading a clandestine movement of teachers but also representing them on the Coordination Committee of the Norwegian resistance movement.

A champion of women's rights and an inspirational speaker, her activism continued after the war.

"Now, when the war is over and the United Nations are trying to build a new world, trying to lay the foundations of peace and freedom for humanity," she said to the UN, "the world cannot afford to do so without the rich resources that women's experience and capacity for work, women's insight and equipment mean for the various nations of the world." Dalen was awarded Norway's King's Merit Gold Medal in 1965.

> "When the nation was in danger the women were called upon and they came, did their jobs, sacrificed and suffered."

30 JANUARY

Amrita Sher-Gil

(1913–1941)

Born on this day in 1913, Amrita Sher-Gil was only nineteen when her oil painting, *Young Girls* won a gold medal at the 1933 Paris Salon. Her work merged influences from East and West, perhaps unsurprising for the daughter of a Hungarian-Jewish opera singer and a Sikh aristocrat. Sher-Gil had learned to paint aged eight when the family moved from Hungary to India. At sixteen, she moved to Paris to study art and began experimenting with her cultural identity, sometimes wearing a sari, sometimes Western clothing.

Despite her gold medal, and her election as the youngest Associate of Paris's Grand Salon, Sher-Gil left France: "Europe belongs to Picasso, Matisse and Braque and many others. India belongs only to me."

It was in 1937, on a three-month trip around India's rural south, that she found her subject and style, creating work inspired by European modernists, traditional Indian schools of painting and the Ajanta cave art of the people she met. Despite her early death at twenty-eight, her art – especially depictions of Indian women – became crucial to India's identity after independence, influencing generations of artists. When her art is sold in India, the government insists the paintings stay in the country. UNESCO declared 2013 the International Year of Amrita Sher-Gil.

31 JANUARY

Jeanne Villepreux-Power

(1794–1871)

When Jeanne Villepreux was eighteen, she walked 250 miles from her home town of Juillac to Paris to become a dressmaker, but we remember her now not as a seamstress but as a scientist.

After a commission to design a royal wedding gown brought her wealthy connections, in 1818 Villepreux married James Power, a merchant. The couple moved to Sicily; Villepreux-Power spent her new-found "leisure time" teaching herself about natural history. She traveled around the island, recording its flora and fauna, also studying fish and cephalopods.

In 1832, in order to observe and experiment with these aquatic organisms, Villepreux-Power invented the aquarium. The British biologist Richard Owen described her as the "Mother of Aquariophily." Her first ground-breaking work, *Physical Observations and Experiments on Several Marine and Terrestrial Animals* (1839), recorded her work with *Argonauta argo*, the common paper nautilus.

In 1843, most of Villepreux-Power's marine collections, written records and scientific materials were lost in a shipwreck. She stopped doing research but continued to write and give lectures. In 1835, she became the first female member of the Accademia Gioenia di Catania (Academy of Natural Sciences).

FEBRUARY

"I've always been concerned but I've never had the guts to do owt about it, but now it's time somebody did and I've made a start. It's up to other people to follow me."
– Lillian Bilocca

Bodies of evidence: archaeology and the default male

Spare a thought for the nineteenth-century Egyptologist, Jean-François Champollion. Working in the tomb of the pharaoh <u>Hatshepsut</u> in 1829, he was confused by hieroglyphics in which the symbol for "pharaoh" was repeatedly followed by a suffix meaning "female." Eventually, Champollion worked it out; Hatshepsut was a pharaoh *and* a woman.

Let's not be too hard on Champollion. Hatshepsut was, after all, shown in many images wearing not only clothing of a male ruler, but a ceremonial beard. A similar assumption was made in 1878, during an excavation of the grave of a <u>Viking Warrior</u>

at Birka, Norway. The grave goods, typically those buried with fighting men, showed that this person was beyond all doubt a warrior. Not unnaturally, it was assumed the body was a man.

In 2017, DNA tests showed that the Birka warrior was female. Suddenly, after 140 years of certainty, her occupation was *not* beyond doubt. Reactions of scholars and the press were exactly like those we mock in our foreword: "The body couldn't have been a warrior, because it was a woman. It couldn't have been a woman, because it was a warrior. If it was a woman, the grave goods must be symbolic, or perhaps they show her relationship to a great male figure. Feminist historians are rewriting history."

Not only was this warrior a woman, the chances of her being the *only* female warrior in Viking history are vanishingly small. She casts new light on the legendary "shield maidens" – female warriors – of Norse myth, reminding us that non-literate societies often keep their histories in a framework of myth and legend. Others in this book, like planter Whakaotirangi and soldier Seh-Dong-Hong-Beh, were likewise remembered in an oral tradition for many years. It is a mantra of modern archaeology that "absence of evidence does not mean evidence of absence": we cannot say that there were no women warriors, or silversmiths, or legislators, at any given time or place, simply because we don't yet have evidence. We can't assume that a person found with cooking equipment is a woman, or that the person found with swords is a man.

We are not saying that there were many women like the Birka warrior. They were always outliers, but they existed in number enough to make a default assumption of maleness unreliable. This Viking woman was honored with a remarkable monument in her own time. In our time, we need to honor her again, and remain open to all possibilities when we look at the past.

1 FEBRUARY

Jóhanna Sigurðardóttir

(1942–)

On this day in 2009, Jóhanna Sigurðardóttir was elected as the first female prime minister of Iceland. She was also the first openly gay head of government in the world; she married her partner in 2010, on the day Iceland legalized same-sex marriage.

"The experience of being a woman in politics was not always easy, especially in the early years," said Sigurðardóttir, who was for a long time the only woman in Iceland's government. Her political life had begun as a union activist while working as a stewardess for Loftleiðir Icelandic airlines. She was elected to the Althing, Iceland's parliament, in 1978, and nine years later became Minister for Social Affairs. Forming a party called National Awakening, Sigurðardóttir later headed a caretaker minority government after Iceland's financial collapse in 2008. Under Sigurðardóttir's leadership, Iceland's cabinet had equal numbers of men and women for the first time.

"Gender equality did not fall into our laps without a struggle, and Iceland did not reach this stage overnight," she said. For Sigurðardóttir, a turning point was the Women's Strike on 24 October 1975, which brought Iceland to a standstill. Sigurðardóttir retired from politics in 2013 as Iceland's longest-serving MP.

Florence Nightingale

(1820–1910)

In February 1858, Florence Nightingale was admitted to the Royal Statistical Society in recognition of her vital work in data analysis. Her contemporaries celebrated her as a pioneering nurse, caring for soldiers in the Crimean War; most later historians have done likewise. However, although this was certainly a part of Nightingale's story, her later campaigning had a much wider impact on healthcare.

Nightingale worked in Crimean field hospitals for only two years but helped to implement a program of hygiene and ventilation, which massively reduced the death rate. One source estimated that deaths in these hospitals fell from 42 percent to 2 percent. On her return to England, Nightingale devoted the rest of her ninety-year life to social and public health reform. In her push for better sanitation and drainage, she became an expert statistician, collecting and presenting data to the highest politicians, developing visual tools including the polar area diagram or "coxcomb."

Nightingale also worked to professionalize nursing, founded a training school in London, and put nurses into the workhouses of Victorian Britain. She was a well-connected and ceaseless lobbyist, using her celebrity to lever funds and legislation from Parliament.

3 FEBRUARY

Eileen Collins

(1956–)

On this day in 1995, American astronaut Eileen Collins became the first woman to pilot a Space Shuttle. Four years later, she was the first to command a shuttle, on the mission which launched Chandra, the world's most powerful X-ray telescope, into space.

Collins decided as a child that she wanted to be an astronaut but kept it to herself – so no one could tell her this wasn't something girls could do. She became one of four women in the first military pilot training class to admit them, and the second, after Sally Ride in 1983, selected as a NASA astronaut. But Collins's path was not a smooth one. As commander of the first mission after the Columbia Space Shuttle disaster in February 2003 – in which seven astronauts died – she felt strongly that it was up to her and her crew to execute their mission perfectly to ensure that the space program wasn't cancelled.

Collins hopes she paved the way for more women to go into space: "Because of [Amelia Earhart], we had more women available to fly in the 1940s to help us get through World War II. And because of these women, women of my generation are able to look back and say, 'Hey, they did it . . . we can do it, too.'"

Mary Wollstonecraft

(1759–1797)

February 1792 saw the publication of a keystone text in the women's movement. Even in that time of revolutionary politics and ideas, Mary Wollstonecraft's *A Vindication of the Rights of Woman* was radical. Wollstonecraft was a free thinker from an early age and moved amongst leading revolutionary philosophers. She had already penned *A Vindication of the Rights of Men*, attacking hereditary privilege and social conservatism, when she turned to the rights of women.

The *Vindication of the Rights of Woman* expresses the frustrations of domestic life. Women were taught, said Wollstonecraft, to settle for love and not to hope for respect; their perceived frivolity resulted from social pressure and poor education. She argued for equal education to equip women with skills and give them a measure of freedom and financial independence. Wollstonecraft had one daughter out of wedlock before marrying the anarchist William Godwin. She died in 1797 from the complications of giving birth to their daughter, Mary Godwin – later Mary Shelley, the author of *Frankenstein* and a remarkable woman of her own generation. After Wollstonecraft's death, Godwin's memoir of his wife revealed her unconventional relationships and illegitimate child; as a result, her reputation nosedived for many years. Politician Horace Walpole called her "a hyena in petticoats." Wollstonecraft herself had hoped to be "the first of a new genus" of women writers. She was; she began a long line of articulate women writing in defense of their rights.

"I do not wish [women] to have power over men; but over themselves."

Twiggy
(1949–)

In February 1966, sixteen-year-old Brit Lesley "Twiggy" Hornby did her first photo shoot for *Vogue* and became the face of a generation. She was soon at the center of a cultural conversation about the representation of women in the media and the fetishization of particular body types. Twiggy's so-called "androgynous" body shape and cropped haircut were a radical departure from the voluptuous, long-haired women who had previously dominated fashion images. She became immensely famous across the world and sat for renowned photographers including Cecil Beaton, Richard Avedon and Annie Leibovitz.

Retiring from modeling after only four years, Twiggy became an award-winning singer and actress, winning two Golden Globes for her 1971 performance in *The Boyfriend*. In her fifties, she returned to modeling, as the frontwoman for a Marks & Spencers' advertising campaign. This was a step forward for the representation of older women in advertising, but this struggle still has some way to go –when Twiggy modeled for an eye cream brand, there were accusations that the photos had been airbrushed. Twiggy is still an iconic figure in the fashion industry, and in 2019 she was appointed a Dame of the British Empire for her services to fashion and the arts.

6 FEBRUARY

Lillian "Big Lil" Bilocca

(1929–1988)

On this day in 1968, cod skinner "Big Lil" Bilocca and other women of Hull, in north-eastern England, held one of the most successful twentieth-century protests over working conditions in Britain. In the "Triple Trawler Disaster" that winter, three Hull ships and their crews totaling fifty-eight men had been lost in the Arctic waters they regularly fished – a high count, even for this dangerous profession. In response, the women of the fishing community publicly protested the hazardous and unregulated working conditions on the trawlers. Over 200 of them marched to the docks to confront ship owners and speak to the press, demanding better safety measures, including a mother ship with medical and radio facilities.

The protest was covered in the national press, dislodging the Vietnam War from headlines, and Bilocca and her friend Yvonne Blenkinsopp met with ministers in London. As an immediate result, eighty-eight safety measures were enacted, including the mother ship provision. A "fisherman's charter" provided for the protection of future trawler crews.

In accounts of this and other strikes, sources often speak of women as "housewives" or as women "leaving the domestic sphere" – partly to commend their activism – but most of these working-class women had always been workers outside the home too.

Beyoncé
(1981–)

On this day in 2016, Beyoncé performed her song "Formation' during the Super Bowl 50 half-time show. Beyoncé transformed the high-profile performance slot into a charged moment of political statement.

"OK ladies, now let's get in formation," she sang. And they did, arranging themselves with military precision into shapes, including a giant X – a reference to Malcolm X, the civil rights leader. Their outfits were military too: Beyoncé's black jacket had a decoration like crossed bandoliers; her dancers wore combat-style boots and their berets were a clear reference to the Black Panther Party uniform.

"Formation" was also an audacious statement of wealth. Beyoncé earns more than most men in the music industry and she told this to the world during the male gladiatorial spectacle that is the Super Bowl: "I just might be a black Bill Gates in the making."

Beyoncé had been publicly political before, as a supporter of Obama and Hillary Clinton and as a self-proclaimed feminist. But "Formation" – and its video, a mesmerizing statement of black anger, pride and power – sparked a particularly intense reaction. Beyoncé's response: "If celebrating my roots and culture . . . made anyone uncomfortable, those feelings were there long before a video and long before me."

Cesária Évora

(1941–2011)

On this day in 2004, Cesária Évora's album *Voz d'Amor* won a Grammy award. According to a 2002 *Guardian* review, she was "the globe's most unlikely superstar: a dumpy, boss-eyed grandmother from a half-forgotten string of islands in the South Atlantic who did not leave her homeland until the age of 46." But it was precisely this lived experience and her rich, supple voice that combined to make her "the Queen of Morna" – the melancholy, lyrical Creole music of the islands of Cabo Verde.

Évora began her career in the 1960s as a bar-room singer. In the 1970s, she withdrew from music, disillusioned by personal unhappiness and the politics of her newly independent homeland. But in the late 1980s, she began to record again in Europe. Évora toured extensively and rode the rising tide of "world music" to find a large international audience. She was particularly well loved in France, where in 2009 she was awarded the Legion d'Honneur. Unusual for a non-Anglophone singer, she also became famous in the US.

Later an ambassador for the United Nations Food Programme, Évora took part in the Drop the Debt campaign to write off the debts of undeveloped nations. Several European streets, a butterfly and even a colorful sea slug have been named after her.

9 FEBRUARY

Margaret Bourke-White
(1904–1971)

In February 1930, Margaret Bourke-White joined *Fortune* magazine as a staff photographer. Her camera captured the great social and political stories of the 1930s and 40s; her images of war zones, social turmoil and world leaders set new standards for photo-journalism.

Born in Brooklyn in 1904, Bourke-White developed an early interest in architecture and industry. Her images of US steel foundries, South African mines and industrial sites in the Soviet Union would win renown; her photo of the Fort Peck Dam was *TIME* magazine's first cover image in 1936. As the Second World War gathered force, Bourke-White had a knack of being in the right (or wrong) place at the right time. She was attached to the US army in North Africa and Europe, flew with combat missions and survived the torpedoing of the troop ship SS *Strathallan*. She was the only foreign photographer in Moscow when it fell to the Germans.

In the last days of the war, she photographed the newly liberated death camp at Buchenwald.

After the war, Bourke-White captured the violence during the partition of India and the fighting in Korea. She photographed Stalin and other leading figures of the time, including Gandhi. Collections of her work are held at the Library of Congress, the Museum of Modern Art in New York and the Rijksmuseum, Amsterdam.

Johanna Westerdijk
(1883–1961)

On this day in 1917, Johanna Westerdijk – "Hans" to her friends – became the Netherlands' first female professor, appointed at Utrecht University. Westerdijk was a pioneer in plant pathology and mycology – the study of fungi. She also worked to promote women in science: half of the fifty-six PhD candidates she supervised were female.

Westerdijk had wanted to become a pianist but inflammation in her arm put an end to her music career. After studying botany at Amsterdam University, she researched moss in Munich and then Zurich, where she got her doctorate in 1906. That same year, aged twenty-three, she was invited to direct a laboratory in the Netherlands. Under her supervision, the International Association of Botanists' fungi collection expanded to over 10,000 strains of 6,000 different species; the fungus causing elm disease was discovered under her leadership.

Also known for her socializing, Westerdijk's motto was, "A dull and monotonous life even kills a fungus." The slogan carved above her laboratory door read: "For fine minds, the art is to mix work and parties." In this spirit, she always insisted on three geese wearing bows to be present at every new doctoral ceremony. A number of fungus species have been named in her honor.

11 FEBRUARY

Lise Meitner

(1878–1968)

Women weren't allowed into higher education in Vienna in the early twentieth century, so Lise Meitner's parents helped her study physics privately. In 1905, she was the second woman awarded a physics PhD from Vienna University. Moving to Berlin, she became Germany's first female physics professor – but lost her job when the Nazis passed the anti-Jewish Nuremberg laws in 1935. She fled to Sweden soon afterwards.

Meitner's breakthrough came while working with her nephew, Otto Frisch, to understand some odd results seen by her Berlin colleague, chemist Otto Hahn. Realizing that a uranium nucleus had split into two different elements with smaller nuclei, she asked Hahn to test this; he found she was correct, then published the results without mentioning her insight.

On this day in February 1939, Meitner wrote a letter to the editor of the science journal *Nature* describing her breakthrough and coining the term "nuclear fission" to describe the splitting of a large nucleus of an atom into smaller ones: the mechanism behind nuclear power plants and nuclear bombs. However, it was Hahn who won the Nobel Prize for fission in 1944; Meitner never won, despite nineteen nominations for chemistry and twenty-nine for physics. In 1997, element 109 was named Meitnerium in her honor.

Elizabeth Wolstenholme Elmy
(1833–1918)

In February 1873, Elizabeth Wolstenholme became the first paid employee of the British women's suffrage movement. Her job was to lobby Parliament about laws that harmed women. The nicknames bestowed on her by MPs – "Parliamentary Watchdog" and "the Scourge of the Commons" – suggest that she was relentless in her work.

Wolstenholme's first interest had been women's education; when she'd received her inheritance at the age of nineteen, she had established a boarding school for girls. But she was passionate about fighting for women's rights in all aspects of their lives. Her friend and colleague Emmeline Pankhurst described Wolstenholme as "the brains behind the suffragette movement."

On Women's Sunday, a suffragette march and rally in London on 21 June 1908, it was Wolstenholme who led the procession of half a million women and men: the largest demonstration in the UK up to that time. However, in 1913 she resigned from the Women's Social and Political Union because she thought the suffragettes' tactics had become too violent.

Wolstenholme died just six weeks after the Representation of the People Act 1918 finally allowed some British women to vote. Her name is inscribed into the plinth of the Millicent Fawcett statue erected in 2018 in Parliament Square, London.

13 FEBRUARY

Hubertine Auclert

(1848–1914)

On this day in 1881, Hubertine Auclert published the first issue of the French feminist monthly newspaper *La Citoyenne* ("The Female Citizen"). She had founded the newspaper with Antonin Levrier, whom she later married. Auclert used the newspaper to demand equal rights for women in education, law, politics and the workplace. *La Citoyenne* ran for ten years and included articles by prominent feminists such as Caroline Rémy de Guebhard ("Séverine").

Auclert had moved to Paris in 1872 to work for women's rights: "I became a crusader not by choice but from duty . . . and went to war like a medieval knight." She founded the Société le droit des femmes (Society for the Rights of Women) in 1876.

In February 1880, on Election Day, Hubertine Auclert and a group of taxpaying women attempted to register to vote in Paris. When they were turned away, Auclert called for a women's tax strike: "I have no rights, therefore I have no obligations. I do not vote, I do not pay."

Auclert's reach went well beyond her home city. In 1883, she met US suffragists Elizabeth Cady Stanton and Susan B Anthony in Liverpool, England: the beginning of an international movement for women's suffrage. In the 1890s she introduced the word "feminism" (first coined by Charles Fourier) into English.

14 FEBRUARY

Bess of Hardwick

(1527–1608)

On Valentine's Day, consider one of the many talented women whose only path to power was marriage. Bess of Hardwick married four times, each time to a more powerful man, but her success as an investor and courtier was all her own.

Throughout the second half of the sixteenth century, England was ruled by queens. For the first time, certain positions close to the monarch could *only* be held by women and these courtiers had privileged access to the source of power. They could petition directly for financial rewards or political office on behalf of their male relatives. Women at court were now lobbyists, representatives of the great political factions and gatekeepers to the monarch's person.

Bess was a contemporary and friend of Elizabeth I. A great landowner and political schemer, Bess husbanded her estates carefully, building grand houses and investing in industries like mining and glass manufacture. She arranged marriage alliances to keep assets in the family and even entertained hopes of her granddaughter, Arbella Stuart, becoming the next queen. Elizabeth I's trust in Bess and her last husband, the Earl of Shrewsbury, was such that she appointed them keepers of the captive Mary, Queen of Scots. Partly as a result of the tensions caused by hosting Mary, Bess and her husband became estranged in later years.

Once certain that her estranged fourth husband was days from death and her inheritance was secure, Bess signed off the plans for a new Hardwick Hall, which still dominates the Derbyshire landscape. On its parapets, visible for miles around, are the enormous initials of a powerful woman: ES, for Elizabeth Shrewsbury.

15 FEBRUARY

Zeb-un-Nissa

(1638–1702)

On this day in 1638, Mughal princess Zeb-un-Nissa was born, a direct descendant of Genghis Khan. Aged seven, she became a *hafiza*, having memorized the Quran in three years. Her father, Aurangzeb, celebrated the occasion with a public holiday. Zeb-un-Nissa went on to learn philosophy, mathematics, astronomy, literature and the languages Persian, Arabic and Urdu. She built up a great library and a scriptorium, where scholars wrote and copied books for her. She wrote poetry in her native Persian, using the pen-name "Makhfi" ("Hidden One"), perhaps a reference to her veil: "The world can see me / Only in my poetry." Zeb-un-Nissa persuaded her father to gather poets to form a literary circle which held a competition for improvized poetry called *mushaira*.

In around 1682, Zeb-un-Nissa was imprisoned by her father. The reasons are not entirely clear: perhaps she had displeased him by taking a lover, or her poetic and musical activities offended his more austere take on religion. She died in prison twenty years later. In 1724, some of her writings were collected under the title *Diwan-i-Makhfi* ("The Book of the Hidden One").

"The rapturous nightingale sings,
Wooing the rose
In the midst of the garden new-born:
But only the gardener knows
Of the labour that brings
To the garden its beauty"

Bessie Smith

(1894–1937)

Known as the "Empress of the Blues," Bessie Smith, the highest-paid black performer of her time, recorded her first hit on this day in 1923. "Down Hearted Blues" went on to sell 800,000 copies and was named one of the songs of the century.

Smith, growing up in poverty in the American South, had lost both parents by the age of ten; she earned money singing on the street while her brother played guitar. At fourteen, she joined traveling performance troupe the Moses Stokes Company as a dancer and met Gertrude "Ma" Rainey, the "Mother of the Blues," who took Smith under her wing. In 1923, Smith signed with Columbia Records. Her enormous popularity was due to a combination of her stage presence and the lyrics of her songs, which dealt with everyday experiences of southern life, independence, fearlessness and sexual freedom. She argued that

working-class women shouldn't change their behavior to earn respect. "I don't want no drummer," she once told a producer. "I set the tempo."

Smith died in 1937 after being injured in a car crash; there were rumors, later discredited, that a whites-only hospital had refused to take her. Her grave was unmarked until 1970 when a gravestone was paid for by the singer Janis Joplin.

17 FEBRUARY

A Viking Warrior
(10th century CE)

On this day we remember an unnamed warrior of the tenth century, whose grave was excavated in Birka, Sweden in 1878. This high-ranking Viking had been laid to rest with two horses in an underground chamber near a fortress. The body was surrounded by weapons: a sword, axe, fighting knife, lances, shields and armor-piercing arrows. A gaming board and pieces – signs of a military leader – were set next to it. There were no household items. The grave was prominent, visible from the nearby lake and settlement and marked with a large boulder.

In 2017, archaeologists revealed that this warlike person had been a woman. The 1878 excavators had not unnaturally assumed that this body must be a man, but new DNA analysis showed that it was undoubtedly female (see Bodies of Evidence). The findings unleashed a storm of incredulity in the international press. Two

years later, the same archaeologists were compelled to publish a second paper, explaining their results further. They reiterated that beyond doubt, the grave belonged to "a woman who lived as a professional warrior and was buried in a martial environment as an individual of rank." Even now, such evidence has to filter through present-day prejudice to become part of the historical record.

If *this* warrior was a woman, then what about other remains – soldiers, sailors, workers – which have long been assumed to be men? There may be more women in all strands of human history than we have imagined.

The findings unleashed a storm of incredulity in the international press.

18 FEBRUARY

Anne Acheson

(1882–1962)

The modern plaster cast, which revolutionized the healing of broken bones, was developed in 1917 by Anne Acheson, a sculptor from Portadown, Ireland. During the First World War, Acheson volunteered with the Surgical Requisites Association (SRA) in London. Seeing soldiers returning home in bandages and basic wooden splints, Acheson, who had won an anatomy book at art school, decided she could do better. Following up on work begun by her SRA colleague, sculptor Elinor Hallé, Acheson created papier maché splints which proved successful. Her next step was to create casts of patients' limbs using the plaster of paris familiar to sculptors, so that anatomically-correct splints could be made for each patient.

Several surgeons had experimented with applying substances, including plaster of paris, to stiffen bandages. But these inventions encountered problems: from heaviness, which immobilized the patient, to the ill-effects from cutting off air to the wounds. "There were many difficulties to contend with," Acheson wrote, "for example the difference between the fleshy and bony surfaces." Solving these, her splints – which not only properly supported limbs but shortened healing times – were described by the *British Nursing Journal* in February 1917 as "perfectly rigid and beautifully light."

In February 1919, Acheson was made a Commander of the British Empire (CBE) for her war work. She would become the first woman elected to the Royal Society of British Sculptors.

19 FEBRUARY

Betty Friedan

(1921–2006)

"Women quite simply were stopped at a state of evolution far short of their human capacity," wrote Betty Friedan in *The Feminine Mystique*, published on this day in 1963 and credited with sparking American feminism's second wave.

Friedan, active in Marxist and Jewish circles as a young woman, began her career as a journalist for left and labor union publications. She had seen her mother give up her own career in journalism when she got married, so, for Friedan's fifteenth college reunion, she decided to survey fellow female graduates about their experiences after college and life satisfaction. She then spent five years interviewing white, middle-class women across America. The passionate responses she received prompted her to expand them into a book.

After *The Feminine Mystique* became a bestseller, Friedan co-founded and was elected the first president of the National Organization for Women (NOW), to bring women "into the mainstream of American society now [in] fully equal partnership with men." In August 1970, on the fiftieth anniversary of the Nineteenth Amendment to the US Constitution, which granted women the right to vote, she organized the nationwide Women's Strike for Equality; 50,000 women joined the march.

20 FEBRUARY

Sophie Germain

(1776–1831)

On this day in 1807, Sophie Germain revealed to German mathematician Carl Friedrich Gauss that he was actually corresponding with a woman. She had been writing to him under a pseudonym, Monsieur Le Blanc, "fearing the ridicule attached to a female scientist."

Her interest in mathematics began at the age of thirteen, however her parents considered her fascination with the math books in her father's library unhealthy for a girl and tried to stop her studying by taking away her warm clothes and the materials to build a fire. When she equipped herself with candles and quilts, they realized she was serious. Under her pseudonym, Germain procured lecture notes from the new École Polytechnique and started writing to several mathematicians, including Gauss. When his Prussian town was threatened by Napoleon's troops, Germain sent a friend to make sure he was safe – and so was forced to reveal her identity.

In 1816, Germain became the first woman to win a prize from the Paris Academy of Sciences, though she was still banned from their lectures. Gauss persuaded Göttingen University to give her an honorary doctorate but she died before it could be awarded. Sophie Germain primes are named after her, as is a street in Paris.

21 FEBRUARY

Pussy Riot – Nadezhda Tolokonnikova (1987–); Maria Alyokhina (1988–); Yekaterina Samutsevich (1982–)

On this day in 2012, Russian feminist punk band Pussy Riot staged a performance called "Punk Prayer – Mother of God, Chase Putin Away!" in Moscow's Cathedral of Christ the Saviour.

Three of the women – Nadezhda Tolokonnikova, Maria Alyokhina and Yekaterina Samutsevich – were arrested. Six months later, they were found guilty of "hooliganism motivated by religious hatred" and sentenced to two years in prison. Their argument – that they did not want to offend believers but were protesting the Orthodox church's support for President Vladimir Putin – was rejected by the judge, Marina Syrova.

The sentencing of the women was seen as a warning to other potential dissidents and a personal revenge enacted by Putin. Dozens of protesters were arrested outside court, including chess grandmaster Garry Kasparov and opposition leader Sergei Udaltsov. The severity of the sentence was widely condemned by foreign leaders and music industry celebrities and there were protests in cities worldwide. Amnesty International called the women prisoners of conscience.

Pussy Riot appealed against their sentence. Samutsevich was freed on probation and her sentence suspended but the sentences of the other two women were upheld. Tolokonnikova and Alyokhina served twenty-one months in jail.

The group continues to hold guerrilla performances and make music videos about issues of police brutality – in both Russia and the US – and judicial corruption.

Amnesty International called the women prisoners of conscience.

22 FEBRUARY

Sophie Scholl
(1921–1943)

On this day in 1943, German student Sophie Scholl, her brother Hans and their friend Christoph Probst were found guilty of treason and condemned to death for distributing anti-Nazi leaflets. Defending their actions, Sophie is recorded as saying in court: "Somebody, after all, had to make a start. What we wrote and said is also believed by many others. They just don't dare express themselves as we did."

Sophie had enrolled the previous year at the University of Munich, where her brother studied medicine. When she discovered that he and his friends had formed a resistance group, the Weiße Rose (White Rose), she persuaded them to let her join. Their strategy was passive resistance; inspired by American students fighting racism, they published leaflets calling for democracy and social justice, distributing them in the university and throughout southern and central Germany. Sophie proved valuable: as a woman, she was less likely to be randomly stopped.

On 18 February 1943, the group was arrested for distributing their sixth leaflet. Four days later, they were tried and beheaded. Sophie was twenty-one years old. Her last recorded words were: "Such a fine, sunny day, and I have to go . . . What does my death matter, if through us, thousands of people are awakened and stirred to action?"

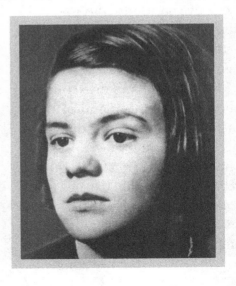

Nancy Grace Roman

(1925–2018)

The Hubble Space Telescope allows us to see further into the universe than ever before, and its existence is thanks to Nancy Grace Roman, the "Mother of Hubble." In February 1959, Roman, who had a doctorate in astronomy, became the first chief of astronomy at the brand new National Aeronautics and Space Administration (NASA). Given responsibility for "planning a program of satellites and rockets," she was the first woman to hold an executive position at NASA – at a time when women had trouble getting bank accounts in their own names.

In 1962, Roman started thinking about sending astronomical instruments into space, though her vision wouldn't be realized for almost thirty years. Although she'd retired in 1979, she returned as a consultant on the Hubble telescope, co-ordinating astronomers and engineers and writing testimony for NASA experts advocating before Congress. The telescope was launched aboard the Space Shuttle Discovery in April 1990. An image released in May 2019, using sixteen years' worth of data, shows around 265,000 galaxies going back 13.3 billion years. "Our view of the universe and our place within it has never been the same," says NASA.

24 FEBRUARY

Naomi Mitchison

(1897–1999)

On this day in 1934, Naomi Mitchison left London for Vienna to distribute aid to families after the Austrian Civil War, when forces commanded by the Austro-Fascist government shelled workers' flats. She wrote *Vienna Diary* (1934) about her experiences in the city, recording the suffering she witnessed and the solidarity she found. It is an important, personal document of a situation that was largely ignored by foreign newspapers at the time and which remains unknown to most people outside Austria to this day.

Mitchison, whose London home was a meeting place for artists, writers, politicians and activists, published over ninety books in various genres. Her best-known novels are *The Corn King and the Spring Queen* (1931) and *The Blood of the Martyrs* (1939). She combined historical and mythological writing with a strong political awareness and a feminist outlook. *We Have*

Been Warned (1935) was censored for its depiction of rape, free love and abortion.

In her sixties, Mitchison became friends with the young chief designate of the Bakgatla tribe, at that time divided between Bechuanaland (now Botswana) and South Africa, and lived with them, receiving the title "mother of the Bakgatla." She worked to help the tribe in various ways including the introduction of contraception.

Nan Shepherd

(1893–1981)

In 1977, Nan Shepherd's pioneering book *The Living Mountain* was published – forty years after she wrote it. A revolutionary text, it placed ecology and spirituality at the heart of the human relationship with nature and was a huge influence on a generation of writers exploring new ways to celebrate landscape and its associations.

Shepherd was a Scottish climber and poet. Her earlier publications had included poetry and novels exploring the lives of Highland women. *The Living Mountain*, her final book, is intimate and moving and hard to categorize – a lyrical mixture of memoir, natural history and philosophy. Writing in praise of Shepherd's book, nature writer Robert Macfarlane says, "Most works of mountain literature are written by men, and most of them focus on the goal of the summit." Shepherd instead spoke of the Cairngorms as a summons to wonder. She addressed climbing not in terms of conquest or "being first," but of humility and attention.

The Living Mountain has been described in the *Guardian* as "the finest book ever written on nature and landscape in Britain." Shepherd appears on the Scottish £5 note with her quote: "It is a grand thing, to get leave to live."

26 FEBRUARY

Caroline Herschel

(1750–1848)

Caroline Herschel might have become a singer had she not moved from Germany to England in 1772 to assist her astronomer brother, William. Helping look after his telescopes, she trained herself in geometry and how to measure time by the stars, and began keeping her own records of objects in the sky. On this day in 1783, she made her first discovery – a nebula or interstellar cloud not included in the widely used catalogue of astronomical objects by Charles Messier.

William built Caroline her own telescope; she discovered eight comets between 1786 and 1797. (Maria Kirch may have in fact been the first woman to discover a comet – in the early 1700s – but it was attributed to her husband.) Caroline updated John Flamsteed's *British Catalogue of Stars*, finding errors and adding 560 stars; her *Catalogue of Nebulae and Clusters of Stars* was published by the Royal Society in 1798.

Caroline was the first woman to receive a salary as a scientist, paid by the king to assist William, and the first, in 1828, to be presented with a Gold Medal by the Royal Astronomical Society, its greatest honor. Seven years later, she and mathematician <u>Mary Somerville</u> became the society's first female honorary members. On her ninety-sixth birthday, the King of Prussia presented Caroline with a Gold Medal for Science.

27 FEBRUARY

Elsa Holzer

(unknown)

On this day in 1943, Elsa Holzer joined a demonstration by "Aryan" German women in Berlin against the imprisonment of their Jewish husbands. The men were being held at a community hall on the Rosenstraße, pending dispersal to forced labor camps. Incredibly, this was the first demonstration on behalf of Jews in wartime Germany.

Elsa's husband, Rudi, was a Catholic, but he had Jewish parents. His former membership of the Communist Party would also have caught the attention of the Gestapo, the powerful secret police. Rudi was declared a Jew in 1939, losing both his job and his German citizenship. In February 1943, he was one of around 1,800 Jewish men who were picked up as part of the Nazis' "final round up" in Berlin.

Elsa Holzer, like other protesters, had been encouraged by the authorities to divorce her husband and had refused. For several days in late February, she and up to 200 other women protested loudly in the Rosenstraße. It was a non-violent action but a conspicuous one, attracting attention and sympathy in a city where some international journalists were still present. Rudi Holzer and his colleagues were released. "We acted from the heart, and look what happened," said Elsa.

The success of the demonstration was limited, however; around twenty-five of the men were sent to Auschwitz and many others were re-arrested within days. Rudi Holzer remained at liberty; he and Elsa stayed in East Germany after the war.

"We acted from the heart, and look what happened."

Catharina van Hemessen
(c.1528–c.1587)

The first self-portrait we know in the familiar "artist at an easel" style is by Catharina van Hemessen, a painter working in mid-sixteenth century Antwerp. It was painted in 1548, when she was twenty years old. She looks solemn and slender; she clutches a bunch of brushes and wears a rather impractical velvet dress.

It was unusual for a female artist to become a professional, but not unique: a handful of other Flemish women were painting professionally at the same time. The standard practice for painters was to study the male nude and to serve a long apprenticeship with an older artist – both of which would be improper for an unmarried woman. Van Hemessen probably served an informal apprenticeship under her artist father. As so often happens, some of her work, including the famous self-portrait (signed by her), has been attributed to him.

Catharina Van Hemessen had financial support from Maria of Austria, regent of the Low Countries. Her portraits were small, intimate and realistic; she also painted religious subjects. She was notable enough to be mentioned by art biographers Guicciardini and Vasari in the 1560s.

In 1554, van Hemessen got married, at the age of twenty-six. No paintings by her are known after this date.

29 FEBRUARY

Ann Lee

(1736–1784)

On this day in 1736, Ann Lee was born to a very poor family in Manchester, England. In her youth, she worked in a cotton factory, then as a hospital cook; she would go on to become the leader of a religious sect.

Lee's family were Quakers. In 1758, she joined a religious society led by former Quakers Jane and James Wardley. The meetings of these "Shaking Quakers" included confessions of sins, which led to singing, shouting, dancing and violent shaking. Lee was often imprisoned for "breaking the Sabbath" with her singing and dancing. While in jail in 1770, she saw a "grand vision" revealing that she was the female successor to Jesus. From then on she referred to herself as "Mother Ann." Convinced that sex was the original sin committed by Adam and Eve, Lee wished to remain celibate, but her father forced her to marry. She had four children, all of whom died in infancy.

In May 1774, Lee, accompanied by eight of her "disciples," emigrated to America. She traveled through New England on horseback, preaching and establishing communities known as "Shakers." Their principles involved simple living, pacifism and celibacy. At the end of the eighteenth century there were 6,000 Shakers; by 2017 there were only two left.

MARCH

"Our meeting today is not a congress but a parliament. A true one! That of women."
– Doria Shafik

Women are people too

While researching for this book and for our Twitter account, we are often inspired by stories we learn of war heroes, innovators, fearless campaigners and ground-breaking musicians, artists and scientists. But we also feature those whose deeds and behaviors were at best unsavory and sometimes downright appalling.

Why? Because women can do – and have done – everything. Our mission is not to illuminate "women's history" but to do our part to rebalance the history of our whole species, which includes those who were cruel, corrupt, murderous. We include women who, when in positions of power, made mistakes, just as men did. Women who killed in the most heinous ways. Women who committed crimes and masterminded (mistressminded?) criminal gangs.

There has been a great deal of very welcome activity recently to celebrate and put women back into history, but much of it centers on the "badass," inspiring women – the heroes and the trailblazers. When we feature female serial killers, say, or corrupt politicians on our Twitter account, we face resistance and hostility. We have to explain that we are not promoting or glorifying these women but that they deserve to be named and put back into the historical record too.

Women are not here to inspire you. Women are not your muses. They are real, flesh-and-blood, often flawed humans. Yes, many of them are astonishing, brave and worthy of celebration, but to highlight only these women would be doing women – and men – a disservice. It is not just men throughout history who have behaved badly, and until we bring these women out of the shadows, history will be incomplete.

1 MARCH

Gwenllian ferch Gruffydd
(c.1100–1136)

On St. David's Day, we celebrate Welsh princess Gwenllian ferch Gruffydd, who died on the battlefield in 1136.

Like many royal women of the Middle Ages, Gwenllian is often portrayed as a romantic beauty who willingly eloped with her prince. In fact, her marriage at around fourteen years old to Gruffydd ap Rhys, prince of Deheubarth in South Wales, was an arranged alliance between powerful families.

The Welsh aristocracy had suffered under the Normans since the 1066 conquest of Britain and retaliated with force. Gwenllian seems to have carried out armed raids with her husband for several years in the 1120s and 30s, sometimes when heavily pregnant. She had at least seven children, and was probably in her thirties when the government of England and Wales was disrupted by a civil war in 1135. During this "Anarchy" period, Welsh leaders saw a chance to win back land and power. Gwenllian raised a small force which camped near Cydweli castle, planning to cut off supplies to the Norman stronghold. A disloyal follower gave away her position to the enemy; Gwenllian was defeated, captured and beheaded on the battlefield. Her death galvanized further resistance against the Normans.

Long after the Normans had conquered Wales and for centuries after, the battle cry of the Welsh was *Ddail Achos Gwenllian!*, or "revenge for Gwenllian." A representation of her is still used in demonstrations for Welsh independence with the slogan *Cofiwch Gwenllian* – remember Gwenllian.

2 MARCH

Claudette Colvin

(1939–)

On this day in 1955, fifteen-year-old African-American schoolgirl Claudette Colvin was arrested in Montgomery, Alabama, for refusing to give up her bus seat to a white woman.

At her segregated school, Colvin had been studying the stories of former slaves who had become leaders: "I felt like Sojourner Truth was pushing down on one shoulder and Harriet Tubman was pushing down on the other – saying, 'Sit down girl!'" Colvin was handcuffed by police, jailed and charged with assault and battery, disorderly conduct and defying the segregation law.

The leaders of the National Association for the Advancement of Colored People (NAACP), including Martin Luther King, had been thinking about how to fight bus segregation for years, but they did not take up Colvin's cause. She became pregnant not long after her arrest and they wanted a test case based on someone morally irreproachable. So, when we think of the Montgomery bus protest, we think of Rosa Parks, who refused to give up her seat later that same year. Nonetheless, Colvin played her part in the fight for civil rights. She was one of five women (with Aurelia Browder, Susie McDonald, Mary Louise Smith and Jeanetta Reese) whose case led to a ruling, on 5 June 1956, that bus segregation was unconstitutional.

Dagmar Overbye

(1887–1929)

On this day in 1921, Danish serial killer Dagmar Overbye was sentenced to death for killing nine children, including her own daughter, in one of Denmark's most notorious trials. Overbye had set herself up in Copenhagen as an intermediary between families looking to adopt and women who had children outside of marriage. Mothers paid her and gave her their newborns but the children were never adopted. She strangled, drowned or burned the babies to death, cremating, burying or hiding the corpses in her loft.

Overbye's appalling crimes were finally exposed when she told a woman who wanted her baby back that she couldn't remember the adoptive family's address and the woman went to the police. Although suspected of killing twenty-five children – she admitted to sixteen – due to insufficient evidence, she was convicted of only nine murders. Her lawyer argued that Overbye had been abused as a child, but that did not sway the judge.

One of three women sentenced to death in Denmark in the twentieth century, like the other two Overbye was reprieved; she died in prison. The trial drew attention to childcare legislation reform; in 1923, as a direct result of the Overbye case, a law was passed establishing public homes for illegitimate children.

Although suspected of killing twenty-five children – she admitted to sixteen – due to insufficient evidence, she was convicted of only nine murders.

Seh-Dong-Hong-Beh

(unknown)

Seh-Dong-Hong-Beh was a nineteenth-century West African warrior – or perhaps more than one warrior with the same name. She led an all-female army of up to 6,000 soldiers, who were later called the Dahomey Mothers.

The kingdom of Dahomey (present day Benin) had a female militia from at least the early eighteenth century. The king was protected by armed female bodyguards; these high-status women escaped the normal domestic life of a wife, being instead nominal "wives" of the king. They also fought in the service of Dahomey's slave trade. In the 1850s, a soldier called Seh-Dong-Hong-Beh was mentioned in the journals of Frederick Forbes, a British Navy commander. She had led an attack on a fortress of the Egba people in the hope of capturing prisoners for the slave market. Forbes' memoirs include an image of her holding the severed head of an enemy.

There is no clear evidence for Seh-Dong-Hong-Beh's later history. Her name has been attached to various campaigns between 1849 and 1894, but as these dates are decades apart, it is unlikely that it's the same woman. Perhaps Seh-Dong-Hong-Beh was actually a title or symbolic name. Nonetheless, the woman known by that name belonged to a long tradition of respected female fighters.

5 MARCH

Ida Cook (1904–1986) and Louise Cook (1909–1991)

In March 1965, British sisters Louise and Ida Cook were named Righteous Among the Nations by Yad Vashem, Israel's Holocaust Remembrance Center, for helping twenty-nine Jewish families escape Nazi Germany before the Second World War.

After friends in continental Europe asked the sisters if they could do anything for their Jewish acquaintances, Louise and Ida began making weekend trips by plane to smuggle valuables such as furs and jewelry out of Germany, so that the refugees – forbidden from taking money or possessions themselves – could meet Britain's financial security requirements for immigrants. Using funds Ida made writing over 100 Mills and Boon romance novels as "Mary Burchell," the sisters then found British people to vouch for those fleeing the Nazis, they assisted the new arrivals with paperwork and even bought a flat for refugees to stay in.

In her autobiography, *Safe Passage*, Ida said they pretended to be "nervous British spinsters who didn't trust our families . . . so we took all our jewellery with us." They stayed at expensive hotels precisely because they were filled with top-ranking Nazis: "If you stood and gazed at them admiringly as they went through the lobby, no one thought you were anything but another couple of admiring fools." They made their final trip just before war broke out, in 1939. "Two girls can often do what one on her own cannot," Ida wrote.

"If you stood and gazed at them admiringly as they went through the lobby, no one thought you were anything but another couple of admiring fools."

Henrietta Swan Leavitt

(1868-1921)

American astronomer Henrietta Swan Leavitt changed the way we see the world. In March 1912, she published a paper that showed for the first time how a star's distance from earth could be measured, and led to the finding that our universe is expanding. Leavitt, who was deaf, worked at Harvard College Observatory as a "computer," one of several women paid thirty cents an hour to scan thousands of photographic plates. Identifying over 2,400 variable stars, which change brightness over time, she became curious as to whether their brightness and their period – the time it takes for them to get brighter, dimmer, then brighter – were connected. If so, this would allow their distance from earth to be calculated.

Focusing on stars in the Small Magellanic Cloud star cluster, Leavitt discovered that brighter stars have longer periods. Her 1912 paper, "Periods of 25 Variable Stars in the Small Magellanic Cloud," enabled astronomers to measure the distance to any Cepheid star. This led directly to Edwin Hubble's discovery that the universe is bigger than had been thought, contains many other galaxies and is still expanding (see Nancy Grace Roman). The tools Leavitt developed for measuring the size and rate of expansion of the universe are still used today.

Kathryn Bigelow

(1951–)

"The winner could be, for the first time, a woman," said Barbra Streisand, before opening the Best Director envelope at the Academy Awards on this day in 2010, and announcing Kathryn Bigelow as the winner. She was only the fourth woman to be nominated for Best Director in the eighty-two-year history of the Oscars. Bigelow's film, *The Hurt Locker*, tells the story of an American bomb disposal team during the Iraq War. Themes of violence and war are generally regarded as the province of male directors; her next film, *Zero Dark Thirty*, continued in this vein, covering the search for al-Qaeda terrorist leader Osama Bin Laden.

Bigelow had originally studied painting but, in 1972, after moving to New York to take part in a program at the Whitney Museum, her focus shifted to film. In 1978, she made her first short, *The Set-Up*, which explored why violence in the cinema is so alluring, before moving on to feature-length projects. "I suppose I like to think of myself as a film-maker – not a female film-maker," Bigelow said at the 2010 Directors' Guild of America Awards, where she was once again the first woman to win a Best Director award.

Nina Simone

(1933-2003)

In March 1964, Nina Simone performed "Mississippi Goddam," which she called "my first civil rights song," to a mostly white audience at Carnegie Hall in New York. She had written it in response to the 1963 murder of black civil rights activist Medgar Evers in Mississippi and the 16th Street Baptist Church bombing in Birmingham, Alabama.

At an early age, Simone (born Eunice Wayton) dreamed of being the first black concert pianist, but after a year at the famous Juilliard School in New York, her application to study at the Curtis Institute of Music in Philadelphia was rejected. She believed that it was because she was black: "I never really got over that jolt of racism." She changed her name so that her religious parents would not know that she was making a living by singing in bars. Her incredible musical ability and versatility brought her success as a performer and recording artist.

Simone said that when she heard the news about Evers' death, she "had it in mind to go out and kill someone." She made her anger into words instead. "Mississippi Goddam," she said, "erupted out of me quicker than I could write it down." When she met Martin Luther King at the Selma to Montgomery civil rights march in March 1965, Simone told him, "I'm not non-violent!" "That's OK, sister," he replied. "You don't have to be."

Hypatia
(c.355–415 CE)

On this day in 415, the great scholar Hypatia was murdered by a Christian militia in Alexandria. She was a mathematician, astronomer, philosopher and adviser to the political class of her time.

Hypatia was particularly famed as a teacher of philosophy and astronomy. She wrote commentaries on important mathematical texts and probably edited Ptolemy's astronomical treatise, *The Almagest*. Hypatia built scientific tools including astrolabes, the device used to identify planets and determine time or location.

A pagan, Hypatia welcomed Christians into her classes and recommended religious tolerance. However, she was a prominent supporter of the politician Orestes. Orestes was a critic of the Christian bishop Cyril, whose henchmen pulled Hypatia from her chariot, dragged her to a temple, stripped her and flayed her to death with jagged pieces of shell. She was dismembered and her remains burned, in a mockery of pagan rites.

No contemporary images of Hypatia exist. The picture we use here shows a recurring problem in the representation of women in history. Even when their achievements are undisputed, they are sexualized for the male gaze. We include Charles William Mitchell's nineteenth-century painting of a famous scholar, nude, as an example of this ongoing trope.

Kym Worthy

(1956–)

On this day in 2014, American lawyer Kym Worthy introduced Sexual Assault Kit legislation in Michigan, US. As a result, rape evidence in the state must now be processed within ninety days. At least seventeen other states followed suit, with more due to follow in the near future.

In 2009, Worthy was the county prosecutor for Wayne County, which includes the city of Detroit. Her assistant prosecutor, Rob Spada, discovered a warehouse full of unprocessed evidence. This included "rape kits" documenting 11,341 sexual assaults and rapes. The kits contained DNA swabs taken from victims or suspects. None of the cases had been investigated after the initial witness statement. Worthy ordered that each kit should be opened, catalogued and matched with historic police records from the original case, sometimes dating back many years. A federal grant of $1.5m was awarded to help her office with the backlog. By the end of 2017, almost 2,000 cases had been investigated, 127 offenders convicted and over 800 serial rapists identified.

Time and resources have sometimes been cited as the reason for sidelining these cases, but institutional sexism, racism and attitudes to class are also to blame. These are key factors in the treatment of any sexual assault claim. Worthy says, "Eighty-six percent of our victims in these untested kits are people of color."

By the end of 2017, almost 2,000 cases had been investigated, 127 offenders convicted and over 800 serial rapists identified.

Lorraine Hansberry

(1930–1965)

On this day in 1959, Lorraine Hansberry's play, *A Raisin in the Sun*, opened in New York: the first Broadway performance of a play written by an African-American woman. The granddaughter of a freed slave, Hansberry wrote in her spare time while working as a waitress, cashier and writer for a progressive black newspaper. *A Raisin in the Sun* tells the story of a black family in Chicago trying to better their circumstances using an insurance payout after the father's death. Translated into thirty-five languages and made into a film, the work made Hansberry the first black playwright – and the youngest, at twenty-nine – to win a New York Critics' Circle award.

The play was inspired by her family's lawsuit against racist housing restrictions. Hansberry remembered her mother "patrolling the house all night with a loaded German Lüger," after they were attacked and forced out of a white neighborhood; her father later won the lawsuit in the Supreme Court. "Lorraine started off my political education," said songwriter and activist <u>Nina Simone</u>. "Through her I started thinking about myself as a black person in a country run by white people and a woman in a world run by men." Hansberry's second Broadway play, *The Sign in Sidney Brustein's Window*, closed the night she died, aged thirty-four, of pancreatic cancer.

12 MARCH

Doria Shafik

(1908–1975)

Aged just sixteen, poet and activist Doria Shafik won a scholarship to study for a PhD at the Sorbonne in Paris. When she came back to Egypt, she was denied a university teaching position because she was "too modern." She became editor-in-chief of *La Femme Nouvelle*, a cultural and literary magazine written in French aimed at Egypt's elite, and in 1945 founded an Arabic magazine, *Bint Al Nil* ("Daughter of the Nile"), to educate Egyptian women.

On 19 February 1951, Shafik gathered 1,500 women at the American University of Cairo, ostensibly for a feminist congress but in reality she had other plans: "Our meeting today is not a congress but a parliament," she said. "A true one! That of women." The women stormed the Egyptian parliament, where they held up proceedings for more than four hours until the president of its upper chamber pledged to take up their demands: the right of women to vote and to hold office.

On this day in 1954, Shafik began a hunger strike protesting the fact that the government had formed an all-male committee to draft a new constitution. She ended her strike when the president committed to a constitution that respected women's rights. In 1956, as a direct result of Shafik's efforts, Egyptian women gained the vote.

Louise Labé

(c.1524–1566)

Today we celebrate Louise Labé, renowned poet of the French Renaissance. In the mid-sixteenth century, she was acclaimed by her peers as "the Tenth Muse." In her writings, she spoke frankly of love and desire – "A woman's heart always has a scorch mark" – and she encouraged other women to write.

In her youth, Labé was a fine horsewoman and archer. Nicknamed "La Belle Cordière" because her husband and father were ropemakers, she dressed in "male" clothing, fought in jousts and perhaps even in battle. She was an accomplished poet by 1555, when she published her *Euvres* ("Works") and hosted a creative salon in her home town of Lyon. Like many female writers, Labé's works have sometimes been attributed to male contemporaries with little reason. In another common experience for women who step outside expected roles, she was accused of promiscuity and unwomanly conduct. Protestant dogmatist John Calvin called her a "common whore" for her supposed loose morals.

Labé is best-known for her love sonnets – daring and plain statements of female sexuality, admired and translated in the twentieth century by Rainer Maria Rilke. Labé scholar Richard Sieburth says, "She moves poetry closer to the drive of speech, as it crosses over into song."

14 MARCH

Hannah More

(1745–1833)

On this day in 1799, Hannah More – teacher, writer, philanthropist and abolitionist – published the first volume of *Strictures on the Modern System of Female Education*.

More had had early success with a drama, *The Search After Happiness*, which proposed that women should use their education at home and be "Fearful of Fame," but she herself became a full-time writer, moving in London's literary circles. She enjoyed intellectual banter, flattery – and fame.

In *Strictures on the Modern System of Female Education*, More – like Mary Wollstonecraft – argued for women to be educated. But unlike Wollstonecraft, she did not challenge male supremacy; More wanted education for women in order that they might be better wives and mothers and better Christians. *Strictures* was immensely successful; seven editions were printed in the first year of publication alone.

More herself gave a lot of time to help others, but though she and her sisters ran schools where poor children could learn to read, they decided not to teach them to write, because it would "encourage them to be dissatisfied with their lowly situation" and perhaps to call for revolution, as had happened in France. As with women's education, More was keen to improve the lives of the poor, but not to disrupt the status quo.

Lady Murasaki

(c.978–c.1014)

In the early eleventh century, a Japanese courtier composed a long, compelling story which became a classic of world literature. The story was *The Tale of Genji*. The courtier's given name is not certain; we know her as Lady Murasaki. Murasaki was born into a family of (male) poets and learned to write Chinese, then the fashionable language of culture in the Japanese court. From around 1005, she had a place in the household of Empress Shōshi.

Although Murasaki's poetry was acclaimed, it was *The Tale of Genji* which became a literary landmark. Written in Japanese, it was completed by 1008. *Genji* is often called the world's first novel but, with its hundreds of characters and complicated storyline, it might equally be called a monumental soap opera. Lady Murasaki probably wrote it piecemeal, to be performed in "episodes" for an intimate circle around the empress.

The story follows a nobleman, Genji, through his changing fortunes and secret loves. One of his lovers is a high-born lady called Murasaki, who eventually marries him. In the Japanese court, where titles and nicknames were routinely used, the name of this character became attached to the real courtier who imagined her.

Genji is often called the world's first novel but, with its hundreds of characters and complicated storyline, it might equally be called a monumental soap opera.

16 MARCH

Katharine Burr Blodgett

(1898–1979)

On this day in 1938, American physicist Katharine Burr Blodgett patented an anti-reflective coating for glass which would revolutionize everything from windshields to camera lenses.

Blodgett had been the first woman awarded a doctorate in physics from Cambridge University and, at the age of twenty, the first female scientist at General Electric (GE). Researching techniques for applying ultrathin "monomolecular" coatings to glass and metal, she discovered that, at a certain thickness, these coatings cancel out reflection. She had invented "invisible glass," the world's first truly transparent glass. Her invention was of enormous benefit, not only for lenses and spectacles but also for submarine periscopes and airborne spy cameras. *Gone with the Wind* was the first movie filmed with "invisible glass" cameras. Blodgett also patented methods for creating smoke screens and for de-icing airplane wings.

On 13 June 1951, "Katharine Blodgett Day" was celebrated in her hometown of Schenectady, New York, where she lived in a so-called "Boston marriage," or lesbian partnership, with Gertrude Brown.

Golda Meir

(1898–1978)

On this day in 1969, Golda Meir was elected prime minister of Israel – the first and, to date, only woman to hold that office. Meir's family had emigrated from Ukraine to the US when she was eight. At eleven, she was already an activist, organizing the donation of schoolbooks to poorer students. In the 1920s, she and her husband emigrated to Palestine, then under British rule, where she became involved in trade unions and wider politics. After the Second World War, she advocated for a Jewish state and traveled around the US raising funds from American Jews. When Israel declared independence on 14 May 1948, Meir was one of only two women to sign the declaration.

Israel's "Iron Lady," she was in office in 1973 when neighboring Arab states launched a surprise attack on Israel on Yom Kippur, Judaism's holiest day. Although Israel defended itself, Meir was criticized by the left and the right for being poorly prepared for attack and resigned the following year. The nation's first prime minister, Ben-Gurion, apparently described Meir as "the only man" in his cabinet. "What amused me about that," she said, "is that he (or whoever invented the story) thought that this was the greatest compliment that could be paid to a woman."

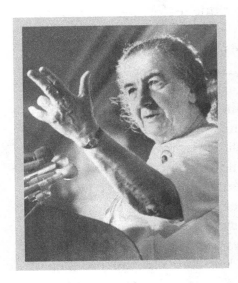

18 MARCH

Charlotte Carmichael Stopes (1840–1929)

In 1868, Charlotte Carmichael Stopes was one of the first women to enroll in university-level classes run by the Edinburgh Ladies' Educational Association, later becoming a Shakespearian scholar. Stopes was an active member of both the Rational Dress Society, which campaigned for dress reform (see "What are you wearing?"), and the National Union of Women's Suffrage Societies.

In 1894, she published *British Freewomen: Their Historical Privilege*, a pioneering work of feminist history. She wrote it to establish a British precedent for women's legal rights – in particular the right to vote. Stopes used and credited research by suffragist and women's rights campaigner Helen Blackburn, who had begun a similar project but had not had time to complete it. When the book was published, Blackburn purchased the whole first print run and sent many copies to members of the House of Commons.

British Freewomen became an invaluable tool for the women's suffrage movement. Activists quoted Stopes' arguments in speeches, in pamphlets and in the courtroom. She herself compared her work to a useful appliance: "Amongst the labour-saving devices of the day, may be classified collections of verified facts. I trust these may reach the hands of those for whom I write, *brave women* and *fair men*."

British Freewomen became an invaluable tool for the women's suffrage movement.

19 MARCH

Ida B. Wells-Barnett
(1862–1931)

African-American Ida B. Wells-Barnett, born into slavery six months before emancipation, became well known in 1884 after suing a railway company for segregating its carriages. She won (though the verdict was later overturned) and began her career in journalism by writing newspaper columns about her lawsuit. In March 1892, she turned her focus to lynching, becoming one of America's first investigative journalists. Her editorial denouncing the myth that black men raped white women – and calling lynching "a means to keep blacks down" – triggered a riot. The office of the Memphis newspaper she co-owned was destroyed and Wells-Barnett fled to Chicago, where she continued her activism.

On this day in 1898, she wrote to President McKinley asking that the murderers of a postmaster and his daughter be punished and the widow be supported. Thirteen white men were charged but a divided jury led to a mistrial.

Wells-Barnett traveled internationally, lecturing on lynching. She founded the National Association of Colored Women's Clubs and was co-founder of the National Association for the Advancement of Colored People. "Virtue knows no color line, and the chivalry which depends upon complexion of skin and texture of hair can command no honest respect."

20 MARCH

Jane Whorwood

(1612–1684)

Jane Whorwood was one of the most active agents for the Royalist cause during the English Civil War of 1642–49. On this day in 1648, she organized King Charles I's attempted escape from Carisbrooke Castle, where he was being held by Parliamentary forces. The attempt failed when the king got stuck trying to get through a window.

Whorwood knew London merchants who supported the king, and she passed information and money from them to the Royalist stronghold of Oxford.

In 1644, helped by an unnamed washerwoman, she smuggled 1,705 lbs of gold into the city in barrels of soap. This money paid for the future Charles II and his mother to escape to France. According to a spy for the Parliamentary side, Jane was "the most loyal to King Charles in his miseries of any woman in England."

After the defeat and execution of Charles I, Jane returned to her violent husband, whose behavior was extreme, even by the standards of the time. In 1657 she left him, securing a formal separation, and began a long legal case for what we would now call alimony. Her husband refused to pay the monies ordered by the court and Jane was left in relative poverty. She died, aged seventy-two, in 1684 – twenty-four years after Charles II was restored to the throne. "My travels, the variety of accidents (and especially dangers) more become a Romance than a letter."

The attempt failed when the king got stuck trying to get through a window.

21 MARCH

Dorothy Ashby
(1932–1986)

On this day in 1958, American harpist Dorothy Ashby recorded her album *Hip Harp*. Her classical instrument was widely seen as an eccentric choice for popular music: "The word 'harp' seemed to just scare people." Through skill and persistence she built up a following, bringing her genteel orchestral instrument into the jazz repertoire.

Ashby began her career as a pianist but found that jazz numbers scored for piano needed a very different approach on the harp. Her instrumentation was innovative and she became a renowned improvisational performer, often playing in bands with her drummer husband, John. Ashby made award-winning records and played with musicians including Louis Armstrong, Diana Ross, Stevie Wonder and Alice Coltrane.

Then, as now, the media expected female musicians to be attractive as well as talented –

"Often the harpists who got write-ups and the media coverage were very pretty, and that seemed to be about all that they were interested in," said Ashby. In a 1983 interview she spoke of the difficulties she faced in achieving recognition: "The audiences I was trying to reach were not interested in the harp, period – classical or otherwise – and they were certainly not interested in seeing a black woman playing the harp."

22 MARCH

Anbara Salam Khalidi

(1897–1986)

Anbara Salam Khalidi was an activist, writer and translator who advanced the cause of women's equality in the Arab world. Born in Beirut, Lebanon, to a family of intellectuals and Muslim scholars, Khalidi was fifteen when she wrote her first editorial, about the vital role to be played by women in the nation's renaissance. Later, with female friends, she founded a society, The Awakening of the Young Arabic Woman, to help girls finance their education.

In 1925, Khalidi moved to Britain. She was struck by how different women's lives were; they were beginning to play a role in public life and some had recently gained the vote. Khalidi translated Homer's *Odyssey* and Virgil's *Aeneid* from English into Arabic: she was the first person to do so. While in Britain she wore Western clothes and no veil.

After two years, Khalidi returned to Lebanon. She had come to see the veil as "a prison, preventing women from advancing in the world." In 1928, invited to lecture at the American University in Beirut, she mounted the speaker's podium and removed her veil; the first Muslim woman in Lebanon to do this in a public place. Her action, an echo of Huda Sha'arawi's famous veil removal in 1923, prompted violent street protests. But Khalidi continued to write and protest for women's rights.

Lizzie Magie

(1866–1948)

For seventy years, the story behind the board game Monopoly was that an unemployed man, Charles Darrow, had invented it, selling it to Parker Brothers and becoming a millionaire. But its real inventor was Lizzie Magie, a secretary, who applied for a patent on this day in 1903 for her *Landlord's Game*, created to demonstrate the evils of monopolies. Intended as "a practical demonstration of the present system of land-grabbing, with all its usual outcomes and consequences," the game became popular across the US, in particular in New Jersey's Quaker community, which is where Darrow got hold of it, passing it off as his own.

The original game had two sets of rules: an anti-monopolist set, in which everyone benefited from the creation of wealth, and a monopolist set, in which a player's goal was to set up monopolies and beat opponents. It was the monopolist set of rules that were used by Parker Brothers. Monopoly became a global sensation, licensed in over 100 countries, but Parker Brothers never gave Magie any credit or royalties. The company later struck a deal with her to purchase her patent and two other game ideas, which were never made. It wasn't until 1973, when Parker Brothers sued someone for producing a game called "Anti-Monopoly," that Magie's role as the game's creator finally came to light.

> But its real inventor was Lizzie Magie, a secretary, who applied for a patent on this day in 1903 for her *Landlord's Game*.

24 MARCH

Mary Ann Cotton

(1832–1873)

Mary Ann Cotton grew up in County Durham, England. Her father, a coal miner, was killed in an accident when she was fourteen. Her mother remarried and opened a school; Mary Ann taught there for a few years before her first marriage, to William Mowbray.

Most of Cotton's children with Mowbray died in infancy, possibly of natural causes. Mowbray himself died young, not long after taking out life insurance, from which Cotton collected £30. This pattern was to be repeated several times over her lifetime. In total, 21 people close to Cotton died, including three of her four husbands and eleven of her thirteen children and stepchildren.

In August 1872, a workhouse overseer became suspicious when a comment made by Cotton about her stepson Charles, "I won't be troubled long," was followed a week later by his death. The post-mortem discovered traces of arsenic in Charles's stomach. When more of Cotton's family members were exhumed and shown to have been poisoned with arsenic, she was charged with murder. As she was pregnant at the time, her trial was postponed until after the birth, finally beginning on 5 March 1873. She was found guilty. On this day in 1873, Mary Ann Cotton was hanged in Durham prison; she took three minutes to die.

25 MARCH

Florence Lawrence

(1886–1938)

On this day in 1910, Florence Lawrence became the world's first movie star to be mobbed by adoring crowds. Only a few weeks before, Lawrence – who starred in over 300 films – had been the first film actor publicly named, having previously been known only as "Biograph Girl," after her studio. Silent film actors had not been named because studio owners thought anonymity would prevent them demanding higher salaries.

Lawrence's unveiling was a stunt concocted by movie mogul Carl Laemmle. Spreading a rumor that Lawrence had died in an accident, he then published advertisements entitled "We Nail a Lie," reassuring the public that Miss Lawrence – using her name for the first time – was fine and would star in his new film. He arranged for her to appear in St. Louis on 25 March; the crowd was so excited they tore the buttons off her coat.

Lawrence was also the first actor to get a film credit, later that year; Florence Turner, the "Vitagraph Girl," was also named at around the same time. Lawrence had been performing since she was three years old. She was also a suffragist, one of the first women with her own production company and an inventor: her "auto signalling arm" was an early version of a car indicator. But with the advent of "talkies," her popularity faded.

26 MARCH

Dorothy Arzner

(1897–1979)

On this day in 1927, Dorothy Arzner's first film, *Fashions for Women*, was released. One of the few female directors during Hollywood's "Golden Age," from the 1920s to the early 1940s, she made three silent movies and fourteen "talkies."

Arzner grew up in Hollywood. After typing scripts for the Famous Players-Lasky Corporation (later Paramount), she worked as a cutter and editor on fifty-two films. Given the opportunity to direct, she made four successful silent feature films – *Fashions for Women* (1927), *Ten Modern Commandments* (1927), *Get Your Man* (1927) and *Manhattan Cocktail* (1928). Arzner was also asked to direct the studio's first sound film, *The Wild Party* (1929), starring Clara Bow, the silent version of which she had edited.

When the Directors Guild of America was established in 1933, Arzner became the first – and for many years, only – woman

member. Her movies often featured strong women. Her final film, *First Comes Courage*, released during the Second World War, told the story of a woman working for the Norwegian resistance and inspired the earliest feminist film criticism.

Arzner, a lesbian, refused to be categorized as a female or gay director. "No one gave me trouble because I was a woman. Men were more helpful than women."

Frieda Belinfante

(1904–1995)

When the Second World War began, Dutch cellist and conductor Frieda Belinfante, who was half Jewish, joined a resistance group, creating forged documents to help Jews escape. On this day in 1943, she took part in the bombing of Amsterdam's population registry to prevent the Nazis from identifying the forgeries. After the attack, which destroyed thousands of files, group members were forced into hiding. Belinfante disguised herself as a man, living with friends for three months before she fled to Montreux, Switzerland, where she was given refugee status.

Belinfante had begun playing the cello at the age of ten; she started conducting after graduating from the Amsterdam Conservatory. In 1937, she had been invited to direct Amsterdam's Concertgebouw, becoming Europe's first female artistic director of a professional orchestra. After emigrating to the US in 1947, she formed and conducted the Orange County Philharmonic Society in California.

In 1962, financial pressures, sexual discrimination and rumors about her sexuality – she was a lesbian – resulted in the orchestra canceling her contract. She withdrew from public life and taught music in private. In 1987, Orange County named 19 February "Frieda Belinfante Day" for "her many contributions to the musical community."

Yaa Asantewaa

(c.1840–1921)

Yaa Asantewaa was a heroic leader who led her people in a great uprising against the British Empire. The African nation then called Ashanti (present-day Ghana) was rich in gold. By the 1890s, the colonizing British were ready to take it by force. They captured and exiled King Prempeh but overlooked the importance of the *asantehemaa*, or queen mother, in Ashanti politics. Yaa Asantewaa was the *asantehemaa* at this time: with the king in exile, she ruled as regent.

In summer 1900, the British Governor-General, Frederick Hodgson, publicly demanded that he should occupy the Golden Stool, sacred throne and symbol of the Ashanti. Yaa Asantewaa now had a pretext to unite her outraged chiefs and spur them on.

In the subsequent war, Yaa Asantewaa directed military operations. Hodgson and his forces were besieged for three months, almost dying of starvation. They escaped, but Yaa Asantewaa continued a guerrilla campaign. The British gained ground, and over sixty Ashanti leaders surrendered or were taken in battle. Yaa Asantewaa remained at large. She was finally captured in November 1900 and her defeated nation became a part of the British Gold Coast. Yaa Asantewaa died in exile in 1921. After decades as a colony, the new nation of Ghana gained its independence in 1957.

Katherine Routledge

(1866–1935)

On this day in 1914, British anthropologist Katherine Routledge first set eyes on Easter Island, one of the most remote settlements on earth. She was the first to thoroughly document the island's statues, people and culture.

Routledge and her husband, Scoresby, had previously studied African communities. Arbitrarily choosing Easter Island for their next project, they built a schooner, crewed it with Devonshire fishermen and traveled for a year and four days to reach it. Once there, Routledge and her team recorded the massive sculptures and carvings. At least once, Routledge was forced to take refuge from the islanders and, after the outbreak of the First World War, the expedition became more precarious still. German cruisers used Easter Island as an occasional base; their crews were a threatening presence, even telling Routledge that Germany had won the war in Europe.

Routledge returned to England in 1916. Her book, *The Mystery of Easter Island*, made the effigies famous but she felt that her work was overlooked by her peers. She became mentally ill, barricading herself into her home. Eventually, her estranged husband, Scoresby, kidnapped her and had her admitted to an asylum, where she died in 1935. Her field notes, lost for many years, are now the subject of ongoing study.

Anne Lister (1791–1840) and Ann Walker (1803–1854)

On this day in 1834, Anne Lister (pictured) and Ann Walker took communion in the tiny medieval church of Holy Trinity, Goodramgate in York, England, in what is now considered the first lesbian wedding. The women had exchanged rings a month or so before; they saw taking the sacrament together as a commitment to each other before God.

We know about this event from Lister's twenty-three-volume diary. Its entries cover her experiences as a landowner, businesswoman and traveler, but also include sections in "crypt hand" in which Lister discusses her sexuality and sexual encounters.

Lister was known as "Gentleman Jack"; she had a "masculine" manner, dressed only in black and lived with a freedom unknown to most women of her day. After their "wedding," Walker, a rich heiress, lived with Lister at her property, Shibden Hall.

Lister died aged forty-nine, leaving Walker a life interest in the Shibden estate. However, the Walker family had Ann declared insane and sent her to an asylum in York. She died at her childhood home, Cliffe Hill, aged fifty-one.

The first legally recognized lesbian and gay marriages in the UK took place on 29 March 2014, almost exactly 180 years after Lister and Walker made their vows to each other.

31 MARCH

Cecilia Payne-Gaposchkin
(1900–1979)

Put off from studying physics in the early 1920s by attitudes towards women in science, Cecilia Payne-Gaposchkin turned to astronomy.

Payne-Gaposchkin passed all her final exams at Cambridge University but, as a woman, was not awarded an actual degree. She later recalled that women were given a certificate saying, in effect, "if you had been a man, you would have got a BA." With no research opportunities open to her in the UK, in 1923 she secured a fellowship at the Harvard College Observatory in the US.

In 1925, Payne-Gaposchkin published her PhD thesis, in which she proposed that stars are made mainly of hydrogen and helium and could be classified according to their temperatures. She concluded that hydrogen is the overwhelming constituent of stars and therefore the most abundant element in the universe. Her research was initially rubbished, but observations eventually supported her work, it was even described as "the most brilliant PhD thesis ever written in astronomy."

In 1956, Payne-Gaposchkin became the first woman at Harvard College to become a full professor and the first to chair a department. To celebrate, she organized a party in the Observatory Library and sent handwritten invitations to all the female astronomy students.

APRIL

"Can't no man play like me.
I play better than a man."
– Sister Rosetta Tharpe

We are not a muse

Women in history books are often defined by their relationships with the men around them. One word in particular is used to describe a creative woman who lives and works with a creative man: she is his "muse." It sounds like praise – a muse exerts her mystical influence on the male artist or writer and helps him to make new work. She is a sort of spiritual battery pack. In fact, many of the people described in this way were actually peers and equals, moving in a circle of artists who informed one another's work. They were not accessories to someone else's talent; they were fellow practitioners.

An excellent example is Elizabeth Siddall, nineteenth-century painter and poet who famously posed for pre-Raphaelite artists and married Dante Gabriel Rossetti. She mixed with male artists and worked alongside them but is almost always described as their muse, not their colleague. There are many such women in this book. Lou Andreas-Salomé, an early psychoanalyst, socialized, studied and sometimes had affairs with men like Rilke, Nietzsche and Freud. Like her friends, Salomé was a key thinker and one of the first to establish psychoanalysis, yet she is usually remembered not in terms of her own work but by her friendships with these equally extraordinary men. Artist Leonor Fini is usually called a muse to Salvador Dali or Picasso, though they themselves recognized her as a fellow artist. Fini was part of their unconventional circle and, like them, had relationships with the people in it. The life story of photojournalist Martha Gellhorn – sometimes described as the muse of Ernest Hemingway, to whom she was briefly married – shows that even he was by no means the most interesting thing in her biography.

Gossip and intimate detail make up one of the most interesting aspects of history – but too often a woman's story is dominated by the men whom she married or worked with in a way which isn't applied in reverse. These women are more than two-dimensional backdrops onto which we can project someone else's life story; they should be remembered for their own work.

Whakaotirangi

(13th century CE)

In the thirteenth century, New Zealand was settled by Polynesian seafarers. Among them was a pioneering gardener called Whakaotirangi, whose experimental planting established new ways to grow traditional crops. Whakaotirangi had been involved in the commissioning and building of the great sea-going canoes and, once in New Zealand, her role in the settlement was vital to its success.

New Zealand's climate was far cooler than the Polynesian islands from which the settlers came. Familiar crops or medicine plants had to be grown in new ways and substitutes found for those that did not thrive. In the canoes, Whakaotirangi stowed a cargo of roots and seeds, including the kūmara or sweet potato, taro root, mulberry and the karaka fruit. She may have established a garden at Hawaiki Nui for trialing new techniques and crops.

Whakaotirangi's importance was overlooked in early histories of New Zealand. Like all historians, including ourselves, the men writing these narratives brought their own prejudices to the task (see The language of history). Modern scholars Diane Gordon-Burns and Rāwiri Taonui explain that, "When European ethnographers asked Māori about their tribal traditions, they tended to question men; colonisation diminished Whakaotirangi's fame as a heroine over time." Nonetheless, her expertise and foresight allowed her to begin feeding a new nation.

"When European ethnographers asked Māori about their tribal traditions, they tended to question men. . ."

Rosa Matilda Richter
"Zazel the Human Cannonball"
(1863–1937)

On this day in 1877, acrobat and tightrope artiste Rosa Richter premiered a new aerial show at the London Aquarium, performing as "Zazel the Human Cannonball." In the show's finale, she was propelled, with a great explosion, some seventy feet into the air. She flew over the heads of the awestruck spectators before landing in a net.

The stunt was the creation of Richter's employer, William Leonard Hunt, the first person to cross Niagara Falls on a high-wire. "Zazel's" flight was caused by mechanics – the explosion of the cannon was pure theatrical effect – but the act was still incredibly dangerous. The show drew audiences of thousands.

In 1880, the House of Commons discussed whether such dangerous stunts should be banned. Richter gave her response: "They'd just no right to take away me living if I loved it. I was ambitious. I wanted to be great. You see, it was me art."

Richter and Hunt left England and toured their show in the US with PT Barnum's circus.

Richter also campaigned for the use of nets as life-saving tools, not just in stunts but also for the safety of people who lived in large buildings; she was thanked for this work by the New York Fire Department. In 1891, Richter broke her back in a tightrope accident, ending her amazing career.

3 APRIL

Georgia O'Keeffe

(1887–1986)

On this day in 1917, Georgia O'Keeffe's first solo show opened at New York's 291 gallery. Her unique painting style made her a force in American art; she has been called the "mother of modernism." Talented from childhood, she was top of her 1905 class at the School of the Art Institute in Chicago.

The art world of the time valued faithful representation of the real world but O'Keeffe wanted new ways of working in a rapidly changing nation – "Nothing is less real than realism," she later said. She sought out new teachers and influences. By 1915, her work was largely abstract. Her paintings became bold, colorful and uniquely American.

O'Keeffe often worked from the landscapes of Texas and New Mexico, or the cityscape of New York, but her best-known works are vivid, close-up abstracts based on flowers and natural forms. One of them, *Jimson Weed*, sold in 2014 for $44 million, vastly exceeding the previous record for any work by a woman. Many have seen these flower pictures as metaphors for the female body, but O'Keeffe consistently rejected the idea.

Troubled by mental illness and the deterioration of her eyesight, she stopped painting in oils around 1972. In 1977 she was awarded the Presidential Medal of Freedom, the highest honor for an American citizen.

> "I've been absolutely terrified every moment of my life and I've never let it keep me from doing a single thing that I wanted to do."

4 APRIL

Raisa Sumachevskaia

(unknown)

In April 1943, Soviet fighter pilot Raisa Sumachevskaia, along with comrade in arms Tamara Pamiatnykh, was scrambled from her air base to deter German "reconnaissance planes," which actually proved to be a bombing mission. There were forty-two enemy aircraft in total, including two groups of bombers and their escort of fighter planes. The fleet's intended target was a railway junction, where Soviet troops and fuel supplies were concentrated. The two women flew into the mass of planes, dispersed the mission and shot down four aircraft.

The Soviet Air Force was the only one known to employ women as fighter pilots in the Second World War; the 586th Fighter Aviation Regiment, to which Sumachevskaia belonged, was nicknamed "Stalin's Falcons." After the war, despite their distinguished service, Sumachevskaia and her fellow female pilots were expected to stay at home and resume their domestic life.

Their commander, Aleksandr Gridnev, reported that the two pilots were sent inscribed gold watches by the King of England as a congratulatory gesture, "but our own people never even found the time to give them the Hero of the Soviet Union medal. I believe this is one of the most distinguished victories of the entire war. They should hang two gold stars on each of them for this."

The two women flew into the mass of planes, dispersed the mission and shot down four aircraft.

5 APRIL

Sister Rosetta Tharpe
(1915–1973)

On this day in 2004, the US Library of Congress added Sister Rosetta Tharpe's recording of "Down by the Riverside" to the National Recording Registry. Tharpe, who began recording hits in the 1930s, is considered the godmother of rock 'n' roll.

Tharpe had mastered the guitar by the age of six when, billed as "a singing and guitar playing miracle," she began performing with her mother in a traveling evangelical troupe. When they moved to Chicago, she became known as a musical prodigy, accompanying her mother – a constant presence throughout her life – as she preached. In 1938, they moved to New York where Tharpe landed a gig at The Cotton Club. She made her first recording in that same year, aged twenty-three, becoming an overnight sensation with songs such as "Rock Me" and "My Man and I."

Tharpe's signature style combined Delta blues, New Orleans jazz and gospel music with powerful vocals, a unique electric guitar sound and lyrics that were often shocking in their openness about sex and love. She was a huge influence on Elvis, Chuck Berry and others.

> "Can't no man play like me. I play better than a man."

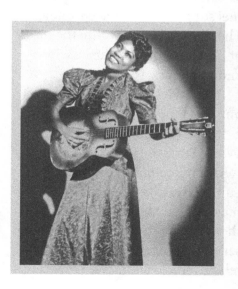

June Tarpé Mills

(1918–1988)

On this day in 1941, comic book hero The Black Fury (later Miss Fury) appeared in print for the first time. She was the first female action hero in comic strips, predating Wonder Woman by a few months. Miss Fury was the work of artist June Tarpé Mills who operated, like her creation, under a pseudonym, using her non-gendered middle name, Tarpé, to escape prejudice in a male-dominated industry. "It would have been a major let-down to the kids if they found out that the author of such virile and awesome characters was a gal," she said later. Mills's earlier creations included The White Goddess, The Blue Zombie and Daredevil Barry Finn.

Miss Fury, who looked very much like her creator, was the first of several "debutante" superheroes. These characters were unmarried and independently wealthy. They had sleuthing skills, physical strength and powers of disguise.

They were not to be "fridged" – killed off – in order to spur a male hero to greater feats of derring-do. These imagined women had opportunities for adventure unmatched by the real women of 1940s America.

Mills had worked in fashion and her characters were always stylishly dressed. Miss Fury's provocative wardrobe included a whip, spiked heels and an enchanted panther suit, but it was her appearance in a bikini that earned her a ban from thirty-seven newspapers in 1947.

These imagined women had opportunities for adventure unmatched by the real women of 1940s America.

Maria Goeppert Mayer

(1906–1972)

In April 1950, German physicist Maria Goeppert Mayer published her revolutionary model of how the nucleus, the heart of every atom, is structured in layers or "shells." Nicknamed the "Onion Madonna," she became the second woman to win a Nobel Prize in Physics for her discovery.

Mayer and her husband, Joseph, a chemist, moved to the US in the 1930s. Johns Hopkins University gave him a job but refused to hire Maria, even though she had a physics PhD. While doing research as a "volunteer associate," she became so highly thought of that, when the Second World War began, she was invited to join the Manhattan Project, working on the atomic bomb (see Chien Shiung Wu). Nevertheless, when the couple moved to Chicago, Mayer could only find part-time work.

Intrigued by the theory of "magic numbers" of particles in the nucleus, Mayer proved that they are arranged in a shell structure, contradicting the prevailing theory of a "soup" of particles. She jointly won the 1963 Nobel Prize with Eugene Wigner and Hans Jensen – after finally becoming a full professor just three years earlier. In a speech to a group of high school girls, she urged them to "become fully educated women and promote the understanding of science . . . My generation has played its part. It is up to you to carry on."

8 APRIL

Lucy Townsend

(1781–1847)

On this day in 1825, in Birmingham, UK, British abolitionist Lucy Townsend and her friend, Mary Lloyd, founded the Ladies' Society for the Relief of Negro Slaves. It quickly found a notable place in the worldwide campaign to abolish slavery.

The transatlantic slave trade had technically been outlawed in 1807. Abolitionists now shifted their focus towards freeing enslaved people in the US and in British colonies. Townsend's society boycotted sugar, which was produced by enslaved labor. It published pamphlets and petitions; its meetings brought together Christian women of all classes and denominations. Following Townsend's example, dozens of similar groups sprang up in the UK and the US. The emancipation campaign brought women together in large numbers to organize, communicate and influence public opinion. They learned much from earlier activists like Mary Fildes and set an example for women in later efforts, such as the suffragette movement and labor unions.

Townsend published a tract, *To the Law and to the Testimony*, in 1832. The following year, the Slavery Abolition Act was passed, freeing over 800,000 Africans in British colonies – though most continued in near-enslavement for many years.

In 1840, Townsend attended the World Anti-Slavery Convention. Despite her prominence, she was not shown in the official painting of delegates. Fellow activist Anne Knight was indignant at her exclusion – Lucy Townsend, she said, was "the chief lady" of the abolitionist movement.

Jane Jacobs

(1916–2006)

On this day in 1956, Jane Jacobs spoke at the Harvard Urban Design conference. It was one routine appearance in an extraordinary career. Jacobs was a theorist who, like many influential women, worked outside the usual professions. Her writings, including her 1961 book *The Death and Life of Great American Cities*, changed the shape of cities across the world.

Jacobs felt that cities in post-war America were losing their sense of community. Developers put up towering buildings with car-friendly architecture and little green space. Cities were designed for industry and transport, not for families and social activity. Although she was not a qualified architect or town planner, she became a celebrated authority on urban design.

In her home city of New York, Jacobs joined others to oppose a destructive highway. She argued for low-rise, pedestrian-friendly streets with a mix of businesses, where people could meet and local neighborhoods flourish. Critics say that Jacobs's style favors the white middle classes and leads to gentrification of working-class areas. Nonetheless, her vision was massively influential; according to writer PE Moskowitz, "She was to her field what Freud was to psychology."

10 APRIL

Elizabeth Nihell

(1723–1776)

Today we remember Elizabeth Nihell, English midwife and one of the earliest known women to write about midwifery. Nihell spent her career working in London in the mid-eighteenth century, at a time when female midwives found themselves in competition with male doctors. Nihell saw these doctors as lacking in empathy and far too eager to intervene in childbirth with instruments such as forceps.

After attending over 900 births, in 1760, Nihell published *A Treatise on the Art of Midwifery Setting Forth Various Abuses Therein, Especially as to the Practice with Instruments*, which advocated for natural births: "Nothing can be more important to the well-being of the patient, than for non-violence to be used to Nature, who loves to go her own full time, without disturbance or molestation." She mocked male midwives, calling them "self-constituted men-midwives made out of broken barbers, tailors, or even pork-butchers." Nihell responded to critics, calling one a "buffoon" in her 1772 book *The Danger and Immodesty of the Present Too General Customs of Unnecessarily Employing Men-Midwives*. After her surgeon husband abandoned her – perhaps because of her dedication to her cause – Nihell spent the final year of her life in poverty, dying in a workhouse.

11 APRIL

Margery Kempe
(c.1373 – after 1438)

Margery Kempe was an English Christian mystic and businesswoman of the Middle Ages. Her life story, *The Book of Margery Kempe*, is the first known autobiography in English. This extraordinary book allows intimate access to a medieval woman's public and inner life.

After having the first of fourteen children, Kempe experienced torments and visions. Nowadays we might recognize this as psychosis, but Kempe understood them as divine revelations. Her marriage was unhappy, partly due to her wish for a celibate life, which she tells us she discussed with her husband. Kempe was briefly a brewer and then a miller, but later followed her spiritual calling. She made long pilgrimages in England, Europe and the Middle East, visiting the famous anchoress, Julian of Norwich, around 1413.

Religious dissent and preaching, especially by women, was harshly punished at this time; Kempe was frequently arrested for her preaching and her incessant public wailing.

The Book of Margery Kempe, lost for centuries, was rediscovered in 1934 by American medievalist Hope Emily Allen. It has suffered the fate of many women's texts in history: its authorship has been doubted and its reliability challenged in ways which are seldom applied to male authors. Some scholars dwell on the fact that Kempe didn't "write" her book but dictated it to a scribe. This is rather like criticizing Ernest Hemingway for writing his novels on a typewriter; like most medieval people of all stations in life, Kempe could not write. She used the available technology to record her moving insights into medieval private and spiritual life.

Rania al-Baz

(1975–)

On this day in 2004, Saudi TV host Rania al-Baz was beaten into a coma by her husband. The next time viewers of *The Kingdom this Morning* saw her was in the newspapers, her face bruised and barely recognizable.

Baz's husband had slammed her face repeatedly against a marble floor until he thought she was dead. When she showed signs of life, he took her to the hospital. While Baz was in a coma, her father took photographs of his daughter's face with its thirteen fractures. When she decided to allow the pictures to be published, it was the first time a woman in Saudi Arabia had so publicly broken the silence around the accepted culture of domestic violence: "I wanted to be some kind of window into what is actually happening to women in my country."

A princess from the Saudi royal family paid Baz's medical bills to show support. But there were also suggestions that Baz had somehow brought this on herself by being a celebrity; that she had "betrayed" her husband by speaking out.

Baz's husband was sentenced to 300 lashes and six months in jail, though his prison term was halved when Baz pardoned him as part of a settlement to gain custody of her children. Without an offer to return to television, Baz nevertheless refused to return to silence; in 2005 she published a memoir and appeared on *Oprah*.

"I wanted to be some kind of window into what is actually happening to women in my country."

13 APRIL

Leonor Fini

(1907–1996)

Leonor Fini was an important artist of the twentieth century who helped to shape the taste of her times. In April 1937, she designed the iconic bottle for Schiaparelli's "Shocking" perfume – a wasp-waisted torso shape revisited by Jean Paul Gaultier in the 1990s.

Fini never called herself a surrealist but was a vital part of the surrealist circle in 1930s Paris. Her own paintings are often fantastical or abstract with an atmosphere of myth and macabre sexuality. Some were hung in the seminal exhibition "Fantastic Art, Dada and Surrealism" at New York's Museum of Modern Art in 1936 alongside works by contemporaries like Georgia O'Keeffe, Magritte and Giacometti. Fini's work appeared in film and theatre design, book illustration and applied arts.

Her private life was as unconventional as her art. Fini was openly bisexual, and for the last forty-four years of her life

lived in a *ménage à trois*. Her wide circle of artist friends included dancer Margot Fonteyn, artist Leonora Carrington and other famous creators. She is frequently described as a "muse," "inspiration" or simply "lover" of fellow artists (Dali, Cartier-Bresson and Picasso in this case) for whom she was in fact a colleague and a friend (see We are not a muse).

Alice Guy-Blaché

(1873-1968)

The forerunner of all modern movies was directed in April 1896 by Frenchwoman Alice Guy-Blaché – one of the first film directors and a pioneer in cinematography. She wrote or produced over 700 films, yet her name seldom appears in lists of early film-makers alongside her male peers.

The first ever moving picture had been made by Louis le Prince in 1888. Since then, film had been used only for real or staged "live action" scenes. Guy-Blaché's April 1896 creation was a short fantasy less than a minute long, called *La Fée aux Choux* ("The Cabbage Fairy"). It is the first film to tell a scripted story. Guy-Blaché also made the first film with an all-black cast – *A Fool and His Money* – which present-day viewers will find full of racist caricatures.

Guy-Blaché was head of production at Gaumont for ten years but, like many working women of the time, was compelled to resign when she married. She moved to America with her husband and co-founded Solax, the largest pre-Hollywood studio in the world. Their venture ended in divorce, bankruptcy and Guy-Blaché's return to France, where she wrote an autobiography. Her creative work was at the heart of a new art form and a global industry. A sign in her office offered advice for all in early film-making: "Be natural."

15 APRIL

Josephine Blatt (1869–1923) and Katie Sandwina (1884–1952)

In the late nineteenth and early twentieth centuries, women were part of the booming entertainment industry in Britain and the US, not only in theatres but also in the circus and music hall. Strongwoman Josephine Blatt – with the stage name "Minerva" – broke horseshoes with her hands and caught cannon balls fired from thirty feet away.

On this day in 1895, at the Bijou Theatre, New Jersey, Minerva harnessed herself to a platform holding twenty-three men. It weighed 3,564 lbs in total and she lifted it off the floor: the greatest weight ever publicly lifted by a woman.

At a time when women were fighting for more influence within society, such spectacles of strength made some uneasy: "The anti-suffragists who [see strongwoman Katie Sandwina] lift her husband and two-year-old son with one arm, tremble . . ." In March 1812, the Suffragette Ladies of the Barnum

& Bailey Circus – the world's first circus suffrage society – staged a rally in Madison Square Garden, New York. Their president was circus rider Josie de Mott, their vice-president was Katie Sandwina (pictured). Suffragists from the Woman's Political Union stated: "There is no class of woman who show better that they have a right to vote than the circus woman, who twice a day prove that they have the courage and endurance of men . . ."

16 APRIL

Aphra Behn

(c.1640–1689)

Much of the early life of playwright and novelist Aphra Behn is a mystery. Perhaps this was deliberate on her part. In the 1660s, working as King Charles II's spy, she was sent to Antwerp to turn an exiled enemy into a double agent. Typically, the king refused to pay her. Behn, sent to debtors' prison after borrowing funds to get home, vowed never to depend on anyone for money again.

The first woman in England to make a living by writing (see Susanna Centlivre), Behn wrote plays, poems and novels, becoming a major literary figure. At a time when respectable women were expected to be modest, she wrote about sex and politics – her novel *Oroonoko* concerns an African prince tricked into slavery and sold to British colonists.

Behn especially valued the power of poetry, "A poet is a painter in his way . . . the pictures of the pen shall outlast those of the pencil, and even worlds themselves."

Buried in Westminster Abbey on this day in 1689, Behn's reputation declined after her death. Her vital role in the development of English literature would be resurrected almost 300 years later by English novelist Virginia Woolf, who said: "All women together ought to let flowers fall upon the tomb of Aphra Behn, for it was she who earned them the right to speak their minds."

Baroness Elsa von Freytag-Loringhoven (1874–1927)

In 2004, *Fountain*, the porcelain urinal which launched the field of "readymades" – sculptures made of items from daily life – was voted the most influential modern artwork of all time. Yet it may not have been created by Marcel Duchamp, the French artist to whom it was attributed. An April 1917 letter from Duchamp to his sister implies that it was actually the colorful German avant-garde artist and poet Baroness Elsa von Freytag-Loringhoven who submitted the urinal, under a pseudonym, to a New York exhibition. Although she never publicly claimed *Fountain*, her piece, *Enduring Ornament* (1913), a rusted metal ring, was labeled as art a year before Duchamp created his first "readymade."

Von Freytag-Loringhoven's life is the stuff of fiction. As a teenager, she ran away to act in Berlin's vaudeville theatres before several affairs took her across Europe, where she helped her second husband fake suicide. After a brief marriage to a baron in New York, she became a vital part of the Dada movement, legendary not just for her sculptures and poetry but also for her outfits and seduction techniques. Her often bizarre sculptures were sometimes incorporated into pieces of clothing. Von Freytag-Loringhoven, who lived in poverty, was frequently arrested for shoplifting.

Émilie du Châtelet

(1706–1749)

Her mother wanted to send Gabrielle Émilie Le Tonnelier de Breteuil, Marquise du Châtelet, to a convent. But her father intervened, allowing her to join his salon of writers and scientists and arranging for her to be taught many subjects. In 1740, du Châtelet published the groundbreaking *Institutions de Physique* ("Foundations of Physics"). Her translation of Isaac Newton's *Principia Mathematica*, with commentary, played a vital part in the scientific revolutions that followed.

Du Châtelet had an affair with French philosopher Voltaire, who encouraged her to focus on science. When du Châtelet published *Institutions de Physique*, she presented it as something she intended to use to teach physics to her son – a typical way for learned women to publish without impropriety (see Maria Gaetana Agnesi). The book caused controversy due to her unique synthesis of ideas from mathematicians and philosophers such as Newton, Descartes and Leibnitz. Tired of responding to criticism, until her death at the age of forty-two du Châtelet focused on translating Newton's *Principia* from Latin into French, making Newton's maths more accessible and extracting the implications for gravity and energy. Einstein's most famous equation, $E=mc^2$, can be directly traced back to her work.

19 APRIL

Dorothée Pullinger

(1894-1986)

Dorothée Pullinger persuaded her father to let her train as an engineer, but in 1914, when she applied to join the Institution of Automobile Engineers, she was refused, on the grounds that "the word person [in their constitution] means a man and not a woman." During the First World War, Pullinger was appointed "lady superintendent manager," responsible for 7,000 female munitions workers making high explosive shells. In 1919, she became a founding member of the Women's Engineering Society; in 1920, she was awarded the MBE for her war work.

Pullinger became director and manager of Galloway Motors Ltd near Kirkcudbright, Scotland, a car factory and pioneering engineering college for women. The factory logo used suffragette colors; there were tennis courts on the roof. In 1921, the first "Galloway" was produced, designed by Pullinger as "a car for women built by others of their sex." Two years later, she was finally accepted into the Institution of Automobile Engineers but by the mid-1920s she was facing hostility in the car industry because of her sex. So, with her husband, she set up White Service Laundries Ltd in Croydon: "I thought washing should not be doing men out of a job."

During the Second World War, Pullinger returned to engineering, managing thirteen munitions factories and supervising the recruitment and employment of female workers; she was the only woman appointed to the Ministry of Production's industrial panel. In 2012, she became the first woman to be inducted (posthumously) into the Scottish Engineering Hall of Fame.

20 APRIL

Gertrude Caton-Thompson

(1888–1985)

It was a trip to Egypt with her mother in 1911, and a British Museum course on Ancient Greece, that inspired Gertrude Caton-Thompson's interest in archaeology. After volunteering as a "bottle washer" at a Paleolithic excavation in France, Caton-Thompson studied Arabic, paleontology, surveying and Egyptology.

In April 1928, she led the first all-female excavation team to study the ruins of a stone city in Zimbabwe. With her were geologist Elinor Wight Gardner, archaeologist Kathleen Kenyon and architect Dorothy Noire. Their conclusions – that the stone city was built by a native African population rather than another people – caused great controversy. Caton-Thompson apparently kept hostile letters from local experts in a file marked "Insane."

Caton-Thompson also pioneered new techniques: she was amongst the first to use air surveys to locate archaeological sites and she took a scientific approach to her digs, excavating in six-inch levels and recording the exact position of each artifact. The first woman to receive the Rivers Medal from the Royal Anthropological Institute, Caton-Thompson became its vice president in 1944.

21 APRIL

Recy Taylor

(1919-2017)

In September 1944, twenty-four-year-old African-American Recy Taylor was walking back from church in Abbeville, Alabama, when she was forced into a car by seven white men armed with knives and shotguns. They drove her to a wooded area and raped her, threatening to cut her throat if she screamed. Taylor and her father reported the rape to the county sheriff. In the following days, one of the men confessed and named the six others involved. None of them was arrested.

When the story reached the Montgomery office of the National Association for the Advancement of Colored People (NAACP), they sent a sexual violence investigator to Abbeville. Her name was Rosa Parks (see Claudette Colvin). The white sheriff didn't want this "troublemaker" around; Parks was told to leave town on several occasions and was once forcibly removed. But Parks launched the Alabama Committee for Equal Justice for Mrs. Recy Taylor and got the story into the newspapers. In response to public outrage, the case was heard twice, but on each occasion the jury refused to formally charge the rapists with their crime.

Sixty-five years later, historian Danielle L McGuire brought Taylor's case back into the news with her book *At the Dark End of the Street*. On this day in 2011, the Alabama Legislature issued an official apology to Recy Taylor for the state's "morally abhorrent and repugnant" failure to prosecute the men who attacked and abused her. She was ninety-one years old.

Nell Gwyn

(c.1650–1687)

Nell Gwyn was a seventeenth-century star actor whose comic performances helped to popularize the work of Dryden and Fletcher. From 1649 to 1660, England's Puritan government banned entertainments including plays, but when Charles II returned to the throne in 1660 the London theatres reopened. For the first time, real women played the female roles which had formerly been acted by men.

Gwyn, an orange-seller at the King's Theatre, trained for the stage; by 1665 she was a star. She was particularly well-loved in "gay couple" plays, which pitted a fashionable bachelor and a clever woman against each other. The diarist Samuel Pepys saw her in *The Maiden Queen* in 1667: "So great performance of a comical part was never, I believe, in the world before as Nell do this."

Soon after, Gwyn began a relationship with Charles II.

Previously involved with two other men called Charles, she joked that the king was her "Charles the Third." They had two sons. The king supported Gwyn and, after his death, his brother James II granted her an enormous pension of £1,500 per year. Gwyn was frank about the source of her wealth. When her servant began fighting a man who had called her a whore, Gwyn stopped him: "Why, you fool, all the world knows it!"

23 APRIL

Lubna of Cordoba

(10th century CE)

In the tenth century, the city of Cordoba in Spain was part of the multicultural empire of the Islamic Golden Age and a world center of invention, science, poetry and philosophy. Lubna of Cordoba was the head of the library in this cultural hub and thus one of its foremost citizens. Cordoba's library, built by the Caliph Abd al Rahman III, was the largest in Europe and one of the most important in the world, containing 400,000 books. Curating it was an astonishing achievement for a formerly enslaved woman who had been scribe and secretary to the caliph and his son before being promoted.

Some histories state that it was also Lubna's job to travel abroad – to Baghdad, Cairo, Damascus – to locate and buy new works for the library. However, writer Kamila Shamsie has suggested that this "Lubna" is the conflation of two women: the historical Lubna and a woman called Fatima, the purchaser of new books. Their identities might have been fused by historians to suggest that a woman having such a learned role was an anomaly. In fact, there were many female scholars – mathematicians, poets, grammarians – in tenth century Cordoba, which was home to 170 female scribes and manuscript copyists. In Shamsie's words, Lubna and Fatima were "neither everyday nor exceptional but somewhere in-between."

24 APRIL

Constance Markievicz

(1868–1927)

On the anniversary of the Easter Rising in April 1916, in which Irish Republicans rebelled against British rule, we remember one of its leaders, Constance Markievicz. In 1918, Markievicz became the first woman elected to the UK House of Commons, as a member of parliament for Dublin. In line with Sinn Féin policy, she did not take her seat.

Born in London, Markievicz trained as an artist before moving to Dublin in 1903. Becoming involved in nationalist politics, she joined the Sinn Féin party and Inghinidhe na hÉireann ("Daughters of Ireland"), a revolutionary women's movement. She was jailed for the first time in 1911 for speaking at a demonstration protesting King George V's visit to Ireland. During the Rising, Markievicz supervised the setting-up of barricades on Easter Monday and was involved in the fighting. The uprising was put down after six days; Markievicz was arrested and sentenced to life in prison. Transferred to jail in England, she was released in 1917 as part of a general amnesty. She was the first woman in Europe to hold a cabinet position, as Minister for Labour in the Irish Republic from 1919 to 1922.

Her advice to female rebels in 1916: "Dress suitably in short skirts and sitting boots, leave your jewels and gold wands in the bank, and buy a revolver."

25 APRIL

Nongqawuse
(c.1841–1898)

In April 1856, a Xhosa teenager called Nongqawuse, living in present-day South Africa, had a mystical vision while scaring birds from the village fields. Her prophecies inspired a strange apocalyptic movement, and a widespread famine.

In her vision, Nongqawuse saw the spirits of two ancestors, who perversely commanded that the Xhosa should destroy all of their own crops and cattle. This would put an end to the lung disease affecting many cattle, said the spirits; the dead would miraculously arise and the British colonizers who had already encroached on much of southern Africa would be wiped out. Nongqawuse's people would be rewarded with better yields, stronger cattle and the defeat of their enemies.

It's hard to understand how such a destructive prophecy gained any following. However, with the support of an influential chief, Nongqawuse's instructions were followed to the letter by thousands of Xhosa people. In the "cattle-killing frenzy" which ensued, they slaughtered up to 400,000 beasts. Having destroyed their own food supply, up to 75 per cent of the people of the region died of starvation. Far from being driven out, the British found that any meaningful resistance had been destroyed. Historian Helen Bradford quotes a Xhosa song lamenting the famine and the young woman whose visions caused it:

"Oh! Nongqawuse! The girl of Mhlakaza She killed our nation."

Jackie "Moms" Mabley
(1894 or 1897–1975)

"Ain't nothin' an old man can do for me but bring me a message from a young man," was one of Jackie "Moms" Mabley's most famous lines. Billed as the "Funniest Woman in the World," with a fifty-year career on stage, television and film, she influenced many of today's best-known comedians, including Whoopi Goldberg and Eddie Murphy.

Mabley, born Loretta Mary Aiken in North Carolina, was one of twelve children with mixed black, Irish and Cherokee heritage. Her showbusiness career began when she ran away from home aged fourteen. "I was pretty and didn't want to become a prostitute," she told audiences. In her twenties, she developed the stage persona that would make her famous: a woman of sixty with flappy clothes and a knitted hat, modeled on her formerly enslaved great-grandmother.

In April 1939, Mabley became the first female comic to perform at Harlem's renowned Apollo theatre, soon becoming a regular. "She was the highest-paid entertainer," said Whoopi Goldberg. "She made crazy money for the time." Her act was raunchy and pulled no punches when it came to commenting on racism and stereotypes. Although onstage she joked about men, Mabley had relationships with women and was called "Mr. Moms" by fellow comedians.

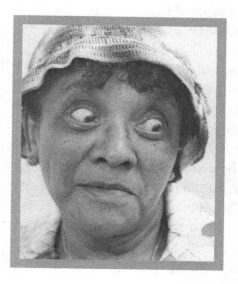

27 APRIL

Betty Boothroyd

(1929–)

On this day in 1992, after seven centuries of parliamentary government in the UK, Betty Boothroyd was elected the first female speaker of the House of Commons.

A working-class Yorkshire-woman and former member of the famous Tiller Girls dancing troupe, Boothroyd served her political apprenticeship in the 1950s. She was an assistant to influential Labour minister Barbara Castle and gained further experience in the US as an observer in John F. Kennedy's 1960 presidential campaign. Boothroyd was elected to Parliament on her fourth attempt in 1973 and was quickly trusted with positions of authority. In the two hotly contested elections of 1974, she was a party whip and she later became a member of the European Parliament.

Boothroyd remained Speaker until 2000, on one occasion using her casting vote to pass a clause of the Maastricht Treaty; she now sits in the House of Lords as Baroness Boothroyd of Sandwell. In a 2004 interview about her political career, she said: "I wanted to make changes. I wanted to have a peaceful revolution in the United Kingdom whereby people who came from my background, people from a "normal' background, hard-working, young people, had opportunities to fulfil themselves."

Anna Ivanovna

(Anna of Russia) (1693–1740)

On this day in 1730, Anna Ivanovna became Empress of Russia, at the age of thirty-seven. Her ten-year reign was described by a foreign minister as "comparable to a storm-threatened ship, manned by a pilot and crew who are all drunk or asleep."

Anna was invited to reign only after signing conditions imposed by the Supreme Privy Council. Once in power, she immediately dismissed the council and ruled as an absolute monarch. Sadly, she was not a talented strategist or politician. Anna's reign is often characterized as a dark age of corruption, cruelty and military failure. The Russian court she presided over was a place of brutal humor, where the powerful made fun of the disadvantaged or physically impaired. In the exceptionally harsh winter of 1739, Anna played an elaborate prank on an offending courtier. He was made to marry one of Anna's maids. The unfortunate bride and groom were dressed as clowns with an entourage of farm animals and so-called "undesirables," such as people with disabilities. They were imprisoned in a mock castle of carved ice, where they were expected to freeze to death; only by bribing a guard did the couple escape.

Sislin Fay Allen

(1939–)

On this day in 1968, Sislin Fay Allen took up her post at Fell Road Police Station, Croydon, becoming the first black policewoman in the UK.

Allen arrived in the UK as a Commonwealth immigrant from Jamaica in 1962. It was a time of extreme racial tension. Nine days before Allen began work, Enoch Powell had given his infamous "Rivers of Blood" speech, disparaging immigration by people of color and quoting a constituent: "In this country in fifteen or twenty years' time, the black man will have the whip hand over the white man." A Gallup poll showed that 74 per cent of the British population agreed with Powell. Thousands of white London dockers marched to protest the influx of "coloured people" to the labour market, brandishing slogans such as "BACK BRITAIN, NOT BLACK BRITAIN" and "CLOSE THE GATE BEFORE IT'S TOO LATE."

Against this background, Allen took up her post as a highly visible presence on the beat. Allen maintained that her colleagues in Croydon were universally welcoming, though her superiors received some racist hate mail. She served first on foot patrol and later at the Missing Persons Bureau. In 1972, she returned to Jamaica and joined the police force there. Before police work, she had been a nurse. "I didn't set out to make history," Allen said, "I just wanted a change of direction."

30 APRIL

Artemisia Gentileschi
(1593-c.1656)

On this day in 2020, a collection of the works of Artemisia Gentileschi was due to open at the National Gallery in London – the first such exhibition of a female artist – but it was postponed due to the coronavirus pandemic.

As her father was a painter, Gentileschi received an artistic apprenticeship – unusual for a woman in this period. When she was seventeen, her tutor, Tassi, raped her. Her father brought charges because she had been "dishonored"; he wanted Tassi to marry her. During the trial, she was tortured to make sure she was telling the truth. Tassi was found guilty and banished but the Pope protected him.

Gentileschi became the first woman to gain membership of the artists' academy in Florence. She brought a personal perspective to her art. Her work, *Judith Beheading Holofernes*, transforms a biblical story of political assassination into an image of a woman enacting violent revenge; it is said that Holofernes' face resembled Tassi.

In her *Self-portrait as Saint Catherine of Alexandria*, Gentileschi identifies with another victim of torture. In her right hand, Catherine/Gentileschi holds a palm leaf – a symbol of victory through martyrdom – as though it were a paintbrush. In 2018, this work became only the twentieth by a woman to enter the National Gallery's collection.

MAY

"You crawl on your stomach for hours and in the end arrive at all sorts of wonders."
– Dorothy Garrod

Revolting women

In 2018, events across the UK celebrated the centenary of the Representation of the People Act 1918, when some British women finally won the vote, thanks to the efforts of the suffragists – who pursued their campaign by lawful means – and the suffragettes, who were more radical. The lengths some women went to in order to secure change – damage to property, hunger strikes – and how they suffered (being force-fed, for example) challenged the traditional picture of womanhood (see <u>Emmeline Pankhurst</u>, <u>Marion Wallace Dunlop</u>).

But the history of British women's involvement in protest goes back much further and the causes they adopted did not just deal with women's rights. In 1381, women led and participated in the Peasants' Revolt in London. Johanna Ferrour – described in court as a "chief perpetrator" – dragged Sir Robert Hales and Lord Chancellor Simon of Sudbury from the Tower of

London and ordered that they be beheaded. In 1649, during the English Civil War, hundreds of female Levellers marched on Westminster to petition for the release of two of their leaders and took up arms to defend their homes and towns. Women were among the demonstrators demanding parliamentary reform on 16 August 1819 in Manchester when the cavalry charged the crowd in the Peterloo Massacre. And many women were active in the nineteenth-century Chartist movement, even though its campaign for "universal suffrage" only sought the vote for men (see Anne Knight).

Women took part in revolutionary movements around the world. One of the most significant events of the French Revolution happened on 5 October 1789, when armed peasant women, angry about the desperate shortage of bread, marched on Versailles, besieging the palace. Nonetheless, when the revolutionary National Assembly was set up, it refused to accept women as equal citizens (see Olympe de Gouges). The start of the Russian Revolution is dated to 8 March 1917 when thousands of women, again protesting food shortages, marched through Petrograd. And women have played active roles in movements campaigning for independence from British rule, from Harriet Tubman in America and Constance Markievicz in Ireland to Huda Sha'arawi in Egypt and Bhikaji Cama in India. On 21 January 2017, when seven million women took part in a Women's March in towns and cities across the world, protesting against the inauguration of Donald Trump as US president, they were standing firmly on the shoulders of their revolutionary foremothers.

Mary Lacy

(1744–1801)

At about six o'clock in the morning on this day in 1759, Mary Lacy ran away to sea: "When I had got out of town into the fields, I pulled off my clothes and put on the men's, leaving my own in a hedge." Lacy's disguise enabled her to have a career otherwise closed to women.

Calling herself William Chandler, she was recruited at Chatham dockyard for a Navy gun ship as the servant to the ship's carpenter, who was violent when drunk. Lacy records that it was "very hard to be struck by a man." But to keep up appearances, she entered into at least one honor fight, with a sailor who had picked on her. In 1763, Lacy was released from the Navy and started an apprenticeship as a shipwright in Portsmouth. She lived on board ship and had a girlfriend called Sarah Chase. In 1770, she became a qualified shipwright, with skills in mechanical drawing, arithmetic and writing.

When Lacy found herself unable to work because of severe rheumatism, a family friend helped her to apply to the Admiralty for a Navy pension. She used her real name, thus revealing her sex, but was still successful, because of "the particular Circumstances attending this Woman's case." In 1773, Lacy published her memoir, *The Female Shipwright . . . Written by Herself*.

"When I had got out of town into the fields, I pulled off my clothes and put on the men's, leaving my own in a hedge."

Mary Barbour

(1875–1958)

In February 1915, Glasgow landlords announced rent increases of 25 per cent, attempting to profiteer on the wartime shortage of housing. In May of that year, carpet printer Mary Barbour led the South Govan Women's Housing Association in rent strikes, encouraging tenants in non-payment. Those threatened with eviction were protected by blockades of women and prams, keeping bailiffs and officers out.

The Glasgow Rent Strike spread throughout the city; on 17 November, thousands of women – nicknamed "Mrs Barbour's Army" – marched to the sheriff's courts. The pressure put on Westminster by the strike and protests resulted in the 1915 Rent Restrictions Act, which kept rents at their August 1914 level.

Barbour's activism didn't stop there. In June 1916, she and two of her rent strike comrades – Agnes Dollan and Helen Crawfurd – founded the Women's Peace Crusade, to speak out against the First World War. They held meetings all over Scotland and produced anti-war literature. It was dangerous work: campaigners often faced physical and verbal abuse and some were sent to prison.

In 1920, Barbour was elected to Glasgow Town Council as their first female Labour councillor. She campaigned for municipal banks, wash-houses, laundries, free milk for schoolchildren, child welfare centers and pensions for mothers.

3 MAY

Mo Mowlam

(1949–2005)

On this day in 1997, Mo Mowlam MP became the UK's Northern Ireland secretary, a job considered a poisoned chalice because of the "Troubles" – the sectarian violence between Protestant and Catholic groups in the province. Over the next eleven months, Mowlam led negotiations which resulted in the signing, on 10 April 1998, of the Good Friday Agreement (GFA). It brought peace to Northern Ireland for the first time in thirty years.

Mowlam's methods were sometimes controversial. She visited Loyalist prisoners at the Maze prison and reversed their opposition to the peace process. She helped restore an IRA ceasefire. She brought both sides to the negotiating table, winning respect from all sides with her integrity and her no-nonsense style – full of both terms of endearment and expletives.

Even when undergoing treatment for a brain tumor, Mowlam continued working.

Unlike her predecessors, she also worked with community groups: men and women from both sides of the conflict. She knew that getting women involved was key to negotiations.

However, Mowlam's vital contribution has begun to be forgotten. On 10 April 2018, Tony Blair gave a speech in Belfast for the twentieth anniversary of the Good Friday Agreement. He didn't mention Mowlam's name.

Margaret Thatcher

(1925–2013)

On this day in 1975, Margaret Thatcher became the first woman to head a British political party, the Conservatives. In 1979, she became the UK's first woman prime minister.

She was a totemic and divisive figure in post-war politics. For the right, Thatcher's premiership is seen as a golden age, reversing the growth of trade unions and the state. To the left, she was corrosive and amoral, a leader who tore apart public welfare provision. Both sides agree that "the Iron Lady" valued individual achievement and enabled a culture of consumerism which has shaped Britain ever since.

The Falklands War of 1982, when UK forces successfully defended British-owned islands in the Atlantic from Argentinian invasion, was a landmark in Thatcher's career. Her subsequent landslide election victory enabled her to carry out deep changes in national culture. Utilities and industries were sold off to large companies; tenants were encouraged to buy their council houses and workers to become shareholders. Her 1985 defeat of the miners' unions was seen as a wider defeat for organized labor.

Thatcher's premiership saw riots, IRA attacks and the end of the Cold War. "There is no such thing as society," she said in 1987. But she changed UK society in profound ways.

Amy Johnson

(1903-1941)

On this day in 1930, Amy Johnson, a young pilot from Hull, set off on her 8,600-mile flight from Croydon to Darwin. The journey took nineteen and a half days and made her the first woman to fly solo from Britain to Australia: "When I sighted Melville Island I stood up and cheered myself." Her achievement brought congratulations from King George V and a CBE.

In 1928, Johnson had joined the London Aeroplane Club; their subsidized lessons made learning to fly affordable on her office-job salary. In 1929, she was awarded not only her pilot's "A" licence but also her ground engineer's "C" license – the first to be issued to a woman. When she undertook her Britain–Australia flight, Johnson had completed less than 100 hours' solo flying; her nerve and determination enabled her to go on to break several long-distance flying records. She also became a member of the Women's Engineering Society (WES) and was its president for three years.

During the Second World War, she worked in the women's section of the Air Transport Auxiliary. Her last flight was on 5 January 1941, in bad weather. It is assumed that she ran out of fuel and baled out over the Thames Estuary. An attempted rescue was unsuccessful. Her body was never recovered.

Dorothy Garrod

(1892–1968)

On this day in 1939, Dorothy Garrod became the Disney Professor of Archaeology at the University of Cambridge, the first woman to hold a chair at either Oxford or Cambridge. She was still not a full member of the university, as women were excluded until 1948.

Garrod had graduated from Newnham College, Cambridge, with a degree in history in 1916, then studied for a Diploma in Anthropology at the Pitt Rivers Museum in Oxford. She had her first experiences of archaeology in France: "You crawl on your stomach for hours . . . and in the end arrive at all sorts of wonders."

She is best known for directing the excavations at the Wadi el-Maghara in Palestine between 1929 and 1934. Her predominantly female crew included Dorothea Bate, Elinor Ewbank, Mary Kitson Clark and Jacquetta Hopkins (later Hawkes). The women first lived in tents and then in tiny mud-brick huts ("tibn") which they named "Tibn Towers." They called themselves the "Tibnites." Garrod was called "the Boss," but all living and working routines were decided by the group at breakfast or tea.

Garrod employed many women from local villages as excavators. One of them, Yusra, acted as overseer in charge of picking out items before the excavated soil was sieved. In 1932, in the et-Tabun Cave, Yusra spotted a tooth which led her to the skull of a female Neanderthal, known as Tabun 1, one of the most important human fossils ever found.

"You crawl on your stomach for hours and in the end arrive at all sorts of wonders."

7 MAY

Aisha Bakari Gombi

(1979–)

In May 2016, Nigerian hunter Aisha Bakari Gombi was the first woman to be crowned Sarauniyar Baka Adamawa, or Queen of Adamawa hunters. Aisha commands a group of male hunters which has rescued hundreds of men, women and children from Boko Haram, a violent sect which wants to create an Islamic state in north-eastern Nigeria.

Aisha has been a hunter since she was a girl. When Boko Haram attacked her town, Gombi, she was working as a seamstress; she sold her sewing machine to buy a bigger rifle. She was the only woman to take part in defending the town: "People . . . said I was a mad woman . . . But now they all appreciate me and love what I do." Aisha and her hunters protect other villages and search for those taken captive by Boko Haram.

Aisha has a special hatred for the Boko Haram leader, Bula Yaga. "He has killed many women and children. He even slaughters pregnant women and drowns little children. His wickedness knows no bounds . . . the male hunters should step aside and allow the women to deal with him. Then we'll cut him into pieces and split his skull open for the whole world to see that we've taken our revenge for what he has done."

She sold her sewing machine to buy a bigger rifle.

143

Joan of Arc

(c.1412–1431)

France and England had been at war for almost a hundred years when Joan of Arc, a seventeen-year-old farmer's daughter, offered Charles, the heir to the French throne, her help to "liberate France from its calamities." She wore "male" clothing and was inspired by visions she saw as divine. Charles accepted, providing her with a small army. In April 1429, "the Maid" and her troops entered a besieged Orleans, bringing supplies and galvanizing resistance. On this day in 1429, Joan led her soldiers into battle. She was victorious and the English retreated. More military successes followed, but in 1430 Joan was captured by the Duke of Burgundy, who sold her to the English.

She was put on trial and accused of transgressing divine law by dressing as a man and fighting, of deceit (claiming to be sent by God) and of heresy and witchcraft. Joan was found guilty and on 30 May was burned at the stake. Twenty years later, her sentence was overturned; in 1920 she was canonized as a Roman Catholic saint.

Dorothy Hodgkin

(1910–1994)

"Oxford housewife wins Nobel" was how the UK's *Daily Mail* reported the news that Dorothy Hodgkin had become the first British woman to win a Nobel Prize for science.

Hodgkin was an X-ray crystallographer, measuring the diffractions of X-rays to determine the 3D structures of molecules. Her first major discovery came in May 1945, when she figured out the molecular structure of the antibiotic penicillin. Despite skepticism from some colleagues, Hodgkin's formula was proved right; her work enabled the synthesis of chemically modified penicillins.

In 1954, she published the structure of vitamin B12, research for which she won the Nobel Prize for Chemistry in 1964. Her breakthrough had proved vital for the treatment of pernicious anemia. Hodgkin's next major discovery, published in 1969, was the structure of insulin. She had begun the research thirty-five years earlier when X-ray crystallography wasn't advanced enough to pursue it. Hodgkin and others developed the technology to the necessary level and their research significantly improved treatment for diabetics. Hodgkin's dedication to her research has saved many lives. "I was captured for life," she said, "by chemistry and by crystals."

Hodgkin also worked for humanitarian causes. A committed socialist, she was nevertheless called upon as an advisor on science and international affairs by a former pupil, Margaret Thatcher, during the latter's time as Conservative prime minister.

> "I was captured for life by chemistry and by crystals."

Ivy Williams

(1877–1966)

Ivy Williams was the third woman to study law at Oxford University. She passed all her exams by 1903 but, like all women at Oxford until 1920, did not receive a degree. Williams challenged this in an article in the UK's *Law Journal*: "Admit us or we shall form a third branch of the profession and practise as outside lawyers." She finally became England's first female barrister on this day in 1922.

However, Williams didn't want to practice law but to offer free legal advice to the poor; Helena Normanton would become England's first practicing woman barrister six months later. The first woman to teach law at an English university and the first to be awarded a Doctor of Civil Laws, Williams paved the way for Dame Elizabeth Lane, the UK's first female High Court judge, and Dame Rosalyn Higgins, the first to sit in the International Court of Justice.

When her eyesight began to fail, Williams taught herself braille and wrote a braille handbook for the National Institute for the Blind in 1948.

> "Admit us or we shall form a third branch of the profession and practise as outside lawyers."

Ida Pfeiffer

(1797–1858)

Ida Pfeiffer had always wanted to travel: "When I was but a little child, I had already a strong desire to see the world." When she was forty-five and her sons had homes of their own, she separated from her husband and made her preparations. In 1842, Pfeiffer set off on her first journey: down the Danube from Vienna to Istanbul, then on to Jerusalem and Egypt. Her account of her travels, *A Viennese Woman's Trip to the Holy Land* (1844), was enormously successful and paid for her next trip – to Scandinavia and Iceland.

Pfeiffer traveled round the world twice. She went hunting in Singapore, visited local homes during Ramadan in Azerbaijan and was in California during the Gold Rush. Her published accounts of each trip were translated into several languages. In May 1857, she traveled to Madagascar and unwittingly became involved in a coup to replace the brutal Queen Ranavalona I. She was expelled from the island, contracting malaria before she left. After a difficult journey, she died at home.

Vienna's Natural History Museum purchased 721 specimens from her final trip, including nine species of mammals, ten species of spiders and 185 species of insects. In 1892, Ida Pfeiffer became the first woman to be buried in the rows of honored dead in Vienna Central Cemetery.

12 MAY

Louisa Garrett Anderson (1873–1943) and Flora Murray (1869–1923)

Louisa Garrett Anderson and Flora Murray were pioneering doctors and passionate suffragettes. In 1912, they founded the Women's Hospital for Children in London. Staffed entirely by women, it took its motto from the Women's Social and Political Union founded by Emmeline Pankhurst: "Deeds Not Words."

At the outbreak of the First World War, the women's offer to work for the war effort was rejected by the British authorities. Undaunted, they founded a Women's Hospital Corps and ran two hospitals in France. In 1915, Sir Alfred Keogh, the Director-General of Army Medical Services, asked them to run a military hospital in London, after receiving "letters from Paris and Boulogne, which stated that the work of women doctors at the Front was beyond all praise."

On this day in 1915, their Endell Street Military Hospital received its first patients. All posts were filled by women: surgeons, anaesthetists, orderlies, dispensers, stretcher-bearers. This was revolutionary; the women were treating not only other women and children but men with war wounds, many of whom had arrived straight from the front. Within a week, all 520 beds were full.

By the time of the hospital's closure in 1919, the women of Endell Street had treated over 26,000 patients, and performed around 7,000 operations. Keogh wrote to them: "I think your success has probably done more for the cause of women than anything else I know of." The possible impact of running the hospital had always been clear to Anderson and Murray, who saw military medicine as "suffrage work . . . in another form."

13 MAY

Louise Bourgeois Boursier (1563–1636) and Angélique-Marguerite du Coudray (1712–1794)

One hundred and fifty years apart, two French midwives made major contributions to their profession. In 1609, Louise Bourgeois Boursier published *Observations*, the earliest known printed work by a midwife. She described her experiences working for the French queen and the 2,000 deliveries she attended. Case histories illustrated diagnosis and treatment and the book was hugely successful. It remained in print in France for fifty years and was translated into German, Dutch and English.

But the situation for French midwives changed in 1743. As in Britain, male surgeons were trying to squeeze women out of practice (see Elizabeth Nihell). The midwives presented a petition urging the University of Paris to give women proper training.

Angélique-Marguerite Le Boursier du Coudray (who may have been related to Boursier) was one of the most vocal petitioners at this time. She made groundbreaking advancements in the field and became one of France's best-known midwives. On this day in 1756, she presented her "machine," a life-size, anatomically accurate obstetrical mannequin of cloth and leather, to the French Academy of Surgery, who approved it for teaching obstetrics and childbirth. Sent by the king to teach midwifery in over forty cities and rural towns, Du Coudray would train thousands of students, as well as male surgeons. In 1769, she published her own textbook, *Abrégé de l'Art des Accouchements*.

One hundred and fifty years apart, two French midwives made major contributions.

14 MAY

Ani Pachen

(1933–2002)

Today we remember Ani Pachen, sometimes called "the Tibetan Joan of Arc," who led a force of around 600 fighters in guerrilla operations against the Chinese.

Pachen was born in 1933, the daughter of a chieftain in the Lemdha clan. When the Chinese invaded Tibet in 1950, the Lemdha and other clans took up arms to resist them. Eight years later, Pachen was preparing for ordination in a Buddhist monastery when her father died. She abandoned her spiritual calling, took over the leadership of the clan and returned to command the Lemdha rebels.

With support from external powers, including the US, Pachen's warriors waged a paramilitary campaign against the invading armies. They traveled on horseback, sometimes even mounting attacks on tank regiments. In 1960, Pachen was captured by the Chinese. She was subjected to torture, including beatings, solitary confinement, being hung by her wrists, and rape. Her captivity lasted for twenty-one years.

When Pachen was released in 1981, she continued to protest the occupation. She was threatened with re-arrest and crossed the Himalayas on foot to take refuge in Nepal. Pachen later published a memoir, *Sorrow Mountain: The Journey of a Tibetan Warrior Nun*, and became a well-known advocate for Tibetan self-government. She died in India, still in exile from her own people, in 2002.

"I remembered Gyalsay Rinpoche's words . . . 'Your enemy is your teacher.'"

15 MAY

(Mary) Beatrice Davidson Kenner (1912–2006)

Mary Beatrice Davidson Kenner – known as Beatrice – grew up in a family keen on inventing. Her father held three patents, and she and her sister liked to design solutions to everyday problems; Kenner invented a self-oiling hinge to stop her mother being woken by a squeaky door. One of her later inventions would make life easier for countless women.

For most of history, women have had to be inventive in order to manage their periods, most commonly using cloth rags (hence the expression "on the rag") which they could wash and reuse. Rags were uncomfortable and prone to leaking; tampons, invented in the 1930s, were considered by some to be "indecent." Many women stayed at home as much as possible when menstruating.

On this day in 1956, Kenner patented a sanitary belt for keeping sanitary towels in place "in a highly efficient and satisfactory manner."

When a company showed interest in her invention she was thrilled, but their racism meant that her happiness was short-lived: "I was so jubilant. I saw houses, cars, and everything about to come my way. Sorry to say, when they found out I was black, their interest dropped."

Big companies such as Kotex did produce the sanitary belt but Kenner never made a lot of money from her invention, which was gradually replaced from the 1970s onwards by the self-adhesive disposable towel.

16 MAY

Junko Tabei
(1939–2016)

On this day in 1975, Japanese climber Junko Tabei was the first woman to reach the summit of Mount Everest. Overcoming not only the physical challenges of her chosen career but sexism in climbing and Japanese society, she was the first woman to summit the highest peak on every continent.

Tabei began to take climbing seriously at university in the 1950s, but her sex barred her from the mountaineering society. Some men simply refused to climb with a woman. In reaction, she formed the Ladies' Climbing Club of Japan.

Tabei built up her experience on peaks including Mount Fuji, the Matterhorn and Annapurna III. The Ladies' Climbing Club made their ascent of Everest in early 1975, with home-made sleeping bags, gloves and other equipment. Tabei, with a three-year old daughter at home, was widely criticized for her choice to climb. In early May, an avalanche buried the whole party and knocked Tabei unconscious, but twelve days later, she stood on the summit.

Tabei continued to climb, adding the highest peak of each continent to her record until, in 1992, with her ascent of Puncak Jaya in Indonesia, she became the first woman to complete all of the Seven Summits. She died in 2016, having seen seventy-three nations from their highest points.

Maria Beasley

(1847–1904)

In May 1882, American inventor Maria E. Beasley patented a "fireproof, compact, safe and readily-launched" life raft. Her first patent had been for a barrel-hooping machine that helped speed up manufacture, making up to 1,500 barrels a day. A local newspaper wrote in 1889 that it earned her "a small fortune," perhaps as much as $20,000 per year.

Her inventions ranged widely, from foot warmers and cooking pans to an anti-derailment device for trains, but it was her life raft design that brought her renown. Where previous life rafts had been made of wood, Beasley's had metal floats, was fireproof, easy to launch and came with protective guard railings.

Twenty of her life rafts were carried by the *Titanic*, which, on its first voyage across the Atlantic Ocean from England to New York, hit an iceberg on 15 April 1912. Half of the 2,000 passengers died but, thanks to Maria Beasley's rafts, 706 survived.

Twenty of her life rafts were carried by the Titanic.

Bertha von Suttner

(1843–1914)

Austrian writer and pacifist Bertha von Suttner may have been the inspiration for the Nobel Prizes. Born into nobility in 1843, von Suttner was forced to find employment due to her widowed mother's gambling losses. She moved to Paris and for a short time was Alfred Nobel's secretary. They stayed in touch until his death. She told him about her activities on behalf of world peace. Nobel, who'd made a fortune from explosives, wrote: "Inform me, convince me, and then I will do something great for the movement."

When she first heard of the International Arbitration and Peace Association, von Suttner said it "electrified her." Two years later, she published her anti-war novel, *Lay Down Your Arms*. The book became a bestseller and von Suttner focused on activism, giving lectures, attending meetings and setting up peace groups. On this day in 1899, von Suttner was the only woman invited to the Hague Peace Conference.

In 1905, four years after the Nobel Prizes were established, she became the first woman to win the Nobel Peace Prize, aged sixty-two. The award was given in great part due to *Lay Down Your Arms*, because, said the Nobel committee, "the impact made on the reading public was tremendous." She died six weeks before the First World War began.

19 MAY

Eglantyne Jebb (1876–1928) and Dorothy Jebb (1881–1963)

On this day in 1919, sisters Eglantyne and Dorothy Jebb launched the Save the Children Fund, which is still working to make children's lives better one hundred years later. They had first been moved by the plight of children suffering in Germany and Austro-Hungary after the First World War, when British blockades badly affected food supplies. After their first appeal for starving children raised £35,000, the sisters set up the International Save the Children Union in Geneva.

In 1923, Eglantyne took her draft Children's Charter to one of its meetings and the result was the Declaration of the Rights of the Child, intended to put children's rights at the forefront of international planning. The charter, adopted by the League of Nations, was one of the inspirations behind the 1989 UN Convention on the Rights of the Child.

"The child that is hungry must be fed, the child that is sick must be nursed, the child that is backward must be helped, the delinquent child must be reclaimed, and the orphan and the waif must be sheltered and succoured."

20 MAY

Kanchhi Maya Tamang
(1988–)

On this day in 2017, self-trained climber Kanchhi Maya Tamang reached the peak of Mount Everest, almost exactly forty-two years after Junko Tabei. If Tabei's climb represented a pioneering triumph, Tamang's was a metaphor for the ongoing struggle of many women in her country against exploitation and enslavement.

Tamang, a twenty-eight-year-old Nepali, had escaped slavery herself. Her home region of Sindhupalchok is a rich source of labor for human traffickers. Its minority Tamang communities are impoverished even by the standards of this relatively poor nation, and they have often sold women into abuse and sexual exploitation.

Tamang was sold into enslavement as a maid in Egypt. After escaping captivity and returning to Nepal, she became a prominent anti-trafficking campaigner. She also advocates for girls' education and involvement in sports. "I have climbed Everest to empower women who are climbing their own mountains."

Tamang is now a sherpa, working as an expedition guide for others seeking to climb the major peaks of the Himalayas.

> "I have climbed Everest to empower women who are climbing their own mountains."

Amelia Earhart

(1897–c.1937)

On this day in 1932, pilot Amelia Earhart landed an airplane in a field near the village of Culmore, Ireland. When an astonished local asked her if she had flown far, she replied, "From America."

Earhart was the first woman to fly solo across the Atlantic, which won her the US Distinguished Flying Cross. She had been instructed by another early airwoman, Neta Snook, and was already a frequent record-breaker. Even before qualifying for her pilot's license (the sixteenth woman in the world to do so) she had set an altitude record for women. Weeks after her famous solo journey, she became the first woman to fly coast to coast across the US.

In 1928, Earhart had been the first female passenger on a crewed transatlantic flight. This well-publicized trip made her globally famous – a celebrity as well as a pioneer aviator. She endorsed clothing lines and travel products, signed sponsorship deals, wrote memoirs and became the aviation editor for *Cosmopolitan*. She also used her notoriety to advocate for women's equality.

In 1937, she attempted a circumnavigation of the globe with navigator Fred Noonan. Their aircraft missed a fuel stop and probably ditched in the Pacific. Many explanations have been suggested and many searches made, but no trace has been found of them or the plane.

22 MAY

(Elizabeth) Leah Manning

(1886–1977)

When the Spanish Civil War began in July 1936, British teacher and former Labour MP Leah Manning went to Spain to help. Her friend Alvarez del Vayo, Spanish Minister of Foreign Affairs, urged her to persuade the British government to send aid. But Manning and her colleagues failed to persuade the Labour Party to oppose the Conservative government's non-intervention policy. So she found another way: setting up the Spanish Medical Aid Committee with anti-fascist Isabel Brown. Manning traveled to Spain several times with supplies, and reports she published helped raise £2 million.

Witnessing the bombardment of the Basque town of Guernica in April 1937 by German and Italian planes – which killed 1,600 civilians – spurred Manning to drastic action. In May, while the British consul was away celebrating George VI's coronation, Manning sent a telegram to London pretending to be the consul, giving permission for an evacuation of Guernica. On 21 May, a yacht with 3,826 Basque children and 95 teachers set sail, arriving into Southampton on this day in 1937. "Perhaps, many years hence, in happier times, they will erect a statue of me, with children, in the Park in Bilbao," Manning wrote. A square in Bilbao was named Jardines de Mrs Leah Manning in 2002.

Audre Lorde
(1934–1992)

In May 1979, Audre Lorde wrote a celebrated letter to white feminist Mary Daly, critiquing Daly's book *Gyn/Ecology* for its approach to black women. Lorde was an important American poet and civil rights activist, an essayist, publisher and a womanist (a feminist focused equally on sexism and racism). Her whole output was a call for society to right injustice.

Lorde's work urged people to respect different categories of gender, race, class or sexuality and, at the same time, to see beyond those categories to a shared humanity. She was a forerunner of today's intersectional thinkers, exploring how different parts of a person's identity – like Lorde's own as a lesbian, black, feminist mother – affect their experience of the world. Even the language in which we describe things is a part of the world Lorde wanted to change: an idea summarized in the title of her essay, *The Master's Tools Will Never*

Dismantle the Master's House.

Lorde's poetry is lyrical, political and fierce. Her prose is precise, articulate and uncompromising. In 1981, she said: "Mainstream communication does not want women, particularly white women, responding to racism. It wants racism to be accepted as an immutable given in the fabric of your existence, like evening-time or the common cold."

Simone de Beauvoir

(1908–1986)

On this day in 1949, French writer, philosopher and activist Simone de Beauvoir published *The Second Sex*; it sold around 22,000 copies in the first week. De Beauvoir argued that, throughout history, man has been treated as the default and woman as the "Other"; that, "Woman is not born but made: out of expectations and customs rather than out of her own desires."

In the 1930s, de Beauvoir had planned on writing an autobiographical work, but then came the outbreak of the Second World War. "History burst over me," she said later. Instead of seeing herself principally as an individual, she saw herself as a historical subject and part of a sex class; she began to ask, "What is a woman?"

To answer this question, de Beauvoir deployed not only philosophy but also anthropology, law, literature, religion and history. English readers missed out: the original English translation cut 10 percent of the text and the names of seventy-eight women de Beauvoir had included to show that, "It is not women's inferiority that has determined their historical insignificance: it is their historical insignificance that has doomed them to inferiority."

In 2011, Constance Borde and Sheila Malovany-Chevallier at last provided readers of English with a full and unabridged translation of the monumental work that triggered feminism's second wave and created networks of female solidarity. De Beauvoir herself was part of this movement, campaigning for abortion rights and birth control throughout the 1970s.

"Woman is not born but made."

Althea Gibson

(1927–2003)

On this day in 1956, American tennis player Althea Gibson won the French Open, becoming the first player of color to win a Grand Slam title. Six years earlier, she had been the first black tennis player in the US National Championships. Before 1950, the US Tennis Association enforced a rigid – though unwritten – ban on black players. As Billie Jean King described it: "Everything was white. The balls, the clothes, the socks, the shoes, the people. Ev-ery-thing." Then-US national champion Alice Marble criticized the ban: "If tennis is a game for ladies and gentleman, it is time we acted a little more like gentle people and less like sanctimonious hypocrites."

In 1950, Althea Gibson was sent an invitation and made her debut at the National Championships on her twenty-third birthday.

A year later, Gibson was the first black tennis player at Wimbledon. In 1957 and 1958, she won singles titles at both the US Championships and at Wimbledon. "Shaking hands with the Queen of England," she wrote, "was a long way from being forced to sit in the colored section of the bus." American tennis star Serena Williams – winner of seventy-three singles titles – has said that Althea Gibson "paved the way for all women of color in sport."

26 MAY

Jacquetta Hawkes
(1910–1996)

In May 1951, British archaeologist Jacquetta Hawkes published her unusual book, *A Land*. It was, she knew, "very difficult to place in any of our recognised categories," as it looked at Britain as a cumulative product of geology, culture, climate and happenstance. The book's author was herself hard to categorize – a public intellectual who followed unconventional paths of thought and occupation.

Hawkes was a specialist in prehistoric archaeology, working with <u>Dorothy Garrod</u> and <u>Dorothea Bate</u>. She took a particular interest in the Minoan culture of Crete; her research suggested that women played an unusually large role in Minoan public institutions. She wrote many popular guides to archaeology and made documentaries.

Hawkes was a literary figure as much as a social scientist. She was increasingly drawn to imaginative writing and society, especially after meeting the writer JB Priestley, who became her second husband. Her wider interests in social history, journalism and the life of the intellect made her a fantastic public communicator and campaigner. In later life, Hawkes was an archaeological adviser to the Festival of Britain, a founder member of the Campaign for Nuclear Disarmament and a governor of the British Film Institute.

27 MAY

Shelagh Delaney

(1938–2011)

On this day in 1958, Shelagh Delaney's first play, *A Taste of Honey*, was performed by Joan Littlewood's radical Theatre Workshop in Stratford, East London. A working-class nineteen-year-old from Salford, Delaney had left school at seventeen. She got a job as usherette at the Manchester Opera House. There, in 1956, she saw Samuel Beckett's play *Waiting for Godot*. It had a powerful effect on her, reinforcing her sense that, "There were other voices that needed to be written and to be heard."

These voices were the voices Delaney had grown up with, the voices of working-class people, particularly women. There were no plays about their lives, lived in factories and shops, or offices; as married women exhausted by domestic chores; as single mothers; as prostitutes.

The program for the first performance of *A Taste of Honey*

described Delaney as, "The antithesis of London's 'angry young men.' She knows what she is angry about." In the play, the white main character, Jo, gets pregnant by her black lover; her mother lives off her various boyfriends; her flatmate is a gay man. Addressing questions of class, race, sexuality and women's choices (or lack of them), Delaney showed that working-class people, even women, have something to say.

Hannah Arendt

(1906–1975)

In May 1963, the *New Yorker* published "Eichmann in Jerusalem: A Report on the Banality of Evil," a report on the trial of Adolf Eichmann, one of the Holocaust's Nazi architects. It was written by Hannah Arendt, who became one of the twentieth century's most famous political philosophers.

Arendt, a secular Jew, fled Germany after being arrested in 1933 for researching anti-Semitism in Nazi propaganda. Later, living in Paris without papers, she was interned as an "enemy alien." She describes being officially stateless for eighteen years in one of her first articles, "We Refugees," published in 1943 after she and her husband escaped to New York.

Arendt wrote on many topics, from freedom and totalitarianism to thought and judgement. The conclusion of her report on the Eichmann trial caused great controversy: "The deeds were monstrous, but the doer was neither demonic nor monstrous . . . Might the problem of good and evil, our faculty of telling right from wrong, be connected with our faculty of thought?" Her writing remains relevant, for example on the danger of "alternative facts": "The result of a consistent and total substitution of lies for factual truth is . . . that the sense by which we take our bearings in the real world . . . is being destroyed."

29 MAY

Sojourner Truth

(c.1797–1883)

On this day in 1851, Sojourner Truth, African-American abolitionist, activist and formerly enslaved person, gave her famous "Ain't I A Woman?" speech at the Ohio Women's Rights Convention. There is debate over the exact wording; this is an extract from one published version:

> I could work as much and eat as much as a man – when I could get it – and bear the lash as well! And ain't I a woman? I have borne thirteen children, and seen them most all sold off to slavery, and when I cried out with my mother's grief, none but Jesus heard me! And ain't I a woman?

Born into slavery in New York, Truth escaped to freedom with her daughter in 1826. In 1828, after discovering her son had been sold illegally to a white slave owner, she went to court and – after months of legal proceedings – became the first black American woman to win a case against a white man to get her son back. Truth was active on many issues, from prison reform and property rights to universal suffrage. Her memoirs were published in 1850. In 2014, she was named as one of *Smithsonian* magazine's "100 Most Significant Americans of All Time."

Germaine Tillion

(1907–2008)

In June 1940, French ethnologist Germaine Tillion was working in Algeria when she learned of France's surrender to the German army. She returned to Paris and became a member of the Resistance, helping Allied prisoners escape and gathering intelligence for Allied forces. In August 1942, she was arrested after being betrayed by a priest who had joined her cell as a spy. In October 1943, she was sent to the women's concentration camp of Ravensbrück, near Berlin, along with other Resistance members, including her mother.

In the camp, Tillion secretly wrote an operetta comedy to entertain the fellow prisoners, *Le Verfügbar aux Enfers* ("The disposable man in hell"). Loosely based on Offenbach's *Orpheus in the Underworld*, it tells the story of a naturalist attempting to describe the alien creatures he encounters in the strange world of the camp.

Tillion herself did an ethnographic study of the camp system, believing that a clear understanding of their situation would help inmates defend themselves and improve morale.

Tillion, whose mother died in the camp, escaped Ravensbrück shortly before it was liberated. In 1973, she published *Ravensbruck: An eyewitness account of a women's concentration camp.*

In May 2007, in the week of her hundredth birthday, Tillion's Ravensbrück operetta was performed in Paris. In April 2010, it was performed on the site of the camp to mark the sixty-fifth anniversary of its liberation.

31 MAY

Tracy Edwards

(1962–)

When twenty-six-year-old Tracy Edwards announced she was entering the first all-female crew to sail in the Whitbread Round the World Yacht Race, competitors started taking bets on how long they would last. The media referred to them as "girls"; one male journalist called the boat a "tin full of tarts." This puzzled Edwards: "I'd already sailed around the world. I was strong enough and smart enough – I'd already learned the skills."

The crew became celebrities, with female fans cheering them at every port and telling Edwards that what she had done had inspired them to change their own lives. The doubters were firmly silenced when, in May 1990, the crew of *Maiden* came second in their class. Edwards – who had been expelled from school at fifteen – became the first woman named Yachtsman of the Year and was awarded one of Britain's highest honors, Member of the British Empire (MBE).

Maiden was sold after the race. In 2018, after buying the yacht back and restoring her, Edwards set off around the world again to raise awareness and funds for girls' education and empowerment. "I have always felt very strongly that you have to stand up and be counted."

JUNE

"I do not intend to give you reasons, [I am] simply not suited to marriage"
– Queen Christina of Sweden

Passing it on

How might a girl or woman learn to do things no girl or woman has ever done? For many in this book it was their parents who made it possible. Objecting to the lack of education for their daughters, they encouraged them into the field in which they would later make their mark. In the 1700s, French mathematician <u>Émilie du Châtelet</u>'s father welcomed his young daughter into his salons, as did <u>Anne Germaine de Stael</u>'s mother and Italian mathematician <u>Maria Gaetana Agnesi</u>'s father. A hundred years later, <u>Maria Mitchell</u>'s father taught her to use a telescope; still later, film star <u>Hedy Lamarr</u>'s career as an inventor began with her father's explanations of how things worked on walks around Vienna.

However, not all were supportive: mathematicians <u>Mary Somerville</u> and <u>Sophie Germain</u> had parents who tried to keep them from their books. <u>Frances Glessner Lee</u>'s parents prevented her from studying medicine; she waited until they had died to pursue her interests.

Even once they entered their chosen field, many women faced – and still face – difficulties; this is where other women's assistance is vital. Many of those we feature here not only broke glass ceilings, they turned around and offered a hand to those coming after. In the 1600s, Italian painter <u>Elisabetta Sirani</u> opened a studio for women artists. American chemist <u>Ellen Swallow Richards</u> launched MIT's Women's Laboratory in 1876; <u>Maria Mitchell</u> made sure her female astronomy students were informed about their rights, inviting feminists to talk to her lab. <u>Helena Normanton</u>, England's first female barrister, was well known for mentoring female students and employing them in her chambers.

American computer scientist <u>Frances Allen</u> was so active in mentoring young women that, in 2000, IBM created the Frances E. Allen Women in Technology Mentoring Award, with Allen as its first recipient. But, as tennis player <u>Billie Jean King</u> said when appointed UNESCO's Global Mentor for Gender Equality in 2008: "There is so much work still to be done when it comes to breaking down barriers to opportunity for women and girls throughout the world."

1 JUNE

Gladys West

(1930–)

In June 1986, American mathematician Gladys West published a paper on processing satellite data which was vital to the development of GPS (global positioning system) technology, now used in everything from mobile phones to cars and social media to tell us where we are and where we're going.

Born into a rural farming community, West realized she "had to get an education to get out." She won a scholarship to study math and, in 1956, was only the second black woman working at Virginia's Naval Support Facility, where she would stay for forty-two years. She worked with the programmers of the brand new, room-sized computers to measure the earth's surface elevations and pinpoint specific locations. In 1986, she published a report, "Data Processing System Specifications for the Geosat Satellite Radar Altimeter," which was instrumental in the foundation of GPS.

West retired in 1998. Despite a stroke, which limited her mobility, hearing and vision, in 2018, aged eighty-eight, she completed a distance-learning doctorate in public administration. In December of that year, she was inducted into the US Air Force Space and Missile Pioneers' Hall of Fame.

Harriet Tubman

(1822–1913)

On this day in 1863, Harriet Tubman became the only woman to lead an armed expedition in the American Civil War. In September 1849, she had escaped from slavery and traveled with the Underground Railroad (a network of safe houses) to Pennsylvania, a free state. She herself then became a railroad "conductor"; nicknamed "Moses," she freed about a hundred people. When the Civil War began in 1861, Tubman worked as a cook and nurse, then as a spy and scout. As commander of a group of scouts, Tubman led raids to liberate enslaved people, partly in the hope that they would fight for the Union cause.

On the night of 2 June 1863, Tubman and her troop of 150 black soldiers piloted down the Combahee River on two paddle-steamers converted to gunboats. The steam whistles blew the signal for liberation; at the front of one of the boats, Tubman stood singing.

The "owners" tried to stop the liberation with the aid of whips and guns but at least 727 men, women and children escaped; Confederate troops were too late to stop them.

Tubman is celebrated by memorials all over the US. Her likeness was due to be printed on the new $20 bill, but this change was postponed by the Trump administration, citing "technical issues."

Pocahontas

(c.1596–1617)

From the early days of the Jamestown colony in Virginia, Pocahontas – daughter of Native American leader Powhatan – helped the English settlers with food supplies. When there were hostilities between the colonists and the Powhatan tribe, Pocohontas was taken hostage. She lived with the colonists for a year, during which she met John Rolfe, owner of a tobacco plantation. Their marriage in April 1614 was instrumental in ending the First Anglo-Powhatan War.

In 1616, Pocahontas and Rolfe traveled to England with their son, Thomas. On this day in 1616, Pocahontas arrived in Plymouth. On 6 January 1617, she went to a masque at Banqueting House, London, attended by James I and Queen Anne. Later that year, Pocahontas became unwell; she died and was buried in Gravesend, Kent.

Pocahontas is now an icon of American history; her story has been told on stage and screen. In the 1820s, she became a heroic symbol for Virginia's colonial history and many of the state's prominent families claimed to be descended from her. When, in 1924, the Virginia Racial Integrity Act forbade interracial marriage, it included a qualification: one could be one sixteenth Native American and still be "white." It was called "the Pocahontas Exception."

4 JUNE

Queen Christina of Sweden
(1626–1689)

On this day in 1654, Queen Christina of Sweden took European society by surprise by abdicating her throne. She immediately left the country, disguised as a man.

A queen from the age of six, Christina was educated to a very high level, studying from five o'clock in the morning. She became an extravagant patron of art, sculpture and music; her court was a port of call for intellectuals, including the philosopher Descartes. Christina founded a national newspaper, encouraged mining, trade and industry, and was unusually liberal in matters of religion and personal freedom.

The queen's sexuality has been much discussed. Today she might call herself genderqueer, but it is difficult to separate fact from court gossip. From childhood, she wore "masculine" clothes; later, she was probably in love with her lady-in-waiting, Ebba Starre, and with at least one man, Cardinal Azzolino.

Christina did not marry and named a cousin as her heir.

A Catholic convert, after leaving Protestant Sweden, Christina spent many years in Rome as the guest of several popes, including Alexander VII, who called her "a queen without a realm, a Christian without faith, and a woman without shame." She is one of only six women buried in the Basilica of St. Peter in Rome.

Harriet Beecher Stowe

(1811–1896)

On this day in 1851, Harriet Beecher Stowe published the first installment of *Uncle Tom's Cabin* in the abolitionist paper, *National Era*. The novel, a sentimental story of an enslaved family, was published in its entirety in 1852 and was an instant sensation on both sides of the Atlantic. Stowe's work influenced worldwide opinion ahead of the American Civil War, which ended slavery in the US.

Stowe was one of thirteen children, many of whom followed their father, minister Lyman Beecher, into Christian activism and social reform. Later, Stowe's marital home was a station on the Underground Railroad, offering shelter to people escaping slavery (see Harriet Tubman). In 1850, the Fugitive Slave Act was passed, allowing Southern "owners" to retrieve escapees from northern free states. Stowe was at risk of heavy fines or imprisonment. This Act was the spur for Stowe to begin *Uncle Tom's Cabin*.

Uncle Tom had an immense impact on white audiences. Its romantic style is certainly flawed: Stowe's melodramatic narrative makes white Christian women role models and Uncle Tom himself is so subservient that his name is still used to describe a servile person of color. As an emotive campaigning narrative for its time, however, it was unrivalled.

Martha Gellhorn
(1908–1998)

On this day in 1944, 150,000 Allied troops landed on the Normandy beaches. Only one woman was amongst them. Legendary American war correspondent Martha Gellhorn had stowed away on a hospital ship to report from the danger zone knowing that, as a woman, she would be forbidden to go.

Gellhorn was publishing newspaper articles in the US by the age of twenty-one. After a stint in Paris, she returned to work for family friends, the Roosevelts, at the White House. They sent her to report on the desperate poverty across Depression-era America with photographer Dorothea Lange; this was the real beginning of a long and peripatetic career.

D-Day was not the first or last time Gellhorn used subterfuge to overcome sexism. She often pretended to be visiting a lover "one last time" to get past checkpoints. She filed reports from conflict zones all over the world, including the Spanish Civil War, Burma, Vietnam, the Middle East and Central America, and she was present at the liberation of the Dachau concentration camp. Aged eighty-one, she entered Panama – posing as a reviewer for the *Daily Telegraph* – in order to report on the US invasion. Shortly afterwards, failing eyesight and cancer brought her career to an end. She took her own life at the age of eighty-nine.

7 JUNE

Annie Smith Peck (1850–1935) and Fanny Bullock Workman (1859–1925)

In June 1911, mountaineer Annie Smith Peck placed a "Votes for Women" banner on the summit of Corupuna in Peru. A year later, Fanny Bullock Workman unfurled a "Votes for Women" newspaper during an expedition she led to the Siachen Glacier in the Himalayas. Co-founders of the American Alpine Club, Peck and Workman were also rivals, competing for altitude records.

Peck became famous in 1895 not only for climbing the Matterhorn but by being scandalously the first woman to do it in trousers, which led to calls for her arrest (see What are you wearing?). Two years later, she climbed Mexico's Citlaltépetl volcano, the highest point in the western hemisphere to have then been reached by a woman. Supporting herself by giving lectures and writing books, Peck wrote: "Climbing is unadulterated hard labour. The only real pleasure is the satisfaction of going where no man has been before."

Fanny Bullock Workman traveled with her husband, a surgeon. During their eight trips to the Himalayas, Workman set three women's altitude records, although some were disputed. The Workmans published books illustrated with Fanny's photographs, including maps and scientific observations.

Competition between Peck and Workman intensified in 1908: after climbing Peru's Mount Huascaran, Peck claimed she'd beaten the world elevation record Workman had set at Pinnacle Peak in the US. But surveyors sent by Workman found that Huascaran was actually a thousand feet lower.

8 JUNE

Zaha Hadid

(1950–2016)

In June 1993, Iraqi-British architect Zaha Hadid completed the Vitra Fire Station in Germany. This small but eye-catching building, with its sharp angles and visually striking planes, was her first major commission. Hadid's work, built just at the time when computer design opened up new possibilities, continued to innovate and surprise for over two decades until her death in 2016.

Hadid's architecture pushes traditional materials into grandiose curves, unexpected gradients and unusual angles; she often used environmentally friendly materials such as recycled concrete or sustainable wood. The word "parametric" was coined to describe these memorable structures. Her buildings include the Riverside Museum in Glasgow, whose zig-zag outline echoes the line of a river, and London's Aquatic Centre, which has streamlined curves like the flanks of a shark. In China, the Guangzhou Opera House looks like a science-fiction spaceport. Even functional constructions like ski jumps and bridges were designed with such flair that they have become impressive landmarks. In 2004, Hadid was the first woman to win the prestigious Pritzker Architecture Prize; she remains the only woman to be awarded the Royal Institute of British Architects' Gold Medal.

"If I was a guy, they would think I'm just opinionated. But as a woman, I'm 'difficult.'"

9 JUNE

Frances Allen

(1932-)

On this day in 2007, computer scientist Frances Allen became the first woman to be awarded the Turing Award – the "Nobel Prize of computing" – for her work in the field of automatic program optimization. Allen had joined tech company IBM as a computer programmer in 1957 to pay off the debt she incurred from her masters degree; she planned to get back to teaching mathematics. But her first task at IBM was training scientists how to use "compilers" – programs which translate software into the fundamental computer language known as machine code that a computer runs on. She was hooked, and from then on she worked to make these compilers better and faster.

In 1989, Allen became IBM's first female Fellow. In 2000, IBM created the Frances E. Allen Women in Technology Mentoring Award to honor her for not only focusing on her own forty-five-year career but mentoring younger women (see <u>Passing it on</u>). Allen herself was the award's first recipient. Computing was a field where women had been dominant until the early 1970s, she said in a 2003 interview, adding:

> "In the technical community [mentoring] has become extremely important, particularly to the women. It's catching on in a wonderful way."

10 JUNE

Hedy Lamarr

(1914–2000)

On this day in 1941, Austrian-born film star Hedy Lamarr, famous Hollywood "sex bomb" of the 1940s, filed a patent for a communication system, developed with her friend, composer George Antheil. This technology – radio signals sent at changing frequencies – is now used in everything from WiFi and Bluetooth to GPS.

"Inventions are easy for me to do," she once said. But her looks led her into acting and at eighteen she appeared in a Czech film, *Extase*, banned by Hitler for its nudity and famous sex scene. Fleeing a controlling husband, Lamarr headed for Hollywood where her friend, the businessman and aviator Howard Hughes, set up a chemistry lab in her trailer. Together they redesigned airplane wings, inspired by the aerodynamics of fish and birds. Lamarr also invented an improved traffic light.

To help the Allies win the Second World War, Lamarr, who was Jewish, and Antheil developed their frequency hopping system to prevent torpedoes from being intercepted. However, their invention was shelved by the US Navy, and the government, declaring Lamarr an "enemy alien," seized the patent. The Navy later developed the technology but neither Lamarr nor Antheil made anything from their invention.

Anne Knight

(1786–1862)

In June 1840, seasoned abolitionist Anne Knight was one of the British delegates at the World Anti-Slavery Convention in London. Female delegates to the convention – including Lucy Townsend from Britain and Lucretia Mott and Elizabeth Cady Stanton from the US – were outraged to find themselves banned from speaking. Perhaps they shouldn't have been so surprised: male abolitionists had a tradition of excluding women from their campaign groups. The large numbers of women involved in the anti-slavery movement had to form their own societies, such as Knight's Chelmsford Ladies' Anti-Slavery Society.

Made aware, once again, that their capacity for public action was limited by their sex, the women were spurred on to campaign for their own rights in the UK and the US. Knight had supported the nineteenth-century British Chartists in their fight for parliamentary and voting reform but became disillusioned when it was clear that the charter's so-called "universal suffrage" excluded women.

In 1847, Knight published what is probably the first leaflet about women's suffrage: "Never will the nations of the earth be well governed, until both sexes, as well as all parties, are fully represented." In 1851, she formed the Sheffield Female Political Association, the first women's suffrage group in Britain.

"Never will the nations of the earth be well governed, until both sexes, as well as all parties, are fully represented."

12 JUNE

Margaret Harrison
(1918–2015)

On this day in 1982, sixty-four-year-old Margaret Harrison and her husband Bobby set up a tent in a lay-by next to the naval base in Faslane, Scotland, establishing what would become the world's longest-running peace camp. Despite several threats to its existence from the authorities and occasional periods of dwindling interest, it survives as a ramshackle collection of caravans to this day.

The Harrisons had protested at anti-nuclear rallies and camps for decades. Early members of the Campaign for Nuclear Disarmament (CND), they took part in the famous 1950s marches from Aldermaston to London. Margaret was first arrested for her activism in 1961 and added a dozen further arrests to her record in a long career of peaceful protest.

Surprisingly, during the Second World War she had worked at a shipyard producing military vessels. Although registered as a conscientious objector, she did not leave the job: "I was living at home with my parents and they would have been very upset."

In the early 1980s, fears of nuclear war were widespread in the UK, and CND enjoyed a second lease of life. Margaret and Bobby continued to campaign against the installation of nuclear missiles and were given the Freedom of Dumbarton in 1985 for their long commitment to disarmament.

Boudica

(c.30–61 CE)

In the summer of 60 or 61 CE, Boudica, leader of the Iceni tribe in eastern Britain, led her people in a revolt against Roman occupiers. Although the Romans built their empire by military force, they often won a workable peace after invasion by honoring local beliefs and culture. In Britain, however, they were heavy-handed. Taxes and conscription were imposed; tribal lands were settled by ex-soldiers; a conspicuous temple was dedicated to the emperor.

The death of Boudica's husband, Prasutagus, brought a further outrage. As a chief of the Iceni and a friend to Rome, Prasutagus left his lands to be ruled jointly by his wife and the emperor. Instead, the Romans seized his whole estate. Boudica appealed the decision. She expected a fair hearing from the authorities; instead, she was flogged like a criminal. Her young daughters were publicly gang raped. This shocking provocation, recorded by Roman historian Tacitus, united the Iceni and their neighbors, the Trinovantes. Their combined forces overwhelmed the Roman Ninth Legion and destroyed Camulodunum (Colchester), Londinium (London) and Verulamium (St. Albans), before being defeated by the Roman army.

As a captured enemy, Boudica knew that she would probably be humiliated in a Roman triumphal procession. Instead, she killed herself. Archaeological evidence of her initial success survives in the soil around Colchester as a "destruction layer" of ash and debris known as the Boudican Layer.

She expected a fair hearing from the authorities; instead, she was flogged like a criminal.

14 JUNE

Marianna Martines

(1744–1812)

"In my seventh year [my parents] began to introduce me to the study of music, for which they believed me inclined by nature." Composer Marianna Martines was a favorite of Austrian Empress Maria Theresa; the Empress's son, the future emperor, turned the teenage musician's pages at concerts and the court composer taught her music theory.

Composers were mostly employed by churches or noble families but these positions were rarely available for women. It was also difficult for women to travel to give concerts or to compose music for patrons in other cities. So Martines remained in Vienna, where she wrote for court and religious events, held music and art salons and established a singing school for young women. She herself had trained as a singer and often sang her own compositions.

Despite staying close to home, her reputation grew throughout Europe and, in 1773, she was the first woman admitted to the Accademia Filarmonica of Bologna. Some scholars think her work may have influenced Mozart. We know from early catalogues that she created 150 works. Only around sixty-five are still in existence; many were destroyed in a fire in 1927.

"In my seventh year [my parents] began to introduce me to the study of music, for which they believed me inclined by nature."

Florence Price

(1887–1953)

On this day in 1933, Florence Beatrice Price became the first black female composer to have a symphony performed by a major orchestra, when the world première of her "Symphony No. 1 in E minor" was performed at a concert in Chicago entitled "The Negro in Music."

Price had studied at the New England Conservatory, where she had initially presented herself as of Mexican, rather than African-American, descent. In 1910, she became Head of Music at what is now Clark Atlanta University. Two years later, she married lawyer Thomas Price and moved back to her hometown of Little Rock. After several local incidents of racist violence, including a lynching, the Prices moved to Chicago.

In the early 1930s, Price – now a divorced single mother – was earning her living as an organist for silent film screenings and by composing jingles for radio ads. In 1932, Price submitted her "Symphony No. 1 in E minor" for the Rodman Wanamaker Competition and won first prize.

Price's classical music training was in the European tradition but many of her compositions use elements from spirituals and folk songs, weaving together traditional structures with contemporary vernacular styles. In 2009, many of Price's scores – including her fourth symphony – were found in an abandoned house in Illinois. The *New Yorker* wrote: "That run-down house . . . is a potent symbol of how a country can forget its cultural history."

The first black female composer to have a symphony performed by a major orchestra.

Valentina Tereshkova

(1937–)

On this day in 1963, Valentina Tereshkova became the first woman to go into space. After the launch, she radioed down from space capsule Vostok 6: "How beautiful the Earth is . . . everything is going well." She orbited Earth forty-eight times over three days. She is the only woman to have been on a solo space mission. After her space flight, Tereshkova received congratulations from around the world. Women in particular were excited about the expansion of women's roles that her achievement seemed to promise.

Tereshkova, a textile-factory worker and amateur parachutist, had been one of five women recruited to the Soviet Cosmonaut Corps in 1962; the aim was to ensure that the first woman in space would be Soviet, not American. But despite Tereshkova's achievement, the female cosmonaut program was shut down in 1969. She was channelled into political positions and roles representing the Soviet Union abroad. In November 1963, she married fellow cosmonaut Andriyan Nikolayev; the marriage was encouraged by the Soviet space authorities as a "fairy-tale message to the country." The couple's daughter, Elena, was the first person with both a mother and father who had traveled into space.

Tereshkova said she would volunteer to go to Mars, even if the trip turned out to be one-way.

17 JUNE

Noor Inayat Khan
(1914–1944)

Born in Moscow to an American mother and a father descended from Indian royalty, Noor Inayat Khan and her family were living in Paris when the Second World War began. After France was occupied by the Nazis, Khan, a poet and harpist, escaped to Britain and joined the Women's Auxiliary Air Force. In 1942, the Special Operations Executive (SOE) recruited her as a radio operator – and on this day in 1943, Khan became the first female radio operator sent by Britain into occupied France to help the French Resistance.

Despite doubts about her lack of experience, Khan, codenamed "Madeleine" and posing as a children's nurse, became radio operator for the "Prosper" Resistance network. When other British agents were arrested, she chose to stay. With dyed blonde hair and constantly on the move, she did vital work, helping airmen escape and allowing critical deliveries to come in. In October 1943, she was betrayed, arrested and tortured, but refused to cooperate. The following September, together with three other female SOE agents, Khan was transferred to Dachau concentration camp and executed.

Khan was posthumously awarded the George Cross in 1949. After a campaign by the Noor Inayat Khan Memorial Trust, a statue of her was erected in London's Gordon Square in 2012 – Britain's first memorial dedicated to a woman of Asian descent.

She was the first female radio operator sent by Britain . . . to help the French resistance.

18 JUNE

Sutematsu Yamakawa Ōyama
(1860-1919)

In 1872, aged eleven, Sutematsu Yamakawa Ōyama was selected as one of "the two most promising girl-students in Japan," as she later said, and sent to America to receive a Western education. She lived with the family of an anti-slavery activist and Congregational minister in Connecticut, near her brother, who was studying at Yale. In June 1882, she became the first Japanese woman with a college degree, graduating third in her class at Vassar College.

Although Ōyama had been class president at Vassar, a member of the Shakespeare Club and president of the theatre group, on returning to Japan she found it hard to get a job. She could still speak Japanese but couldn't read or write in her native language. After marrying the minister of war, she became Princess Ōyama through his promotions. Together with Alice Bacon, the daughter of the Connecticut family she had grown up in, and Tsude Uma, one of the other girls sent to the US, Ōyama founded a private language school for women in 1900, which would produce many of Japan's leading feminists.

She became the first Japanese woman with a college degree.

19 JUNE

Emily Hobhouse

(1860-1926)

In 1900, reports started to reach Britain that, as part of the Anglo-Boer War in South Africa, the British Army was imprisoning women and children in "concentration camps." British suffragist and pacifist Emily Hobhouse traveled to South Africa to investigate conditions in the camps and to distribute aid; she witnessed the disease and deaths caused by overcrowding, lack of food, poor hygiene and limited medical facilities.

In June 1901, in defiance of official hostility (the secretary of state for the British colonies called her a "hysterical spinster of mature age"), Hobhouse delivered a report which included photos of (white) Boer women and children imprisoned in the camps.

Forced to respond, the British government set up a committee of inquiry, whose members, uniquely for its time, were all women. Chair Millicent Fawcett initially claimed

that the camps were "necessary from a military point of view." But having seen them, she changed her mind and the recommendations of the Ladies' Committee echoed those made by Hobhouse a year earlier. As a result, the camps were reformed; the death rates for Boer inmates dropped significantly. Neither Hobhouse nor Fawcett visited any of the camps for black prisoners.

Hobhouse's ashes are ensconced at the base of the National Women's Monument (Vrouemonument) in Bloemfontein, South Africa: a memorial for the 27,000 Boer women and children who died in the camps. There is no memorial to the 20,000 South Africans who died in the black camps.

20 JUNE

Lucy Wills

(1888–1964)

On this day in 1931, Lucy Wills published her paper on pernicious anemia (a vitamin B12 deficiency) in pregnant women in the *British Medical Journal*.

After qualifying at London's Royal Free Hospital School of Medicine for Women, Lucy Wills worked in its department of pregnant pathology. In 1928, she joined the Maternal Mortality Inquiry in Bombay, India. There, Wills observed an apparent correlation between class, diet and anemia during pregnancy; poor Muslim women were most susceptible. Wills demonstrated that this could not be pure pernicious anemia because it didn't respond to the standard cure: Vitamin B12, found in liver extracts.

In experiments on rats, Wills discovered that those fed on the same diet as the Muslim women became anemic but that this could be prevented or cured by adding yeast to their diet. She repeated the findings in clinical trials with women. Fortunately there was a cheap source of yeast extract available: Marmite. The newly-discovered B vitamin in Marmite was named the "Wills Factor" – we know it as folic acid. We know now that it doesn't just save pregnant mothers from anemia but also helps the fetal brain to develop, preventing birth defects such as spina bifida.

In her later career, Wills became Head of Pathology at the Royal Free Hospital and established the first hematology department there. In retirement, she traveled the world, continuing her research on the links between nutrition and illness.

21 JUNE

Elizabeth Wilkinson/Stokes

(1700s, active 1722–1728)

In June 1722, Elizabeth Wilkinson fought Hannah Hyfield in the first recorded women's boxing match. The *London Journal* reported: "Two of the Feminine Gender appeared for the first Time on the Theatre of War at Hockley in the Hole, and maintained the Battle with great Valour for a long time, to the no small Satisfaction of the spectators."

The papers often printed the original challenges issued by Wilkinson, providing wonderful examples of boxing "trash talk." In 1728, accepting a challenge from Anne Field, an ass-driver from Stoke Newington, she wrote that, "The blows which I shall present her with will be more difficult for her to digest than any she ever gave her asses."

Wilkinson's fame was at least equal to that of her male contemporaries until the end of the nineteenth century, but in 1880 the Amateur Boxing Association of England banned female fighters.

Women continued to go to boxing clubs but the official ban was only lifted in 1996. The first appearance of women boxers in the Olympics came in 2012.

"I; Elizabeth Wilkinson of Clerkenwell, having had some Words with Hannah Hyfield, and requiring Satisfaction, do invite her to meet me on the Stage, and Box me for Three Guineas."

Maria Gaetana Agnesi
(1718–1799)

In June 1748, Italian mathematician Maria Gaetana Agnesi published the first mathematics textbook, *Analytical Institutions for the Use of Italian Youth*. It explained the brand new field of calculus. Like her French colleague <u>Émilie Du Châtelet</u>, Agnesi came from a wealthy family who held gatherings of intellectuals at their Milanese home. These were a showcase for Agnesi, a child prodigy known as the "Seven-Tongued Orator" – she was fluent in several languages by the age of eleven – to talk on various philosophical topics.

The eldest of twenty-one children, Agnesi asked to enter a convent. Her father forbade it but allowed her to live in seclusion and keep doing research as long as she taught her siblings. Her two-volume textbook, which she said was written for them, brought her fame and attention. She was elected to the Bologna Academy of Sciences and appointed the University of Bologna's second female professor, after Laura Bassi, although she never took up the position. Ironically for a devout Catholic, Agnesi is known for a mathematical curve usually called the "witch of Agnesi" because of a mistranslation. She later turned her home into a refuge for the poor and became director of the women's ward of a Milan hospital.

23 JUNE

Rachel Carson

(1907–1964)

On this day in 1962, the second part of *Silent Spring*, American biologist and writer Rachel Carson's article on pesticides, was published in the *New Yorker* magazine. Her book of the same title, published later that year, became a bestseller, inspiring the creation of the environmental movement.

Carson studied zoology and was the second woman hired by the US Bureau of Fisheries, as editor-in-chief of all Fish and Wildlife Service publications. *Silent Spring* was sparked by a letter from a friend about the effect of pesticides on birdlife. In her book, Carson discusses pesticides' potential to cause cancer in humans and accuses the chemical industry of misleading the public. "Nature has introduced great variety into the landscape, but man has displayed a passion for simplifying it. Thus he undoes the built-in checks and balances by which nature holds the species within bounds."

Although chemical companies tried to label her a Communist and "hysterical woman," 15 million people watched the 1963 TV special *The Silent Spring of Rachel Carson*, and President Kennedy's Science Advisory Committee validated her research. The pesticide DDT was banned for agricultural use and the resulting environmental movement led to the creation of the Environmental Protection Agency in the US.

24 JUNE

Clärenore Stinnes

(1901–1990)

When a woman is mentioned for her achievements, it is often as the *first* woman to do something, as if she was singular, an aberration. Today we celebrate German car racer Clärenore Stinnes, who, on this day in 1929, arrived back in Berlin after her 47,000 km journey, the *second* woman to circumnavigate the globe in a car. Canadian <u>Aloha Wanderwell</u> had made it into the record books after completing her journey two years earlier.

Stinnes took part in her first car race at the age of twenty-four and became one of the most successful racing car drivers in Europe, with seventeen wins. She set off on her round-the-world trip on 25 May 1927, accompanied by two mechanics, a freight vehicle with spare parts and equipment and Carl-Axel Söderström, a Swedish cinematographer she'd met a few days earlier. They drove through twenty-three countries, arriving back in Germany by ship from New York. In 1931, Stinnes and Söderström, who had married and settled in Sweden, released a documentary about the trip, *Im Auto durch zwei Welten* ("Across Two Worlds by Car").

"The automobile makes the big world small."

Elena Cornaro Piscopia
(1646–1684)

On this day in 1678, Venetian philosopher Elena Cornaro Piscopia became the first woman in the world with a doctorate. Piscopia, a child prodigy, had become known for her translation of the Spanish book, *Colloquy of Christ*. She wanted to study for a theology doctorate but, when the bishop objected because of her sex, switched to philosophy. Her doctoral examination attracted such interest it had to be moved to a larger venue, Padua Cathedral. After talking for an hour in classical Latin about Aristotle, she was granted the degree immediately, without the usual vote.

Piscopia devoted the rest of her life to charity. She was so well known that after she died memorial services were held in four cities. Although the University of Padua created a medal in her honor, Piscopia's achievement did not open doors for women: when a second female student applied to take the doctoral examination, the university changed its rules to ban women. This is a common pattern, in which one pioneer woman is admitted to an institution and the rules are then changed to prevent further women following. It wouldn't be until 1732 that a second woman received the degree.

26 JUNE

JK Rowling

(1965–)

On this day in 1997, an unknown British author called JK Rowling published her first book, *Harry Potter and the Philosopher's Stone*. Twenty years later, she was the UK's bestselling living author with a personal fortune estimated at £600 million. A global influence survey named her the tenth-most influential "thought leader" in the world.

Before publication of her books, Rowling survived with help from state benefits. The years since have brought her not only wealth, but a substantial impact on popular culture. The seven Harry Potter books are the fastest sellers in history and they are read in over sixty languages. They generate revenue not only for Rowling but for many involved in spin-off films, theme parks, merchandise, shows and other projects. Rowling has put her wealth to good use, with philanthropic donations including £15.3 million to research multiple

sclerosis, the disease which killed her mother at the age of forty-five.

It is largely because of Rowling that young readers are now seen as a serious market force, and "crossover" fiction, read by all age groups, has come into being. A 2012 survey found that 55 per cent of young adult fiction in America is read by adults; JK Rowling is largely responsible for this shift.

Helen Keller

(1880–1968)

Today is Helen Keller Day in the US, marking the birthday of this humanitarian campaigner and disability activist.

Keller was a brilliant child who, when left blind and deaf by illness, was frustrated by her inability to communicate. Once armed with sign language – taught to her by tutor and friend Anne Sullivan – she flourished. In 1904, she graduated *cum laude* from Radcliffe College, Harvard, as the first deaf-blind woman to earn a degree. Realizing that her disabilities made her especially memorable to able-bodied audiences, Keller pressed this unwanted celebrity into the service of campaigns for social justice. She published a memoir and undertook speaking tours across the world.

Keller was a powerful advocate for disabled people, but also a suffragette, pacifist and supporter of birth control. Recognizing that many people acquired disability through poor working conditions, she became a prominent socialist.

She called out unsympathetic editors who refused to print her articles, saying of one: "[Formerly] the compliments he paid me were so generous that I blush to remember them. But now that I have come out for socialism, he reminds me and the public that I am blind and deaf and especially liable to error."

In 1920, when radicals in the US were being unlawfully arrested, Keller co-founded the American Civil Liberties Union (ACLU). It remains a dynamic and important organization for many kinds of social justice campaigning.

Theresa Kachindamoto

(1959–)

In June 2015, Theresa Kachindamoto, the Inkosi or paramount chief of Dedza, Malawi, annulled 330 child marriages in her district and returned the children to school. Kachindamoto convinced local leaders to ban child marriage on the grounds that young Malawians need education and better opportunities.

Malawi has one of the highest rates of child marriage in the world. The cultural tradition is deep-rooted and, where dowries are exchanged, it is an important transaction. In some communities, up to half of the girls under eighteen are married. Some are expected to have sex as a "cleansing" ritual after their first period, often with a sex worker hired for this purpose. In a country with poor rates of education and high rates of HIV infection, the Malawi government recognized this as a problem. It outlawed marriage for under-eighteens in 2015.

However, many Malawians look to traditional leaders rather than national government for jurisdiction, therefore Kachindamoto stepped up. She worked with local people, religious organizations and the UN to uphold the change. By 2019, Kachindamoto had overseen the reversal of over 3,500 child marriages. In 2016 she was recognized with the Hrant Dink International Award for human rights activists.

29 JUNE

Vigdis Finnbogadóttir

(1930–)

On this day in 1980, theatre director Vigdis Finnbogadóttir became president of Iceland. She served for sixteen years and remains the longest-serving elected female head of state so far. Her presidency started a domino effect of social change in Iceland and across the world.

Finnbogadóttir was encouraged by the Woman's Day Off in 1975, when 90 per cent of Iceland's women withdrew from all work including domestic chores. "Everything came to a halt . . . [It was] a day of joy, a day of much laughter and singing. And extremely intelligent speeches." After the protest, men and women alike began to call for more women in Iceland's political life.

Other women followed in Finnbogadóttir's footsteps, and so too did legislation on issues primarily concerning women and the balancing of gender roles. Laws were passed on parental leave, paid childcare and equal pay; on prostitution, domestic violence and gender quotas for company boards. These reforms have led to Iceland being consistently ranked the most gender-equal country in the world by the World Economic Forum.

In a BBC interview, Finnbogadóttir told the story of a little boy in Iceland who saw Ronald Reagan on TV and asked, "Mummy, mummy, can a *man* be president?" The power of example and role models cannot be overestimated, as Finnbogadóttir said: "Women thought: if she can, I can."

30 JUNE

Maria Sibylla Merian

(1647–1717)

In 1679, German naturalist, illustrator and explorer Maria Sibylla Merian published Volume I of *The Wondrous Transformation of Caterpillars*, the first book to show insects' life cycles and animal-plant relationships. Bringing together art and science, her observations transformed scientific thinking. At the time, many naturalists believed that insects emerged spontaneously from rotten meat, mud or even rain.

"I noticed that much more beautiful butterflies and moths would emerge from other caterpillars," Merian wrote. "This inspired me to collect all the caterpillars I could find and observe their metamorphoses." In Volume II of *The Wondrous Transformation*, Merian's illustrations documented this metamorphosis for the first time.

Leaving her husband, Merian moved with her daughters to Amsterdam, where women were allowed to own businesses. Using money from sales of her drawings, in June 1699, she and her daughter, Dorothea, sailed to Surinam in South America to collect specimens. Merian employed indigenous people to bring her insects and clear paths for her through the jungle. The result was *The Metamorphosis of the Insects of Suriname*, published in 1705.

After her death, Merian's reputation was sullied by accusations about lack of scientific training and inaccuracy; it seems that publishers were adding errors, including imaginary insects, into new editions. Dismissed at the time as "nothing more than an artist," she is now considered the first ecologist.

JULY

"It's gotten me into a lot of trouble. But . . . speaking out has sustained me and given meaning to my life."
– Hazel Scott

Tea

When we think of tea in history, we may picture ladies in drawing rooms, sipping from china cups and discussing the price of muslin or improvements to their garden. In fact, afternoon tea has often been the setting for more revolutionary plans. It was at afternoon tea on 9 July 1848 that five women – Jane Hunt, Lucretia Mott, Martha Wright, Mary Ann McClintock and Elizabeth Cady Stanton – planned the first women's rights convention in the US, which took place just ten days later at Seneca Falls, New York.

The 1848 Seneca Falls "Declaration of Sentiments" – the first US statement of women's rights – was written and signed at Stanton's now iconic traveling tea table.

In Canada, in the early twentieth century, suffragists organized "Pink Teas" to which only women were invited. Tables with frilly "feminine" pink decorations were topped with cakes. The discussion, however, was not sugary but subversive:

how to campaign for the vote. It was also at Pink Teas that the Famous Five gathered support for their petition to have women considered "persons."

The first tearoom in the UK was opened by a female manager of London's Aerated Bread Company in around 1864, whose name, sadly, has gone unrecorded. By the end of the nineteenth century, there were thousands of tea rooms: places in which women of all classes could appear in public, unchaperoned. Parkers in Manchester and the Gardenia in London were key venues for women organizing campaigns for the vote, whether the more law-abiding suffragists or the radical suffragettes.

Not only is tea often to be found in the stories of women, women are often to be found in the stories of tea, as inventors and merchants. In 1879, Mabel Cabell Tyree published the first recipe for iced tea in her *Housekeeping in Old Virginia*. Roberta Lawson and Mary Molaren of Milwaukee, Wisconsin, were the first to patent the tea bag ("Tea-Leaf Holder"), in 1901. In eighteenth-century Britain, Mary Tuke of York was one of the first tea merchants; Mary Twining ran the Twinings tea import business and shop in London for twenty-one years after her husband's death in 1762. Oura Kei from Nagasaki was responsible for the massive growth of the Japanese tea export business in the 1800s.

In the present day, most tea-pickers are women, some of them carrying their babies as they work. The breadline wages make families vulnerable to people traffickers who offer their daughters a well-paid job. In 2018, around 400,000 tea-plantation workers in Bengal went on strike and secured pay rises. The connection between tea and revolution lives on.

1 JULY

Fanny Mendelssohn

(1805–1847)

In July 1846, German pianist and composer Fanny Mendelssohn wrote in her diary: "I have now decided to publish my things," defying her brother Felix, who had published her compositions under his name. They had both been taught to play the piano by their mother and, in 1820, had joined the Sing-Akademie zu Berlin, led by Carl Friedrich Zelter. In letters to German author Goethe, Zelter described Fanny as "something special," saying she "plays like a man." She would go on to write more than 460 pieces of music, including a piano trio and several books of solo piano works.

Some now believe that the "Songs Without Words" genre her brother became famous for may have been started by her. "It must be a sign of talent," Fanny wrote, "that I do not give up, though I can get nobody to take an interest in my effort."

Publishing Fanny's work as his own caused some embarrassment for Felix when he had to confess to Queen Victoria that her favorite song of his had actually been written by his sister. In 2010, an American musicologist, Angela Mace Christian, recognized that a work signed "F Mendelssohn" and attributed to Felix was actually by Fanny. It had its first performance under her name on International Women's Day, 8 March 2017.

2 JULY

Fanny Schoonheyt

(1912–1961)

In July 1936, Fanny Schoonheyt began fighting against the fascists in the Spanish Civil War, the only Dutch woman to take up arms for the Republican cause. She became famous for her technical knowledge and bravery and was called *la reina de la ametralladora* – "the queen of the machine gun" – by Barcelona newspapers.

In 1934, Schoonheyt had left the Netherlands because it was "dusty, musty, flat and boring." A year later, she stood out at Communist Youth Meetings in Spain: tall, blonde and smoking a cigarette. In 1936, she worked as a press agent for the planned People's Olympiad, which was canceled because of Franco's coup. Schoonheyt fought in the defense of Barcelona against Franco and later became an officer in the Spanish Republican Army.

In 1937, all of the 600–800 Dutch citizens who fought for the Republicans were declared stateless by their government; many ended up in concentration camps. Schoonheyt, helped by the Emigration Service for Spanish Republicans, moved to the Dominican Republic, where the dictator Trujillo was welcoming white European immigrants.

For the rest of her life, Schoonheyt spoke little of her radical youth. It was her biographer, Yvonne Scholten, who first informed Schoonheyt's daughter of her mother's actions in Spain: "When I told her that her mother had been famous as 'queen of the machine gun' and the bravest girl of Barcelona, she was flabbergasted."

3 JULY

Hazel Scott

(1920–1981)

At the New York home she shared with her musician mother, Alma Long Scott, Hazel Scott was mentored by jazz greats. At just nineteen, Scott became the new headline act for Café Society – the first racially integrated nightclub in the United States – when Billie Holiday had to cancel a gig and insisted on Scott as her replacement.

Scott was one of the first black entertainers to stipulate in their contract that they would never play for segregated audiences. When she began acting in Hollywood, she refused to take subservient roles: "It's gotten me into a lot of trouble. But . . . speaking out has sustained me and given meaning to my life." Her outspokenness put paid to her film career, but she was then offered her own TV show. On this day in 1950, Scott became the first African-American to host a US network television series – *The Hazel Scott Show*.

This was the McCarthy era in America, when left-wing citizens were suspected of communism. Because of her connection with Café Society, Scott was under suspicion. She appeared voluntarily in front of the House Un-American Activities Committee and spoke her mind. Afterwards, she moved to Paris with her son, where her apartment became a hangout for musicians and artists.

4 JULY

Susan B. Anthony (1820-1906); Matilda Joslyn Gage (1826-1898); Sara Andrews Spencer (1837-1909); Lillie Devereux Blake (1833-1913); Phoebe Wilson Couzins (1842-1913)

On this day in 1876, American suffragists Susan B. Anthony, Matilda Joslyn Gage, Sara Andrews Spencer, Lillie Devereux Blake and Phoebe Wilson Couzins crashed the celebration of the hundredth anniversary of American independence in Philadelphia.

After listening to the 1776 Declaration of Independence being read out by Senator Thomas Ferry, the five women made their way to the platform. Looking rather pale, Ferry accepted their "Declaration of Rights of the Women of the United States," making the women's guerrilla action seem part of the official proceedings. As the women walked back down the aisle in Independence Square, they scattered printed copies to audience members, who were keen to take them.

The women then made their way to a platform in front of Independence Hall, where Anthony read out the declaration while Gage held an umbrella to shield her from the sun: "We ask of our rulers, at this hour, no special favors, no special privileges, no special legislation. We ask justice, we ask equality, we ask that all the civil and political rights that belong to citizens of the United States, be guaranteed to us and our daughters forever."

The suffragists' request took a long time to be heard; the Nineteenth Amendment to the United States Constitution, giving women the right to vote, was finally passed by Congress in May 1919, almost forty-three years later.

5 JULY

Marion Wallace Dunlop

(1864–1942)

On this day in 1909, sculptor and illustrator Marion Wallace Dunlop began the first modern hunger strike as a protest against the authorities' refusal to recognize her, a suffragette, as a political prisoner. She was released after three and a half days of refusing food.

Wallace Dunlop had been involved in the suffrage movement from 1900. From 1908, she was active in <u>Emmeline Pankhurst</u>'s Women's Social and Political Union (WSPU). She was arrested and imprisoned in Holloway for the first time in July 1908 for "obstruction," and again in November of that year.

On two occasions in June 1909, Wallace Dunlop stamped an extract from the Bill of Rights on the wall of St Stephen's Hall in the Palace of Westminster. She was arrested and sent back to Holloway where she began her hunger strike. Her action, though not official WSPU policy, was adopted by many other suffragette prisoners over the summer of 1909. It had a much wider influence too.

At the end of July 1909, Mahatma Gandhi attended a WSPU meeting in London: "We have a great deal to learn from these ladies and their movement." He later used fasting as a part of his non-violent resistance to British rule in India. Irish republican James Connolly named the suffragettes' actions as the inspiration for his hunger strike in 1913.

6 JULY

The Edinburgh Seven

(1860s-1890s)

On this day in 2019, the trailblazing students known as "the Edinburgh Seven" were posthumously awarded medical degrees, 150 years after they entered Edinburgh University. They were represented at the ceremony by seven women currently studying medicine.

In 1869, women in Britain were not allowed to take a university degree, but Sophia Jex-Blake wrote to ask if she might at least attend medical lectures at Edinburgh University. She was refused after 200 male students petitioned to keep her out. Nevertheless, Jex-Blake persisted. Later that year, she enrolled with six other women – Mary Anderson, Emily Bovell, Matilda Chaplin, Helen Evans, Edith Peche and Isabel Thorne. The "Edinburgh Seven" were the first women registered at any UK university.

The discrimination they suffered, like that faced by other pioneers, was stressful and humiliating. They were compelled to organize their own lectures. They were bullied; doors were shut in their faces and male students bayed at them. What happened when they arrived for their anatomy exam is now known as the Surgeons' Hall Riot. Hundreds pelted them with mud in the streets and a live sheep was driven into the exam hall. The women were not allowed to graduate. Several went to Paris or Ireland to earn qualifications that would allow them to practice medicine. All seven worked in or established new women's hospitals, from London and Edinburgh to Bombay and Tokyo.

The University of Edinburgh's first female doctors graduated in 1896. They still had to organize their own tuition.

Mary Harris "Mother" Jones
(c.1837–1930)

Mary Harris "Mother" Jones knew suffering and injustice throughout her life. In Ireland, she saw people starve while food was exported. After emigrating to the US, she lost her husband and children to yellow fever: "The rich and the well-to-do fled the city . . . One by one my four little children sickened and died."

Her activism began in the 1890s. The success of her work for miners' unions and their families earned her the title of "the most dangerous woman in America." Her slogan was "Pray for the dead and fight like hell for the living."

In June 1903, Jones came to Philadelphia to support 75,000 textile workers – at least 10,000 of them children – striking for a fifty-five-hour working week and a ban on night work by women and children. Told that newspapers were ignoring the outrage of child labor, which affected at least two million children across the US, because they didn't want to upset stockholders, she said, "I've got stock in these little children, and I'll arrange a little publicity."

On this day in 1903, the March of the Mill Children set off from Philadelphia, led by Jones. When the young marchers arrived in New York, around 30,000 people turned out to welcome them. In 1904, the National Child Labor Committee was formed.

8 JULY

Melitta Bentz

(1873–1950)

We have a woman in Dresden, Germany, to thank for the invention of the coffee filter. Fed up with lukewarm gritty coffee, Melitta Bentz started to conduct experiments in her kitchen to improve it. One day, she took blotting paper from her son's school notebook, folded it and stuck it into an old tin pot in which she had punched some holes. She put ground coffee in the cone of paper and poured hot water over it. The coffee that dripped into the cup was still hot, free of grounds and easy to clean up afterwards.

Bentz hosted coffee afternoons to try out her *Perfekter Kaffeegenuß* (perfect coffee enjoyment) on her friends and acquaintances. Recognizing its commercial potential, she patented her "coffee filter with a domed underside, recessed bottom and inclined flow holes." On this day in 1908, Bentz was awarded the patent for her invention.

In December 1908, Bentz started a company for the marketing of Melitta coffee filters. Its starting capital was seventy-two Reichspfennig; its address was the Bentz family flat. The family business waxed and waned through two world wars but survived, and now employs more than 4,000 people across the world. Most Melitta locations still have a photograph of their founder on the wall.

Catherine the Great

(1729–1796)

On this day in 1762, a German-born woman of thirty-three was enthroned as Empress of Russia. Catherine the Great, as she became, had usurped her husband, the eccentric and unpopular Peter III, in a palace coup; he mysteriously died eight days later. Catherine reigned over her enormous empire for thirty-four years. According to Voltaire, she was an "enlightened despot."

At home, Catherine took over church property, created new towns to build trade and crushed rebellion. Abroad, she annexed Ukraine, Poland and other territories, adding over 200,000 square miles to her empire and almost doubling the Russian population. Catherine was interested in the European enlightenment and social reform but knew that her own power depended on the deeply conservative aristocracy. Her reforms gave them more, not less

control over their workers.

The Empress was a patron of education and culture. Her court became a calling point for European intellectuals. She founded a girls' school, the Smolny Institute; her private art collection was the basis of the Hermitage Museum.

Like male monarchs with their *maîtresses en titre*, Catherine's lovers were installed as official favorites. The capable ones were given important positions. One was established as King Stanislas of Poland and her long-term partner, the legendary general Potemkin, became effective ruler of southern Russia. When Catherine the Great died, she was succeeded by her son Paul, whose father was probably her lover Count Orlov, and not her former husband.

10 JULY

Lise Cristiani

(1827–1853)

In early July 1849, Lise Cristiani played her cello to whales in the Pacific Ocean. She wrote in her diary: "One of the enormous cetaceans passed silently under our ship . . . Stradivarius was casting the most touching Bach melodies on the wind and the waves . . ."

Cristiani is the earliest known female solo cellist, at a time when this was considered scandalous because the cello was held between the legs – most women played "side-saddle" for modesty's sake. After a successful concert tour of Europe in 1844, she bought herself a Stradivarius cello. She called it "Lord Stradivarius, my noble husband."

Lord Stradivarius became her companion on an extraordinary, dangerous tour of the remotest parts of Russia. She transported her precious cello in a steel case, sealed with lead and covered with wolfskins: "I travelled by sleigh, cart, litter – pulled by horses, reindeer, dogs . . . I played in places where no artist had hereto set foot . . . I was more at ease than in the salons of St Petersburg."

We know that Cristiani played in Pyatigorsk in July 1853 because Tolstoy wrote about her performance in his diary. This may have been her last concert. She died of cholera three months later; her cello "husband" was with her. Now in the Stradivarius museum in Cremona, he bears her name: "the Cristiani."

Kate Edger

(1857–1935)

On this day in 1877, Kate Edger became the first woman in New Zealand to be awarded a university degree – and perhaps the first in the British Empire with a Bachelor of Arts. Over a thousand people came to the ceremony and the *New Zealand Herald* wrote, "Let us hear no more about the intellectual inferiority of women."

Born in England, Edger's family emigrated to New Zealand in 1862. The only girl at Auckland College and Grammar School because there was no equivalent girls' school, when she applied to university she mentioned her age and qualifications but not her gender. She was accepted; her graduation with a BA in maths and Latin in 1877 put an end to female students being fobbed off with a "certificate" instead of a degree.

Edger became headmistress of a girls' school, teaching subjects ranging from English to mathematics, geography – and even club swinging. After getting married, she ran a private school from her home. In her 1923 article, "The First Girl Graduates," when asked if women's higher education had proved itself, she wrote: "It is too soon yet for a complete answer to be given to this question, but thousands of university women are proving by their lives that it has not unfitted them for home-making, the noblest sphere of women's work."

"Let us hear no more about the intellectual inferiority of women."

12 JULY

Teofania di Adamo; Francesca la Sarda; Giulia Tofana; Girolama Spara (1600s)

On this day in 1633, Teofania di Adamo was executed in Palermo, Sicily, for using an arsenic-based poison of her own invention – Acqua Tufània – that killed its victim in three days. Her partner and sales assistant, Francesca la Sarda, had been executed the previous year. The manufacture and sale of poisons was part of what historian Lynn Wood Mollenauer has described as a "criminal magical underworld" in early modern cities, whose services also included love potions, toothache cures and abortion methods.

Following the executions in Palermo, associates of di Adamo and la Sarda fled to Rome where they set up a similar operation. It was led by one Giulia Tofana, who may have been di Adamo's daughter. Tofana worked with Girolama Spara – who may have been her own daughter – to recruit gang members with local knowledge. The gang made Acqua Tufània using arsenic they obtained from a priest; they bottled it as "Manna of St Nicholas," a healing oil said to drip from the saint's bones. Their customers were women of all social classes who wanted to be rid of their husbands, at a time when divorce was unavailable and most single women were nuns, beggars or prostitutes. When the gang was finally caught in 1659, five ringleaders and one of their clients were hanged. The priest who had supplied the arsenic escaped punishment.

Their customers were women of all social classes who wanted to be rid of their husbands.

Charlotte Corday

(1768–1793)

On this day in 1793, Charlotte Corday stabbed Jean-Paul Marat, a leader of the French Revolution, in his bathtub. He died instantly.

Corday held Marat responsible for the September Massacres in 1792, when around 1,100–1,500 prisoners in Paris were executed. The great majority of those killed were non-political prisoners and included women and children.

Believing that Marat's death would prevent France descending into civil war, Corday decided on a plan of action. On 9 July 1793, she left her hometown of Caen for Paris. During the next few days, she wrote an "Address to the French People" to explain her motives. She also bought a kitchen knife.

Corday had planned to assassinate Marat in public but discovered that he no longer attended meetings because of ill-health. So she went to his home, gaining admittance by claiming to want to warn him of an uprising from a rival faction. After her arrest, she wrote to her father from prison: "I avenged many innocent victims, I prevented many other disasters . . . the cause is beautiful." She was guillotined in the Place de Grève four days later.

Corday's violent, political act shocked those who thought women incapable of violence. Some believed a lover must have incited her to murder but an autopsy proved her virginity – so it must have been her idea after all.

Corday's violent, political act shocked those who thought women incapable of violence.

Sarah E. Goode
(1850 or 1855–1905)

After the American Civil War, Sarah E. Goode – born into slavery and later freed – got married and moved to Chicago, opening a furniture store. At a time when average sizes of tenements were 25 feet by 100 feet, she invented a cabinet bed which folded easily like a desk, with storage. On this day in 1885 – more than twenty years before the popular Murphy Bed – Goode received patent #322,177 for her invention. She was the first African-American woman named in a patent.

Goode was not the first woman awarded a US patent: Mary Dixon Kies received one in 1809 for a process of weaving straw with silk or thread for the hat industry. The first African-American woman known to have received a patent was Judy W. Reed in 1884 – but Reed signed her patent, for a dough kneader and roller, with an X and not her signature. Until around 1840, twenty other patents are known to have been issued to women for inventions related to clothing, tools, stoves and fireplaces. There may have been more who didn't sign their patents and whose names have been lost to history.

Goode received patent #322,177 for her invention. She was the first African-American woman named in a patent.

15 JULY

Calamity Jane

(1856–1903)

On this day in 1876, the *Black Hills Pioneer* headline was "CALAMITY JANE HAS ARRIVED!" The Wild West celebrity rolled into the town of Deadwood in a wagon train with Wild Bill Hickok and others.

Calamity Jane was born Martha Jane Canary or Cannary in 1856. Her parents came to Montana during the 1860s gold rush and died soon after. Thereafter, she lived hand to mouth. Much of her reputation as a gunwoman, guide and "cowboy" comes from a pamphlet Jane produced for sale at Wild West shows. Her biographer James D. McLaird says that "she arrested no outlaws, robbed no banks, and killed no Indians . . . she worked as a dance hall girl, prostitute, waitress, bartender and cook." Contemporaries remembered her as a generous, charismatic alcoholic. "The way she got that name was this," said her friend George Hoshier, "she was always getting into trouble."

However, the burgeoning small newspapers of the west had readers to entertain. Their sensational stories helped to build a collective sense of identity and heritage in the young United States. Eccentric and conspicuously female, Calamity Jane became famous for being famous and joined Western legends like Wild Bill, Buffalo Bill and Geronimo. That her myth is largely untrue doesn't make it meaningless. In the words of McLaird: "Rather than displaying legendary ingredients, her life illustrates a part of western history not often told, the existence of the poor."

"CALAMITY JANE HAS ARRIVED!"

16 JULY

Miriam Makeba

(1932–2008)

On this day in 1963, Miriam Makeba, South African singer and civil rights activist, spoke to a UN Special Committee against apartheid. She had begun singing professionally in the 1950s and was soon an international star. She won innumerable awards and performed with <u>Nina Simone</u>, Dizzy Gillespie and her sometime husband Hugh Masekela. Makeba sang at the 1962 birthday party for J.F. Kennedy and at the Organisation of African Unity for Haile Selassie. She also performed at independence ceremonies in Kenya, Angola and other African nations shaking off colonial rule.

Makeba was always opposed to the white supremacist government in South Africa, but when two of her relatives died in the 1960 Sharpeville shootings, she became its outspoken and high-profile enemy. She sang in African languages and styles, while numbers like "Soweto Blues" were explicitly political. Her South African citizenship was revoked.

Briefly stateless, Makeba was issued passports by Algeria, Guinea, Belgium and Ghana, and ultimately held honorary citizenship in ten countries. Her pan-African identity crossed borders. At one point, she was both a diplomat for Ghana and a UN delegate for Guinea; she was known as "Mama Africa." Makeba returned to South Africa only in 1990, after the fall of apartheid.

Egeria

(4th century CE)

Egeria, or Etheria, was an early Christian traveler of the fourth century. From Galicia in present-day Spain, she traveled widely on pilgrimages to Jerusalem, Constantinople and Mesopotamia. Egeria recorded her journeys in a letter addressed to her "sisters" – probably fellow Christians back home. "Ladies, light of my eyes, deign to remember me, whether I am in the body or out of the body," she wrote. Religious tourism took many European women to the Middle East, but Egeria's letter, probably written in the 380s, is by far the earliest account to survive. Its middle section was preserved in an early medieval collection, the *Codex Aretinus*. In 2005, a scholar, Jesús Alturo, identified further fragments.

Egeria tells her friends about visits to holy sites including Jerusalem, Jericho, Mount Sinai and Constantinople. She mentions local people and religious communities; she touches on liturgy, religious processions and building styles at a time when important changes were happening in the early church. Egeria's letter gives us precious data about transport in the ancient world, the freedom of women to travel long-distance routes and the network of hostelries and monasteries where they stayed. It gives us valuable clues to the development of Latin in late antiquity; most of all, it gives us the voice of an early woman traveling vast distances to explore her world.

"Ladies, light of my eyes, deign to remember me, whether I am in the body or out of the body."

Nadia Comăneci

(1961–)

On this day in 1976, at the age of fourteen, Romanian gymnast Nadia Comăneci became the first to score a perfect 10 at an Olympic Games. Because the scoreboard could only display up to 9.99, Comăneci's record-breaking achievement had to be shown as "1.00." She received six more perfect 10s and three gold medals that year. Comăneci is also the youngest Olympic gymnastics all-around champion: a record that can never be broken because the sport's minimum age has been revised to sixteen years.

In her memoir, Comăneci writes about how she was considered lucky by her family after a series of near misses and miraculous recoveries. The family mythology continued when she became a gymnast; her mother said that she could "fly" because the first meat she ate came from a bird. At the age of six, Comăneci started gymnastics while still in kindergarten. She trained with Márta Károlyi and then with her husband Béla, who was her coach through all her Olympic successes. After he defected to the United States in 1981, Comăneci was forbidden to leave Romania: "I started to feel like a prisoner." In 1989, she also defected, traveling mostly on foot through Hungary and into Austria, before flying to the US. Now both a US and a Romanian citizen, she funded the Nadia Comăneci Children's Clinic in Bucharest.

Sarah Biffin

(sometimes Beffin, Biffen) (1784–1850)

Sarah Biffin was born without arms or legs, a condition now called phocomelia. By the age of twelve she had learned how to sew, use scissors, write, draw and paint – all with her mouth. Her family was not wealthy (her father was a shoemaker) and when her skills caught the eye of a traveling showman, she was entered into a contract with him.

Biffin became a sideshow attraction, "The Eighth Wonder!", painting miniature watercolors; her employer pocketed all the money. In 1808, the Earl of Morton introduced himself to Biffin after seeing her at a fair. He became her patron and arranged for her to receive training from a royal artist. In 1816, Biffin was released from her sideshow contract and set up a studio in the Strand, London.

In 1821, Sarah Biffin was awarded the silver medal of the Society of Arts for a miniature. She received commissions not only from within

Great Britain, but also the Belgian royal family and exhibited two miniatures at the Royal Academy.

Around 1842, Biffin, now divorced, moved to Liverpool and set up a studio. Despite initial success, her situation and health gradually declined. In 1847, a philanthropist set up a public subscription to raise funds for her. Contributors included her former royal patrons and the "Swedish Nightingale," singer Jenny Lind.

Sofya Kovalevskaya

(1850–1891)

Sofya Kovalevskaya was born into nobility and mathematics ran in the family: her nursery was papered with calculus lecture notes. After she taught herself trigonometry at the age of fourteen, in order to understand a physics book written by a neighbor, the neighbor convinced Kovalevskaya's father to let her go to school in St. Petersburg. However, she ran into difficulties when she wanted to pursue her studies further: no Russian universities accepted women.

Travel abroad was impossible for a single woman on her own, so, in 1870, she entered into a marriage of convenience. The couple moved to Berlin, where Kovalevskaya persuaded mathematician Karl Weierstrass to teach her by solving a math problem he sent her.

In July 1874, Kovalevskaya became the first woman with a doctorate in mathematics. Her examination contained her now-famous work on partial differential equations, the Cauchy-Kovalevskaya theorem. But despite her qualifications, Kovalevskaya couldn't find a job, so she returned to Russia. In 1883, she was finally offered a lectureship at Stockholm University, where, six years later, she became the first woman appointed to a full professorship in Europe. Kovalevskaya also wrote novels, essays and plays. "It is impossible to be a mathematician without being a poet in soul."

Alice Bacon

(1909–1993)

In July 1945, Alice Bacon was elected to the UK Parliament as Yorkshire's first woman MP. Bacon's father was a miner and her whole family was politically active, involved in the National Miners' Union and the Miners' Welfare Institute – which she later described as "a small NHS."

Bacon passed the eleven-plus exam and went to a grammar school. Grammar school children – more likely to be middle class – were taught until they were eighteen. Secondary modern pupils – more likely to be working class – had no education beyond the age of fifteen.

When Bacon became a teacher, she was convinced of the injustice of a system of education which divided children at the age of eleven, supposedly by academic aptitude, but in practice as successes or failures.

As an MP, Bacon was a key member of the Labour governments who established the post-war welfare state. She wanted its ethos of equality to include education and pushed for the introduction of non-selective "comprehensive schools" for all children, regardless of aptitude or background. Her determination transformed the party's attitude: by the 1960s, comprehensive schools were Labour Party policy. As Minister for Education, Bacon was responsible for enacting this policy. By 1979, over 90 per cent of pupils across Britain went to comprehensives.

Alessandra Giliani

(1307–1326)

Italian scientist Alessandra Giliani is the first woman recorded as practicing anatomy and pathology. Around 1323 – when education for men was rare, and for women almost non-existent – Giliani studied at the University of Bologna. She became an assistant to one of Bologna's most famous anatomy teachers, Mondino de Luzzi; working as his "prosecutor," Giliani would demonstrate the techniques being described while he sat on a high chair overlooking the proceedings.

Giliani was not just an assistant but also an innovator, developing a method – the technical details of which were, unfortunately, not recorded – of replacing a cadaver's blood with a colored dye. The dye hardened without destroying the veins, allowing students to see the vascular structure.

Giliani, who died at the age of nineteen, possibly from an infection, is one of 1,038 women celebrated by American artist Judy Chicago in her art installation *The Dinner Party*: thirty-nine women have place settings at the table with 999, of which Giliani is one, inscribed on the "Heritage Floor" underneath.

Eugénie Brazier

(1895–1977)

Orphaned at the age of ten, Eugénie Brazier worked as a farmhand in eastern France before moving to Lyon. There she worked in the kitchen of celebrated French chef Mère Fillioux, one of whose famous dishes included chicken cooked in a bladder. In 1921, Brazier used her savings to buy a grocery store, which she turned into La Mère Brazier, her first restaurant. She later opened a second, cooking at both, and, in 1933, became the first female chef to be awarded three Michelin stars, the restaurant world's highest accolade. Known as the "Mother of French Cooking," Brazier was also the first chef to simultaneously hold six Michelin stars for her two restaurants, a record that remained unbroken for thirty-six years.

Both restaurants are run today by Brazier's granddaughter, Jacotte, who still offers her grandmother's menu. Two of her famous dishes are "beautiful dawn lobster," with brandy and cream, and "poultry in half mourning," where truffle slices are inserted between meat and skin. Brazier turned down the French Legion d'Honneur, saying that the medal "should be given out for doing more important things than cooking well and doing the job as you're supposed to." Her only recipe book, *La Mère Brazier*, was published posthumously.

The first female chef to be awarded three Michelin stars, the restaurant world's highest accolade.

Doreen Spooner
(1928–2019)

On this day in 1963, a photograph of two young women, meeting privately over a drink in a London pub, was splashed across the front pages of the UK press. Christine Keeler and Mandy Rice-Davies had been snapped during a break from testifying in the scandalous Profumo trial at the nearby Old Bailey courts. The photographer – who took the shot surreptitiously from the doorway of the ladies' toilets – was Doreen Spooner. Spooner was one of the world's first paparazzi and the first woman staff photographer on national UK papers.

Spooner started work in 1949 at the *Daily Mirror*. Male colleagues assumed she was a canteen worker or typist. Her first photos were credited to "Camera Girl Doreen Spooner," until she complained: "If I were a man, would you call me Camera Boy?" Early in her career, she worked at the famous Magnum agency in Paris, learning from photographic greats Henri Cartier-Bresson and Robert Capa. In the next five decades, Spooner built a portfolio which included portraits of Queen Elizabeth II, Margaret Thatcher, Einstein and pop culture figures like Twiggy and Mary Quant. She covered news stories including the Yorkshire Ripper murders, IRA terrorist attacks and the miners' strike: "I like to think I played a small part in changing attitudes – never waving a feminist flag, just by getting on with my job."

25 JULY

Jean Purdy

(1945–1985)

On this day in 1978, the world's first "test tube baby," Louise Brown, conceived through *in vitro* fertilization (IVF), was born in Oldham, England. Although British nurse and embryologist Jean Purdy was one of the three scientists involved in the breakthrough, she was overlooked for thirty years.

Purdy had joined embryologist Robert Edwards and gynecologist and surgeon Patrick Steptoe as a lab technician in 1968, but was far more important than the job title implied. She not only co-authored twenty-six scientific papers but witnessed the cell division of the embryo that became Louise Brown. In 2010, the Nobel Prize was awarded to Edwards for the development of IVF, which has enabled the birth of around eight million children. Steptoe had died in 1988, and Purdy in 1985: Nobel Prizes are not awarded posthumously. But Purdy's early death only partly explains why she was overlooked.

Edwards fought unsuccessfully for her name to be included on a plaque in Oldham: "I regard her as an equal contributor to Patrick Steptoe and myself," he wrote. In July 2019, Oldham Royal Hospital announced it would commission a second plaque to honor both Purdy and Sister Muriel Harris, superintendent of the clinic's operating theatre.

Jean Purdy was one of the three scientists involved in the breakthrough.

Phoolan Devi
(1963–2001)

On this day in 2001, "Bandit Queen" and Indian MP Phoolan Devi was assassinated by rivals of her former gang. Born into a low-caste village in Uttar Pradesh in 1963, Devi was given in marriage by her family at the age of eleven, in return for a bicycle and a cow. To escape an abusive husband, Devi ran away and joined a gang of bandits who committed violent robberies and took hostages. During one attack, Devi returned to her husband's village and stabbed him.

Captured by a rival gang, she was held in a locked room in the village of Behmai and gang raped repeatedly for three weeks. She escaped, returned with a new gang of her own and shot twenty-two men dead in revenge. In 1983, Devi was arrested for kidnap, murder and banditry. She served eleven years in prison, where she was given an involuntary hysterectomy. Astonishingly, two years after her release, Devi stood for parliament and was elected. She continued as an MP until 2001, when she was shot dead at the gate of her house by three men seeking revenge for the massacre at Behmai.

She had already been the subject of a sensational biopic, *Bandit Queen*, in 1994. She disliked the film: "I'm portrayed as a snivelling woman, always in tears, who never took a conscious decision in her life."

27 JULY

Pamphila of Epidaurus
(1st century)

Sometimes history *is* written by women. Pamphila of Epidaurus – who lived in Greece in the first century, during Nero's reign – wrote the *Historical Commentaries*, an anecdotal history of Greece in thirty-three books. Although the books themselves have been lost, her work is quoted by many ancient authors. In the introduction, Pamphila explains that the author is a woman and claims that she gathered her material from listening to discussions between her husband and his friends. She explains that she decided not to organize her work by any set system, but to write in a "variegated" manner, weaving anecdotes to make it more enjoyable for her readers.

Pamphila is described in the tenth-century Byzantine encyclopedia, the *Suda*, as also having written many "epitomes," or summaries of other historians' works, as well as treatises on disputes and sex. Classical scholar Deborah Levine Gera believes she may also be the author of the anonymous surviving Greek treatise *Tractatus De Mulieribus Claris In Bello* ("Treatise on Women Famous in War"), which gives brief biographical accounts of fourteen famous ancient women, including Semiramis, regent of the Assyrian empire, and Dido, the first queen of Carthage.

Sometimes history *is* written by women.

28 JULY

Hillary Clinton

(1947–)

On this day in 2016, progressive politician Hillary Clinton became the Democratic Party nominee for President of the United States. She was the first woman nominated by a major party – one of many firsts in a five-decade career. Clinton has held the highest offices of state, redefined the role of First Lady and consistently campaigned on issues of social justice.

Her political career began with doorstep canvassing at the age of thirteen. By the time she met Bill Clinton at Yale, Hillary had a strong record in social justice activism and family law. In the following decades, she worked consistently for child welfare and healthcare improvements. She continued this work as First Lady from 1993 to 2001. Effectively the world's best-placed lobbyist, she chaired the task force on healthcare reform.

Post-White House, Clinton pursued office in her own right. She was the first female senator to represent New York and, in 2009, took the highest office yet held by a woman, as Secretary of State under President Obama. Here she carried out a swathe of progressive reforms to US foreign policy and diplomacy. Finally nominated as Democratic candidate for the presidency in the bitter election of 2016, she lost to Donald Trump, whom she has described as a "corrupt human tornado."

29 JULY

Mabel Purefoy FitzGerald

(1872–1973)

After their parents' deaths, Mabel Purefoy FitzGerald and her five sisters – all educated at home, unlike their brothers – moved to Oxford. In 1896, FitzGerald started to study physiology at the university. As a woman, she wasn't awarded a degree, but went on to do research in Oxford, Copenhagen, New York and Toronto, in fields including histology, physiology and bacteriology.

In 1911, FitzGerald was invited by her mentor, physiologist John Scott Haldane (grandfather of <u>Naomi Mitchison</u>) to join a team of researchers on an expedition to Pikes Peak, Colorado. Rather than go with the men to the comfortable living quarters and laboratory at Summit House, FitzGerald traveled alone on horseback, collecting data from residents of remote mining towns in order to determine the long-term effects of altitude. Her observations that altitude increases blood levels of hemoglobin and oxygen are cited to this day.

FitzGerald took a job at the University of Edinburgh in 1915, deputizing for a clinical pathologist who had been called up for military service. She worked and taught at the medical school until 1937. In later life, FitzGerald cared for her elderly sisters and was all but forgotten by the scientific community. In 1972, at the age of 100, she was finally awarded a degree: an honorary MA from Oxford University.

30 JULY

Marie Tharp
(1920–2006)

Born on this day in 1920, Marie Tharp was the first to map the sea floor, in 1953, proving the theory of plate tectonics: that the earth's shell is made of several plates. The chances of Tharp being able to study geology were slim: less than 4 per cent of earth sciences doctorates were awarded to women between 1920 and 1970. However, the war provided an opportunity, as it did for many women in the 1940s, and she was accepted to an accelerated geology master's degree because of a lack of male students .

With drafting skills – and another master's degree, in math – Tharp started work at Columbia University's Lamont Geological Laboratory. Due to Navy regulations, she couldn't go out on research trips with her male colleagues, so she stayed at the drafting table, collaborating with geologist Bruce Heezen on a map of the ocean floor. "The whole world was spread out before me," she later wrote. When she showed Heezen evidence of a rift valley she'd found in the middle of the mid-Atlantic ocean ridge he brushed it off as "girl talk." But in 1956, he published the finding – crucial proof of plate tectonics and continental drift – under his own name. In 1997, Tharp finally received her due when the Library of Congress named her one of the four greatest cartographers of the twentieth century.

"The whole world was spread out before me."

Christine de Pisan

(c.1364–c.1430)

Christine de Pisan was the first woman in France, and perhaps in Europe, to earn a living solely by writing. She began writing professionally at the age of twenty-five, when the death of her husband left her with three young children to support. One of her best-known works is *The Book of the City of Ladies* (1404), a medieval dream poem and early feminist text, written in response to the misogyny of much courtly literature. In the poem, Christine falls asleep and is visited by three women – Reason, Rectitude and Justice – who tell her that she has been chosen by God to set the record straight about women. They direct her to build a metaphorical city which will house a group of worthy heroines from history.

Women were not de Pisan's only subject: over a thirty-year career she produced forty-one works – political treatises, epistles, poetry – with topics ranging from education and morality to the arts of government and war. Many of these converge in her last work, *The Song of Joan of Arc*, which she finished on this day in 1429. Two months after Joan of Arc led the French army to end a siege in Orleans, de Pisan's lyrical verse celebrated her victory and her heroism. The poem is the only contemporary record of Joan of Arc apart from the records of her trial in 1431.

AUGUST

"I like the smell of gunpowder, grapeshot flying through the air, but above all, I'm devoted to the Revolution."
– Louise Michel

What are you wearing?

Trousers. If you're a woman, they could really get you into trouble. Take <u>Annie Smith Peck</u>. In 1895, the American mountaineer was only the third woman to climb the Matterhorn in Switzerland – but there were calls for her arrest because she was the first to do it wearing knickerbockers.

A *New York Times* editorial of 1876 wrote jokingly of women's "abnormal and unconquerable thirst for trousers" – but is it any wonder, when this type of clothing allowed women to do what they wanted to do?

Surgery, for example. Mary Edwards Walker, the first woman awarded the Congressional Medal of Honor for her work as a surgeon in the US Civil War, was often arrested for wearing "men's clothing"; trousers allowed her to move around freely while she operated. Who would want to climb mountains or perform surgery with "pounds of clothing hung on the hips, the limbs cramped with skirts," as American suffragist Elizabeth Cady Stanton wrote in 1881. Not to mention corsets and other contraptions women squeezed themselves into, which could be hazardous to their health. Not only physically liberating, dressing "as men" allowed women entrance into professions and areas traditionally banned to them, from medicine, the army and the navy to the stage.

The "dress reform" movement gathered strength in Europe and the US in the mid to late nineteenth century. One of its most vocal proponents was American suffragist and temperance reformer Frances Willard, who called on mothers not to make their daughters wear tight corsets, which, she wrote, "deliberately deform[ed] a body that came fresh and fair from God's hand, and manacled a soul made in His image." Although women had worn trousers for activities such as gymnastics, the dress reformers introduced the "bloomer suit," named for Cady Stanton's friend, Amelia Bloomer: a shorter skirt with modest trousers underneath.

And the fight goes on. Only in 2013 was the 1799 French law requiring women to request permission from the police "to dress as men" finally scrapped. (Artist Rosa Bonheur had been one of only a dozen women who had in fact received such permission in the 1850s.) Three years earlier, the French government passed a law banning Muslim women from publicly wearing a full face veil. Last year, a 30,000-signature petition was delivered to Japan's labor minister for a change to the law that allows employers to force Japanese women to wear high heels – and even prevent them from wearing glasses. Elizabeth Cady Stanton's words echo down to us: "How can [women] . . . ever compete with man for equal place and pay, with garments of such frail fabrics and so cumbrously fashioned?"

1 AUGUST

Bíawacheeitchish

(c.1806–1858)

Bíawacheeitchish was a nineteenth-century chief and warrior of the Crow people, in the northern United States. Her name is actually a title meaning "woman chief." The Crow identify at least four genders and have a tradition of "Two-Spirit" people, whose gender and sex are at variance. These people are different but equal, marrying according to their chosen identity. Bíawacheeitchish was a Two-Spirit, a woman whose chosen lifestyle fitted better with the male culture of her tribe. Born a daughter of the Gros Ventres people around 1806, she was kidnapped as a child and adopted by Crow raiders who had no sons. She took over the household of her adoptive father when he died.

In a raid by the Blackfoot people, Bíawacheeitchish won a reputation as a brave fighter, killing enemies and taking horses. She subsequently led raiding parties herself. One European trader who met her said: "She looked neither savage nor warlike . . . She sat with her hands in her lap, folded, as when one prays. She is about forty-five years old; appears modest and good natured." Bíawacheeitchish became a significant chief, rising to third place in the 160-strong Council of Chiefs and taking four wives. She was not alone: other female chiefs, some of whom also married women, include Kaúxuma Núpika, Chipeta, Kwilqs, Akkeekaahuush and Biliíche Héeleelash.

Bíawacheeitchish won a reputation as a brave fighter, killing enemies and taking horses.

2 AUGUST

Andrée de Jongh

(1916–2007)

"Our lives are going to depend on a schoolgirl," one soldier said on meeting Andrée (Dédée) de Jongh. In the summer of 1941, de Jongh, a Belgian artist, set up the Comet escape line for Allied servicemen stranded in Nazi-occupied Europe. She was twenty-four, but looked younger; her youthful appearance may have saved her own life.

When the Second World War began, de Jongh volunteered for the Belgian Red Cross. After Belgium surrendered to the Nazis, she found safe houses for Allied airmen who had been shot down – but, remembering childhood stories about Edith Cavell's heroism during the First World War, she wanted to do more. In August 1941, she did a test run, taking three soldiers along a smuggling route across the Pyrenees to Spain. De Jongh would eventually escort 118 servicemen to safety; 300 escaped in total via the Comet line. Incredulous intelligence officers called her "the Postman."

De Jongh was captured in 1943 and interrogated. When she finally confessed, the Germans didn't believe someone so young could have run the operation. Taken to Ravensbrück concentration camp, she survived the war, later working in leper colonies in the Congo and Ethiopia. She was awarded the US Medal of Freedom, the British George Medal, the French Légion d'Honneur, the Belgian Croix de Guerre and was made an honorary lieutenant-colonel in the Belgian Army.

Incredulous intelligence officers called her "the Postman."

Maggie Kuhn

(1905–1995)

After being forced to retire on this day in 1970, her sixty-fifth birthday, Maggie Kuhn founded the Gray Panthers to fight against ageism and other social injustices: "Old age is not a disease. It is strength and survivorship, triumph over all kinds of vicissitudes and disappointments, trials and illnesses." Kuhn had long been an activist – in college for the Young Women's Christian Association and later for New York's United Presbyterian Church. Originally called the "Consultation of Older and Younger Adults for Social Change," her group was nicknamed the "Gray Panthers" by a journalist comparing them to the African-American political organization the Black Panthers, and the name stuck.

The group promote their cause in many ways, from commissioning a study of nursing homes to battling the portrayal of elderly people on TV. They have staged protests at American Medical Association meetings about doctors' treatment of older patients and tackled larger issues such as the environment. Kuhn often shocked the public by candidly discussing older people's sexuality, declaring that older women could have relationships with younger men – or even each other. Twenty-five years after her death, the Gray Panthers continue her legacy.

"Speak your mind – even if your voice shakes. When you least expect it, someone may actually listen to what you have to say. Well-aimed sling-shots can topple giants."

4 AUGUST

Erricka Bridgeford

(1972–)

On this day in 2017, African-American mediator Erricka Bridgeford instigated the first seventy-two-hour ceasefire in Baltimore, Maryland, a city with one of the highest murder rates in the US, with a death every nineteen hours. "I've been raped twice. My brother got killed . . . I've lost my stepson. I've lost cousins. Two weeks ago, I lost somebody. Some years I go to two funerals in one day," Bridgeford told the BBC. "It's not that I'm naïve. It's just that my optimism is gangster."

Inspired by hip-hop artist Ogun, Bridgeford put out a call in May 2017 for the first ceasefire weekend, with the slogan "Nobody Kill Anybody." From 4 to 6 August, thousands of people attended community events and Baltimore went sixty-seven hours without a murder. When two people were killed on the second day of the ceasefire – and more during the second ceasefire weekend that November – Bridgeford asked residents to show up to the locations of the deaths, creating sacred space rituals as part of a "Don't Be Numb" campaign.

The third ceasefire weekend, in February 2018, saw a record eleven days without homicides. That year, Bridgeford was named Marylander of the Year. The ceasefires continue to be held: "It is about being purposefully peaceful."

241

5 AUGUST

Helen Thomas

(1966–1989)

After receiving her history degree, Helen Thomas decided to take a year off, working for several charities in Cardiff, Wales, including Women's Aid. When she heard about the women who had camped since 1982 at the RAF military base at Greenham Common in Berkshire, England, campaigning for the removal of American nuclear missiles, she decided to join them. Despite her family's concerns, Thomas traveled to Greenham in early 1989. When her mother suggested she come back and find work, she wrote back that "working for peace and justice was not a part-time job."

Tragically, on this day in 1989, aged twenty-two, Thomas was knocked over and killed by a police vehicle while waiting to cross a road near the airbase. The coroner ruled the death an accident; the Thomas family challenged the decision but it was upheld.

The Greenham Common protest – which attracted up to 70,000 women – led to the cruise missiles being removed in 1991 and the closure of the air base two years later. The peace camp remained until 2000, when protestors were permitted to erect a memorial at the site, including a plaque commemorating Helen Thomas, the campaign's only fatality.

"Working for peace and justice was not a part-time job."

Sappho

(c.620–570 BCE)

Sappho, one of the most celebrated women in literature, was born on the Greek island of Lesbos. Little of her work survives, although nine of her "books" or scrolls of poetry were held in the famous ancient library at Alexandria. From the surviving fragments, we know that Sappho's poems spoke of personal, erotic relationships. Many writers have admired her: Donne, Byron, Shelley and, most recently, Canadian poet Anne Carson have all translated her work. New discoveries of Sappho's poetry are still being made, including major finds in 2004 and 2013, preserved on waste papyrus which had been re-used in book-binding.

Because she wrote about love between women, Sappho is the source of words to describe such love – Sapphic and lesbian (originally "a person from Lesbos"). Christian leaders had her works banned or burned and Victorian editors censored them. Readers have tended to agree either with the ancient historian Strabo, who called her "a marvel," or with second-century Christian writer Tatian, who called her "a whore who sang about her own licentiousness."

Sappho's work remains fresh and moving. In her 2002 translations, Anne Carson gives us these lines: "Once again Love, that loosener of limbs, bittersweet and inescapable, crawling thing, seizes me."

7 AUGUST

Alice Coachman

(1923–2014)

On this day in 1948, American athlete Alice Coachman became the first black woman to win an Olympic gold medal. Born in segregated Georgia, US, Coachman was banned from many sports fields. Training on unmade tracks with improvised equipment, she won a sports scholarship to the Tuskegee Institute, Alabama. She had already broken national high jump records for her age, competing barefoot. By 1946, Coachman was a national champion in four track and field events. She won thirty-four national titles during her sports career.

Unfortunately, due to the Second World War, the 1940 and 1944 games were cancelled, but in 1948 her high jump of 5 feet, 6⅛ inches secured the gold medal at the London Games. On her return to America, she was fêted as a celebrity and met President Truman, yet the local white mayor refused to shake her hand. Some fans sent gifts anonymously, not wanting to be known as having corresponded with a woman of color.

In 1952, Coachman became the first African American to sign a product endorsement contract, for Coca-Cola. At the 1996 Summer Olympics in Atlanta, she was honored as one of the hundred greatest ever Olympians. She was the forerunner of today's African-American athletes. "I think I opened the gate for all of them," she said.

Louise Michel

(1830–1905)

The illegitimate daughter of a serving-maid, French radical Louise Michel was raised by her grandparents, then trained as a teacher. In 1865, she opened a school in Paris, which became known for its progressive methods, and was a founder member of the feminist group *Société pour la Revendication du Droits Civils de la Femme* (Society for Demanding Civil Rights for Women).

In 1871, Michel took a leading role in the Paris Commune – a radical socialist government – fighting with the 61st Battalion of Montmartre, the "first all-female military formation in modern history." In her memoirs, she wrote: "I like the smell of gunpowder, grapeshot flying through the air, but above all, I'm devoted to the Revolution."

Around 20,000 Communards were summarily executed. Michel – nicknamed "The Red Virgin" – was one of 10,000 sentenced to penal deportation. On this day in 1873, she was deported to New Caledonia in the South Pacific. During her seven years of imprisonment, Michel became friends with some of the indigenous Kanak people and took their side in their 1878 revolt against French colonial rule. After her return to Europe, in July 1881, she attended the Anarchist Congress in London; on later visits she went to meetings at the home of <u>Emmeline Pankhurst</u>.

9 AUGUST

Fanny Blankers-Koen

(1918–2004)

Fanny Blankers-Koen became a legendary star of the track at the same Olympics in August 1948 where <u>Alice Coachman</u> won gold. Nicknamed "the Flying Housewife," the Dutch woman won four gold medals. It was later revealed that she was pregnant at the time.

Blankers-Koen already held world records in six track events. She was thirty years old with two children and faced the usual criticism of all women who stray far from home – that she should have stayed at home to look after them. Tearful and emotional after her first medal win, Blankers-Koen did in fact offer to return.

Her coach (the children's father, her husband Jan) encouraged her to stay and compete in further events. Blankers-Koen won in the 100m, 200m, 80m hurdles and 4 x 100m relay. She was the first woman to win four gold medals in a single Olympic tournament. In the 200m, her winning margin was 0.7 seconds, which has not yet been matched. On her return to the Netherlands, the city of Amsterdam gave her a bicycle.

Blankers-Koen continued in athletics until she was thirty-seven, winning a total of fifty-eight titles in the Netherlands, and held (or equaled) twelve world records. In 1999, Fanny Blankers-Koen was voted Female Athlete of the Century by the International Association of Athletics Federations.

Hatshepsut

(1507–1458 BCE)

Hatshepsut was a pharaoh who ruled Egypt for over twenty years, from around 1478 BCE. She is "the first great woman in history of whom we are informed," according to historian James Henry Breasted.

Officially co-ruler with her toddler stepson, Hatshepsut was an executive ruler whose policies seem to have brought security and commercial success. We know that she sent traders to the land of Punt for live myrrh trees and frankincense, and war parties to other parts of the Middle East. Her great genius was for architecture, commissioning hundreds of official buildings, temples and statues.

Hatshepsut's own mausoleum was the first built in the Valley of the Kings; its scale, symmetry and grandeur went unrivaled for a thousand years. In 2007, a mummy found in the same tomb as her childhood wet nurse was confirmed as Hatshepsut's.

Like other early monarchs,

Hatshepsut projected her power through images – in her case, showing her in "male" clothes and trappings. Nineteenth-century Egyptologist Jean-François Champollion was confused by hieroglyphics in the tomb: "wherever they referred to this bearded king in the usual dress of the Pharaohs, nouns and verbs were in the feminine, as though a queen were in question. I found the same peculiarity everywhere . . ." The solution was simple enough. The pharaoh, wearing the symbolic beard and dress of a god-king, was a woman. (See Bodies of evidence.)

Her great genius was for architecture, commissioning hundreds of official buildings, temples and statues.

Nanaia Mahuta

(1970–)

In August 2016, Nanaia Mahuta became the first woman to wear the *moko kauae*, or Māori chin tattoo, in the New Zealand parliament. The tattoo is a symbol of gravitas and standing for Māori women. The Labour MP and sometime cabinet minister is a member of the Waikato-Maniapoto tribe: "I am ready to make a clear statement that this is who I am, and this is my position in New Zealand," she said afterwards.

Mahuta was one of fourteen women who had the tattoo at the same time, celebrating ten years of King Tuheitia Paki's reign and showing respect for ancestors. It was intended to set an example of tradition for younger Māori, and also to reclaim the facial tattoo from gang culture in New Zealand. Perhaps most importantly, Mahuta's tattoo was a public expression of *rangatiratanga*, or self-determination. Like other colonized peoples, the Māori have suffered the erosion of their culture. One of the tattooed group, Huritau Muru, said: «When Nanaia took her *moko* back to parliament for all to see, she was taking thirteen other women with her, too. She was taking her life story and our life story as well. She was declaring herself a proud Māori woman – it was a very public statement."

Cleopatra VII

(c.69 –30 BCE)

On this day in 30 BCE, the last pharaoh of Egypt, Cleopatra VII, committed suicide in Alexandria to escape humiliation at the hands of the Roman emperor Octavian.

Ancient Egypt was immensely wealthy in resources and a vital supply of grain for the Roman Empire. Cleopatra became its absolute ruler before she was twenty. By that age, she had already been crowned, deposed and reinstated, had married two of her own half-brothers and had a half-sister killed. As pharaoh, Cleopatra was a shrewd builder of alliances: her affairs with Roman leaders Julius Caesar and Mark Antony were political as well as sexual associations, helping her to consolidate power in Egypt. Both liaisons were unpopular in Rome, where they were taken as undue influence on the government by a foreign power, and a woman to boot. Mark Antony in particular was seen to be over-dependent on Cleopatra's support. On this pretext, his rival Octavian made war on Cleopatra and Antony. He defeated their forces at Actium in 31 BCE and took Cleopatra captive in Alexandria the following year.

Octavian's triumphal procession would have seen Cleopatra paraded through Rome and publicly strangled. Like Boudica ninety years later, the pharaoh preferred suicide, famously allowing an asp to bite her. She was thirty-nine when she killed herself, having defied Octavian in a face-to-face meeting: "I will not grace a triumph."

As pharaoh, Cleopatra was a shrewd builder of alliances.

13 AUGUST

Virginia Hall

(1906–1982)

In August 1941, Virginia Hall entered occupied France, posing as a *New York Post* reporter. She was in fact an Allied spy and became a key player in defeating the Nazis.

Hall was living in Paris when war broke out. She volunteered for Britain's Special Operations Executive (SOE), for whom she coordinated Resistance campaigns. She provided cover as the "wife" of an English spy and ran the crucial HECKLER citizen spy network. In 1942, Hall fled France as the Nazis advanced, walking over a mountain pass to Spain – particularly difficult for Hall who, after a shooting accident, had a wooden leg which she nicknamed "Cuthbert."

Hall returned in 1944 as an agent for the US Special Operations Branch, working at the highest level of the Resistance. She coordinated air drops, safe houses and guerrilla training. One report, according to *Smithsonian* magazine, relayed that, "Her team had destroyed four bridges, derailed freight trains, severed a key rail line in multiple places and downed telephone lines. They were also credited with killing some 150 Germans and capturing 500 more."

The UK awarded her an MBE; France, the Croix de Guerre with Palme. The US gave her the Distinguished Service Cross (DSC), rewarding extreme gallantry: the only one awarded to a civilian woman in the Second World War.

Ella Negruzzi

(1876–1948)

In 1920, on her third attempt to register for the Bar exam – after six years and moving cities twice – Ella Negruzzi was finally permitted to take it in Bucharest. She passed, becoming the first woman to practice law in Romania. Throughout her career, Negruzzi fought for women's education and employment rights. She co-founded the Association for the Civil and Political Emancipation of Romanian Women (AECPFR) to demand women be allowed to participate in all areas of public life. In 1929, when some Romanian women won the vote, she was elected as one of the first female city councillors. (It would be another seventeen years before all Romanian women could vote.)

When the Romanian government, attempting to tackle rising unemployment, tried to stymie women's rights to paid work and pensions, Negruzzi spoke at the AECPFR Congress about the double bind that women face: alongside enormous difficulties in their professions, they are also the first to be fired in times of crisis. She later founded the Women's Front (Front Feminin) to train women to defend their rights.

In 1936, Jewish-Romanian politician Ana Pauker – who in 1947 would become the world's first female foreign minister – was accused of being a Soviet agent. Receiving death threats for being part of Pauker's defense team, Negruzzi retired from public life.

15 AUGUST

Marie-Angélique Josèphe Brûlon (1772–1859)

On this day in 1851, seventy-nine-year old Marie-Angélique Josèphe Brûlon became the first woman to receive the Legion d'Honneur for her courage in a military action more than fifty years earlier.

At the height of the French Revolution, Brûlon married a soldier, disguised herself as a man and enlisted to fight with him, but he died soon after. Brûlon remained in the army fighting against the 1794 rebellion in Corsica. Soldiers in a besieged garrison explained:

> Brûlon, acting sergeant, commanded us in the action at Gesco; that she fought with us with the courage of a heroine . . . that she received a sabre blow on her right arm and . . . a wound on the left; that seeing us running out of ammunition at midnight, she left, though wounded, for Calvi, half a league away: where, through the zeal and courage of a true Republican, she had about sixty women roused and loaded with ammunition.

In 1804, Brûlon was granted a pension and recommended for the Legion d'Honneur. Her commendation lay dormant until, forty-seven years later, she received her medal from Napoleon III. She spent the last sixty-one years of her life as an honored pensioner at the Hôtel des Invalides.

16 AUGUST

Mary Fildes

(1789–1876)

On this day in 1819, a crowd of around 60,000 gathered at St Peter's Fields in Manchester, UK, to hear campaigners for parliamentary reform. Mary Fildes, president of the Manchester Female Reform Society, was on the speakers' platform when cavalry viciously charged the crowd, killing at least eighteen people. The massacre was christened "Peterloo," an ironic reference to the battle of Waterloo.

An estimated one in eight of the Peterloo protesters was a woman. Though few would have hoped for female suffrage at the time, they knew that better representation for working-class men would bring social benefits. Some women met violence with violence: an eyewitness said that, "One of the Yeomanry was dangerously wounded, and unhorsed, by a blow from the fragment of a brick; and it was supposed to have been flung by [a] woman." Four of the dead and 168 of the 654 wounded were women.

Fildes was amongst these wounded protesters. Coshed when she refused to let go of her pro-reform banner, she jumped from the platform but her dress was caught on a nail. As Fildes hung helpless in mid-air, a mounted soldier slashed at her. She survived, but her flag was captured and displayed as a trophy in a shop on Oldham Road. Her supporters broke the windows.

An estimated one in eight of the Peterloo protesters was a woman.

17 AUGUST

Fatima al-Fihri

(c.800–880 CE)

In 859, Fatima al-Fihri founded the first educational institution in the world to award degrees – the University of al-Qarawiyyin in Fez, Morocco. It is the oldest continually operating university. Born into a well-educated family in Tunisia in the early ninth century, al-Fihri moved to Fez. Using the fortune she inherited on her father's death, she founded a mosque and educational institution for the benefit of her local community, which later became the University of al-Qarawiyyin. Students studied a wide range of subjects, from languages and natural sciences to astronomy. During medieval times, it was a major intellectual center.

Now the university focuses mainly on Islamic religious and legal sciences, with other subjects, such as English, French and information technology also available. Although it was founded by a woman, the university only began to admit female students in the 1940s. The university library, one of the world's oldest with over 4,000 manuscripts, reopened in 2016 after being renovated by Moroccan architect Aziza Chaouni.

"I sincerely hope that by opening the library doors to the public that I did justice to the visionary mission of the library's founder and patron, Fatima al-Fihri," Chaouni said, "who wanted to make knowledge available to everyone in her city."

She founded a mosque and educational institution for the benefit of her local community, which later became the University of al-Qarawiyyin.

Mabel St Clair Stobart

(1862–1954)

"If women desired to have a share in the government of the country," British suffragist and writer Mabel St Clair Stobart wrote in her 1935 autobiography, *Miracles and Adventures*, "they ought to be capable of taking a share in the defence of their country." To that end, and without any formal medical training, Stobart set up the Women's Sick and Wounded Convoy Corps (WSWCC), an all-woman medical unit.

The WSWCC saw action in 1912 during the Balkan War, despite British Red Cross objections. After the First World War broke out, Stobart took her unit to Brussels on this day in 1914, setting up a field hospital as the German invasion began. She was almost shot for spying but returned to Belgium to establish a hospital staffed by women. Stobart then traveled back to the Balkans to command a Serbian army hospital unit. Here, she became the first woman with the rank of major in any national army – and acquired her nickname, the Lady on the Black Horse, as most of her days were spent on horseback. When the US joined the war in 1917, Stobart gave a lecture tour across America. She later published *The Flaming Sword in Serbia and Elsewhere* about her experiences. "To go through the horrors of war, and keep one's reason – that is hell."

19 AUGUST

Grazide Lizier

(14th century)

On this day in 1321, a French peasant called Grazide Lizier gave evidence to a Catholic inquisition, along with some of her neighbors from the village of Montaillou. The church authorities were investigating the last traces of the Cathar heresy, which still survived in this part of France.

In her lively answers to the Bishop of Pamiers, Lizier was frank about her beliefs and her sex life. In her mid-teens, Lizier testified, she had begun a sexual relationship with the local priest, Pierre Clergue. After her marriage, the affair continued with her husband's consent. Lizier repeatedly professed that sex was not sinful, so long as it was consensual and pleasurable: "I did not believe that this could be displeasing to anyone, that I slept with this priest, because it was pleasing to us, to him and to me."

This was heresy. Lizier was held in prison for seven weeks, receiving religious instruction. She agreed that she now followed Catholic teaching and was set free.

Whether Lizier's repentance was real or purely practical, we cannot know; some of her neighbors were burned at the stake for failing to recant. But her testimony and that of other illiterate women, speaking about their lives in Montaillou, is remarkable precisely because the voices of ordinary women are usually absent from historic records.

> "I did not believe that this could be displeasing to anyone, that I slept with this priest, because it was pleasing to us, to him and to me."

Herta Oberheuser

(1911–1978)

On this day in 1946, Herta Oberheuser was sentenced to twenty years in prison for her horrific medical experiments on concentration camp prisoners. She had joined the Nazi Party in the 1930s and soon became assistant to Karl Gebhardt, the personal doctor of SS leader Heinrich Himmler.

In 1942, Oberheuser arrived at the women's concentration camp at Ravensbrück. With Gebhardt, she conducted appalling experiments on inmates with the stated aim of finding better ways to treat the infected wounds of German soldiers. Of the eighty-six women experimented on, seventy-four were Polish political prisoners known as the "Ravensbrück Rabbits." On 3 February 1945, fellow prisoners learned that the SS had decided to execute the sixty-three surviving "Rabbits" to eliminate evidence of war crimes. The women staged a rescue and kept the "Rabbits" hidden and alive until the camp was liberated.

Four of the "Rabbits" testified at the Nuremberg Doctors' Trial. Herta Oberheuser – the only woman among the twenty-three defendants – was found guilty, but served only five years of her sentence before returning to work as a family doctor. In 1958, she lost her licence after she was recognized by a Ravensbrück survivor. The surviving "Rabbits" continued to meet and support each other for many years.

21 AUGUST

Nettie Stevens
(1861–1912)

Nettie Stevens began her scientific career at the age of thirty-nine, studying for a PhD in cytology, the structure of cells. In 1903, during a research assistantship in Washington to investigate how the sex of an animal or plant is determined, she noticed that, although female and male mealworm beetles both had twenty large chromosomes, the male's twentieth chromosome was smaller than the other nineteen.

In August 1905, Stevens published a paper in the *Journal of Experimental Zoology* on her discovery, solving a millennia-old argument about how sex is determined. Previous theories had included the effect of the father's body temperature during sex, or poor versus good nutrition. It is the male sperm, which contains the smaller chromosome, that makes the difference, explained Stevens. However, the "Matilda effect" reared its ugly head again and it was her male colleague and mentor, E.B. Wilson, who until recently was given credit for the discovery.

In 1910, Stevens was included in the list of 100 American "Men of Science" [sic]. A teacher as well as a scientist, when a student seemed unsure about asking a question, she said, "How could you think your questions would bother me? They never will, so long as I keep my enthusiasm for biology; and that, I hope, will be as long as I live."

Bhikaji Cama

(1861–1936)

On this day in 1907, Bhikaji Cama unfurled the first Indian flag at the International Socialist Congress in Stuttgart. "Behold, the flag of independent India is born!" she declared. In 1902, Cama had moved from India to Britain to recuperate from bubonic plague, contracted from patients she nursed in Mumbai. Discovering the suffragette movement's occasionally violent methods in the fight for women's rights, Cama wondered what lessons she might apply to the struggle for Indian independence from British rule. Joining the new Indian Home Rule Society, she planned to return to India, but the British authorities forbade it unless she signed a statement promising to stop her nationalist activities. She refused and moved to Paris, co-founding the Paris Indian Society.

Cama carried on helping the revolutionaries, distributing literature and raising funds. Traveling widely to spread her message, at a conference in Cairo in 1910, she said: "Where is the other half of Egypt? I see only men, who represent half the country! Where are the mothers? Where are the sisters?" Cama was finally allowed back to India in 1935. Known as "the Mother of the Indian Revolution," she died soon after, eleven years before India achieved independence in 1947.

23 AUGUST

Molla Bjurstedt-Mallory

(1884–1959)

On this day in 1926, Norwegian tennis player Molla Bjurstedt-Mallory set a record yet to be broken, winning her eighth US Open singles tennis title. She was also the oldest winner, at the age of forty-two. Eight US National Women's Singles Championships, won against eight different opponents, make Bjurstedt-Mallory one of the greatest players tennis has ever seen.

Few people had known who Bjurstedt-Mallory was when she arrived in New York twelve years earlier, even though she'd won a bronze medal at the 1912 Summer Olympics. All that changed when she won the US Indoor Championships. A *New York Times* article credited much of her success to "her powerful forehand drive . . . not the usual stroke of the woman in tennis. It is the stroke rather of the man." Bjurstedt- Mallory herself said, "I believe in always hitting the ball with all my might, but there seems to be a disposition to 'just get it over' in many girls whom I have played. I do not call this tennis."

> "I believe in always hitting the ball with all my might . . ."

Mildred Ella "Babe" Didrikson Zaharias (1911–1956)

In August 1950, Mildred Ella Didrikson Zaharias, or "Babe," won the grand slam of golfing: the US Open, Titleholders' Championship and the Women's Western Open. One of the greatest sporting competitors of all time, golf was only one of the sports in which she excelled.

Nicknamed "Babe" after Babe Ruth for her childhood baseball skills, by twenty-one she held multiple world records. She won two gold medals and set or equaled four world records at the 1932 Olympics in events including hurdles, javelin and high jump. She was a three-time All-American basketball player and set five world records at the Amateur Athletic Union championships. Her lifetime Olympic haul was three golds, one silver, two bronzes.

In 1931, Zaharias somehow found the time to take up golf. In training, she bandaged blistered hands to hit up to 1,000 balls a day.

She won seventeen tournaments in a row, often by huge margins. Famously sardonic, she explained her technique: "I just loosen my girdle and let the ball have it."

Even in her hobbies she excelled, winning first prize for sewing at the 1931 Texas State Fair and spending a few days as a professional harmonica player. One sports journalist wrote: "She operates like a woman whose life is a constant campaign to astound people."

25 AUGUST

Jayaben Desai

(1933–2010)

In August 1976, Jayaben Desai led a strike of 137 mainly South Asian women workers at Grunwick film processing plant in Willesden, north London, in protest against degrading, unreasonable treatment. Desai told factory manager Malcom Alden: "What you are running here is not a factory, it is a zoo. In a zoo, there are many types of animals. Some are monkeys who dance on your fingertips, others are lions who can bite your head off. We are those lions, Mr Manager."

She had no guarantee of union support. It wasn't uncommon for "unskilled" immigrant workers to be treated in this way and trade unions did little to fight for equality when workers were non-white and non-male. But the Grunwick strike struck a chord. Busloads of workers arrived to join the women; sometimes as many as 20,000 people stood in the streets around the plant. When the Union of Postal Workers came out in support,

victory seemed possible; Grunwick's mail-order photo processing service was completely reliant on Royal Mail. But the right-wing National Association for Freedom supported Grunwick's management and sued the postal workers' union.

After two years, the women's union withdrew support and the strike was called off. But Desai and her colleagues had put paid to the idea that South Asian women were passive and subservient.

26 AUGUST

Mary Frith

(1584–1659)

On this day in 1600, notorious thief Mary Frith, also known as "Moll Cutpurse," first entered the historical record. Aged sixteen, she was arrested for stealing 2s 11d from a man in Clerkenwell, London. Her uncle then tried to ship her to safety in America but she jumped overboard and swam home.

Queen Elizabeth I had been on the throne for over forty years by then. Her reign was seen by some as encouraging "masculine women," which Frith's criminal career and cross-dressing might have confirmed. "Moll" was a nickname for disreputable women and "Cutpurse" referred to the purses she stole. Frith was also called a "roaring girl" – a roaring boy was an aggressive young man. One of England's first female smokers, often pictured with a pipe, she was as famous for what she wore as for her crimes. Like many other women in history, Frith seems to have preferred "male" clothing to allow her access to places and opportunities barred to women (see What are you wearing?).

An actor who bantered with the audience, Frith was also a pimp, procuring women for men, and vice versa. Frequently arrested, she was once sentenced to do public penance wearing a white sheet during the Sunday sermon. Two plays were written about her and an "autobiography" was published three years after her death.

Eunice Newton Foote

(1819–1888)

American scientist Eunice Foote's greatest discovery came when she conducted a series of experiments that demonstrated the interactions of the sun's rays with different gases. Of the gases she tested, carbon dioxide trapped the most heat, reaching a temperature of 52C (125F). She had identified the gradual warming of the Earth's atmosphere – what we today call the "greenhouse effect."

In August 1856, Foote's paper, "Circumstances affecting the heat of the sun's rays," was presented at a conference of the American Association for the Advancement of Science. Because women were not allowed to present papers, Professor Joseph Henry of the Smithsonian Institution spoke on her behalf. His introduction included the remarks: "Science is of no country and of no sex. The sphere of woman embraces not only the beautiful and the useful, but the true." Three years later, physicist John Tyndall published similar results to Foote's and, until recently, his work has been viewed as the foundation of modern climate science. But Foote's work is beginning to be recognized; she has been dubbed the "Mother of Global Warming."

Foote was not only a scientist but also a suffragist; she was a member of the editorial committee for the 1848 Seneca Falls Convention for women's rights, and one of the signatories of its "Declaration of Sentiments" (see Tea).

She had identified the gradual warming of the Earth's atmosphere – what we today call the "greenhouse effect."

28 AUGUST

Josephine Baker

(1906–1975)

As a homeless teenager, Josephine Baker made money by dancing on street corners in St. Louis, Missouri; later, she was part of the Harlem Renaissance in New York. In 1925, Baker moved to Paris and became a sensation for her exotic dancing and daring costumes, like the "banana skirt" she wore for her "Danse Sauvage," turning racist stereotypes to her advantage. She was the first African-American to star in a major motion picture – the 1927 silent film *Siren of the Tropics*.

During the Second World War, Baker worked for French military intelligence, gathering information about German army movements from officials she met when performing in ministries and embassies. She passed the information along by writing on sheet music in invisible ink. In 1961, she was awarded the Legion d'Honneur, one of France's highest military honors, for her Resistance work.

In the 1950s, when Baker returned to the US to perform, she faced the kind of racist discrimination she had not experienced for twenty-five years.

She became active in the civil rights movement, writing articles and giving speeches. On this day in 1963, wearing her French Resistance uniform, she was one of two women (the other was Daisy Bates) to speak at the March on Washington, where Martin Luther King gave his "I Have a Dream" speech.

> "When I get mad, you know that I open my big mouth. And then look out, 'cause when Josephine opens her mouth, they hear it all over the world."

Lucy Evelyn Cheesman

(1881–1969)

Lucy Evelyn Cheesman wanted to work with animals, but veterinary schools didn't admit women. After working for the king's canine veterinarian, she was appointed London Zoo's assistant curator of insects in 1917. In three years, she turned the neglected insect house into one of the zoo's most popular attractions and became its first female curator.

Not just an entomologist, Cheesman was also an explorer: in 1924, she went on an insect-collecting mission to French Polynesia, the first of many solo expeditions funded by the sixteen books she wrote about her trips. Battling local bureaucracy, tropical disease and difficult terrain – she once freed herself from a spider web with a nail file – Cheesman sent 70,000 specimens to the Natural History Museum. In 1955, she received an Order of the British Empire (OBE) and a Civil List pension. Cheesman worked until her death; fifty years later, scientists are still making discoveries from her specimens and at least sixty-nine species are named after her. In *Hunting Insects in the South Seas*, she writes: "The insects are the serious part of existence; all the rest is just a joke – a bad joke at times, but not worth worrying about."

30 AUGUST

Margaret Mead

(1901–1978)

In August 1928, twenty-seven-year-old American researcher Margaret Mead published her first book, *Coming of Age in Samoa*. It made her the most famous anthropologist in the world and revolutionized Western thinking about sex, society and the teenage mind.

To 1920s readers, the book seemed not only to document but also to promote a relaxed attitude to sex and sex education. Mead had lived alongside the Polynesian islanders, not only to study their culture but in order to compare it with US society. Her comparative approach influenced the whole field of anthropology. Mead remained deeply interested in the social roles of men and women. Later titles such as *Male and Female* (1949) explored the "nature vs nurture" debate, concluding that men and women are shaped both by biology and by the culture around them. She understood too that an individual's sexuality

could be somewhat fluid. Her own experience confirmed this: she was romantically involved with both men and women. Such ideas were not only ahead of their time but helped to define the times. Mead became a progressive figurehead speaking on women's rights and social issues.

In 1979, President Jimmy Carter awarded Mead a posthumous Presidential Medal of Freedom.

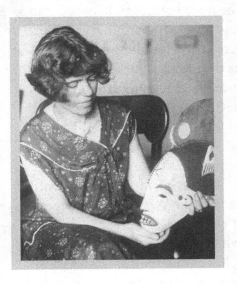

31 AUGUST

Linda Burney

(1957–)

On this day in 2016, Linda Burney – the first indigenous woman to win a federal seat in the Australian House of Representatives – delivered her first speech, wearing a kangaroo skin cloak decorated with her Wiradjuri clan totem. She spoke about the day in February 2008 when she had been one of the people standing in the gallery of that same parliamentary chamber to hear a long-awaited apology for the forced removal, between 1910 and 1970, of Aboriginal children from their families, now known as the Stolen Generations. She remembered how "around the perimeter of this chamber sat some of those children, now old people, still wearing the scars of forced removal on their faces."

Burney's half-sister Lynette Riley sang in the Wiradjuri language, then Burney spoke of an incident when a man from her home town told her that the day she was born was one of the town's "darkest days" because her father was Aboriginal.

After her white mother abandoned her, Burney was brought up by maternal relatives and then by the parents of a friend. She didn't meet her Wiradjuri father until she was twenty-eight. Burney stated her aim for her first term in Parliament: recognition of the First People in the Australian constitution. The extent of this recognition, and what form it should take, are still contested issues.

SEPTEMBER

"That brain of mine
is something more
than merely mortal;
as time will show."
– Ada Lovelace

How far can you go?

Women have faced many obstacles to involvement in public life. As well as battling to overcome the idea of "unladylike" behavior – public speaking, for example – there was a practical hindrance: public toilets. Before their advent, how far women could venture from their house – and for how long – was limited by the fortitude of their bladder: a limitation now referred to as the "urinary leash."

Innovations in plumbing brought the first public lavatories to Britain in the 1850s – but only for men. When the Ladies' Sanitary Association and the Union of Women's Liberal and Radical Associations were set up to campaign for toilets for women of all classes, they faced opposition. A model female toilet on a London high street was deliberately driven into by taxi drivers. It took women in positions of power to bring about change; before becoming New Zealand's first female MP in 1933, Elizabeth McCombs had women's public toilets built in Christchurch city center. But progress was slow: in 1985, the first woman appointed to the County Court of Victoria, Australia, discovered that toilets for judges were labeled "Gentlemen" and ones marked "Women" were for cleaners.

Lack of facilities was often used to justify why women couldn't possibly be lawyers, say, or politicians. But achieving political representation for women was itself affected by toilet provision: where could women gather to organize? Women's presence provoked consternation in pubs or restaurants even at the beginning of the twentieth century. Suffragette Kate Fry wrote in her diary in 1911 about lunch in a country hotel: "Men come in here and, seeing me, shoot out again . . . Awfully funny – they might never have seen a woman before." The late nineteenth century saw the establishment of tea rooms, coffee houses and department stores – many designed with women in mind, and equipped with toilets – which welcomed groups of women, providing them with a place to meet (See Tea).

In developed countries, there are usually designated toilets for women – although, unlike the men's, they often have long queues. However, the problem of the urinary leash hasn't disappeared, especially in developing countries. World Toilet Day, held annually on 19 November, has been campaigning for adequate sanitation since 2001. On International Women's Day, 8 March 2012, women stormed men's public toilets in the city of Nagpur, India, in protest at the lack of adequate facilities for women.

1 SEPTEMBER

Phillis Wheatley
(c.1753–1784)

On this day in 1773, Phillis Wheatley, a nineteen-year-old enslaved African, published *Poems on Various Subjects, Religious and Moral*. The first African-American to publish a book, she became one of America's best-known poets.

Wheatley's birth name is unknown; she was named for *Phillis*, the ship that brought her from West Africa, and for the Wheatley family of Boston, who bought her "for a trifle." Unusually, they schooled her in literacy and literature. Her first poem was published in 1767, and by 1771, her work was circulating in London. English abolitionists seized on her as proof that enslaved people were equal to those who enslaved them.

Wheatley's most famous poem, "On Being Brought from Africa to America," while protesting slavery, also protects the view of Christianity as the force which "refin'd" ignorant Africans.

Such contradictions were commonplace. For instance, Wheatley's correspondents included George Washington and Benjamin Rush, co-signatories to the Declaration of Independence. It stated that "all men are created equal" with "an unalienable right to life, liberty and the pursuit of happiness"; yet both men "owned" slaves. Freed in 1774, Wheatley married an African-American man. They lived in poverty through the revolution and into American independence.

Dorothea Bate

(1878–1951)

In September 1898, Dorothea Bate, aged nineteen and with no qualifications, asked for a job at London's Natural History Museum. She eventually persuaded the curator of birds, Richard Bowdler Sharpe, to employ her sorting bird skins. The museum's first female employee, she stayed for fifty years – sometimes paid piece-work according to the number of fossils she prepared – and became a trailblazer in paleontology, ornithology and archaeozoology, traveling to Palestine, Sudan, Syria, China and Egypt.

One of Bate's specialisms was elephant fossils. In 1902, a Royal Society grant enabled her to dig in Cyprus, where she found a new species of dwarf elephant, *Elephas cypriotes*. In 1934, on her way to Dorothy Garrod's Mount Carmel dig, Bate was asked to investigate a find in Bethlehem, which she identified as an elephant tusk, now considered the remains of one of the earliest true elephants outside of Africa, *Elephas planifrons*. She was furious when archaeologist James Starkey took control of the dig, forcing Bate and her colleague Elinor Gardner to work under his command.

In January 1938, after Starkey was killed by an armed mob, the dig was closed. Archaeologists have never returned to the site; Gardner and Bate's records are the only information we have about ancient elephants, horses and tortoises living in the area 2.5 million years ago.

The museum's first female employee, she stayed for fifty years . . .

3 SEPTEMBER

Ada Lovelace

(1815–1852)

In September 1843, British mathematician Ada Lovelace published "Notes on Charles Babbage's Analytical Engine," emphasizing the difference between Babbage's invention and previous calculating machines. Now seen as "the prophet of the computer age," Lovelace realized the engine could be programmed.

Lovelace was the only legitimate daughter of poet Alfred Lord Byron, who left her mother a month after her birth. Lady Byron, a mathematician, encouraged Lovelace to study math and logic to protect her from her father's "insanity"; <u>Mary Somerville</u> was one of her tutors and mentors. However, Lovelace's approach was all her own, what she called "poetical science": using imagination and mathematics to explore "the unseen worlds around us." She often focused on interdisciplinary projects, combining math and biology, for example, to think about "a calculus of the nervous system." She was not unaware of her brilliance: "That brain of mine is something more than merely mortal; as time will show." Unrecognized in her lifetime, she is now the figurehead for an annual international celebration of women in science, technology, engineering and math (STEM): Ada Lovelace Day, held on the second Tuesday in October.

4 SEPTEMBER

Jessie Tarbox Beals

(1870–1942)

On this day in 1900, Canadian Jessie Tarbox Beals became America's first female photojournalist, with a photo credit in the *Windham County Reporter*. She became staff photographer on several newspapers and was popular with editors for writing good copy to accompany her work. Her first scoop was a portrait of visiting tea merchant Sir Thomas Lipton.

Beals had won her first camera at the age of eighteen, as a sales bonus. Later, she went to great lengths to get her pictures, in spite of the unwieldy glass-plate cameras and restrictive dress of the time. At Edwin L Burdick's murder trial, she bypassed a veto on photographers by climbing up a bookcase to snap a covert picture. She often used ladders to secure a good viewpoint and even rode in a hot air balloon as official photographer at the 1904 St. Louis World's Fair. This event brought indigenous people from around the world and Beals took many striking pictures, both of the "exotic" exhibitors and of President Roosevelt's visit. Her portfolio varied: she recorded society figures, street scenes with slum children, celebrities like Mark Twain and the gardens of the wealthy. Her photographs appeared in major exhibitions; samples of Beals's work are now held in national collections at the Library of Congress, Harvard University and the American Museum of Natural History.

5 SEPTEMBER

Olympe de Gouges

(1748–1793)

On this day in 1791, playwright and activist Olympe de Gouges published her *Declaration des Droits de la Femme et de la Citoyenne* ("Declaration of the Rights of Woman and of the Female Citizen"). A supporter of the French Revolution of 1789, which promised social justice and equal rights, Gouges soon realized that these rights – laid down in the National Assembly's *The Declaration of the Rights of Man and of the Citizen* – didn't include women. She wrote her *Declaration* in response: "Woman is born free and remains equal to man in rights. Social distinctions may only be based on common utility."

Gouges wrote two novels, forty plays and seventy political pamphlets. Her plays are notable for giving agency to women of all ages – with women as supporters of each other, not rivals – and for connecting abuses of women to structural injustices. An early abolitionist, Gouges insisted on the humanity and rights of the marginalized to be equal citizens. She opposed capital punishment, condemning the execution of Louis XVI, and continued to write pamphlets and posters even after the National Assembly banned women's participation in politics in 1793. That summer, during the revolution's "Reign of Terror," she was arrested, convicted of sedition and beheaded by guillotine.

6 SEPTEMBER

Katherine Johnson

(1918–2020)

In 1939, Katherine Johnson was one of just three African-Americans accepted into West Virginia's newly integrated graduate school to study math. In 1953, she was offered a job in NASA's Flight Research Division and in September 1960 she co-authored a report – the first time a woman was cited as author on a NASA publication: "The whole idea of going into space was new and daring. There were no textbooks, so we had to write them."

When Alan Shepard became the first American to travel into space in 1961, it was Johnson who calculated the landing trajectory that brought him safely back to earth. The following year, astronaut John Glenn, wary of trusting the calculations for his mission to the new, erratic IBM machines, told engineers to get Johnson. "If she says [the numbers are] good, then I'm ready to go."

Johnson also helped calculate the trajectory for the 1969 Apollo 11 flight to the Moon, as well as working on projects including the Space Shuttle program and plans for a Mars mission: "I loved going to work every single day."

In 2015, President Obama awarded her the Presidential Medal of Freedom. Johnson is one of the African-American NASA women, along with Dorothy Vaughan and Mary Jackson, whose story is told in the film *Hidden Figures* (2016).

7 SEPTEMBER

Grace Darling

(1815–1842)

On this day in 1838, Grace Darling, a lighthouse-keeper's daughter, helped rescue nine survivors from the shipwrecked *Forfarshire*, which had run aground off the coast of Northumberland in north-east England. Darling became a national heroine, receiving awards including the Royal Humane Society's Gold Medal of Bravery and £50 from Queen Victoria.

But celebrity was also a burden; so many artists wanted to paint or sculpt Darling that she and her family were overwhelmed and had to limit visits. The Duke of Northumberland – who had met the family when their lighthouse was being built – offered to be her guardian to protect her from unscrupulous people trying to exploit her. But in spite of the Duke's protection, the constant public attention took its toll on Darling's health and she became anxious. In 1842, she fell ill and had nightmares of staring eyes;

the Duchess of Northumberland's physician diagnosed tuberculosis. Darling died soon afterwards; according to her sister Thomasin, she "went like the snow."

In 1938, the Royal National Lifeboat Institution opened the Grace Darling Museum in Bamburgh, Northumberland, to commemorate her heroism. Its display includes the coble fishing boat used by Darling and her father during the rescue.

Gertrude Bell

(1868–1926)

Gertrude Bell was an English explorer, writer, archaeologist, spy and administrator. She is best remembered – not always with admiration – as an architect of present-day Iraq. Leaving Oxford in 1892 after studying modern history, Bell traveled Europe, becoming such an accomplished mountaineer that one Alpine peak, the Gertrudspitze, is named after her. She then roamed the Middle East, recording customs, tribal politics and archaeological remains.

After the First World War, Bell worked with Lawrence of Arabia and the British task force to set policy and national boundaries in Iraq. The decisions to allow government by the Sunni minority and to enclose large Kurdish populations inside Iraq caused lasting problems. She wrote presciently from Basra in 1916: "We rushed into the business with our usual disregard for a comprehensive political scheme . . . When people talk of our muddling through it throws me into a passion. Muddle through! Why yes, so we do – wading through blood and tears that need never have been shed."

Bell's white paper for the British Parliament, establishing the basis of the Iraqi state, was the first to be written by a woman. She established the Iraqi National Museum and helped set up the National Library. Bell died of an apparent overdose and is buried in Baghdad's British cemetery.

9 SEPTEMBER

Wilma Rudolph
(1940–1994)

In the 1940s, healthcare for African-Americans was very limited in Wilma Rudolph's hometown of Clarksville, Tennessee. So when she lost strength in her left leg after contracting polio, she and her mother traveled by bus to Nashville, a round trip of 100 miles, for treatment. "My doctor told me I would never walk again. My mother said I would. I believed my mother." With hospital therapy and help from her family, Rudolph regained the use of her leg.

After being homeschooled due to her many childhood illnesses, it was at high school that Rudolph first demonstrated her athletic talents; later she joined the track team at Tennessee State University. At the Rome Olympics in August and September 1960, Rudolph became the first American woman to win three gold medals at a single Olympiad. The fastest woman in the world, she was nicknamed "The Tornado" and "La Gazzella Nera" ("The Black Gazelle").

Clarksville staged a "Welcome Wilma Day" on 4 October 1960: over a thousand people went to the banquet and watched the parade which, at Rudolph's insistence, were both fully racially integrated – a first for a municipal event in Clarksville. Rudolph's autobiography was published in 1977; in 1981, she set up the Wilma Rudolph Foundation in Indiana to support young athletes.

10 SEPTEMBER

Annette Kellerman

(1887–1975)

As a child, Australian swimmer and entertainer Annette Kellerman had to wear steel leg braces. To help her muscles develop, her parents took her swimming. She began to swim competitively and also gave aquatic performances as a mermaid swimming with fish at an aquarium. On this day in 1905, Kellerman came equal third in a swimming race down the Seine, the only woman alongside seventeen men. By 1907, holding many world records, she moved into entertainment, popularizing synchronized swimming with her 1907 performance of the first water ballet.

In the same year, Kellerman was arrested on a Boston beach for wearing her invention: a swimsuit whose tight fit enabled her to swim freely. The publicity helped relax rules around women's swimwear and Kellerman lent her name to a swimwear brand. The first Australian woman to become a Hollywood star, Kellerman played a mermaid/action hero in several films and, in 1916, was the first major actress to appear nude in a Hollywood production (*A Daughter of the Gods*). In 1908, a Harvard professor announced that, having measured the bodies of 10,000 women, he had found Kellerman's to be most similar to the Venus de Milo; he declared her "the perfect woman." Her response is said to have been, "But only from the neck down."

11 SEPTEMBER

Nontsikelelo Albertina "Ma" Sisulu (1918–2011)

On this day in 1944, Nontsikelelo Albertina "Ma" Sisulu was the only woman to attend the founding conference of the African National Congress (ANC) Youth League. Four years earlier, while training to be a nurse in the "non-European wing" of Johannesburg General Hospital, she'd witnessed how white nurses were treated as superior to black ones, regardless of seniority or experience. Her political consciousness was further raised when she married Walter Sisulu, activist and ANC member, and joined the ANC Women's League.

In August 1956, Sisulu helped organize a demonstration of over 20,000 women, protesting against the government ruling that all African women must carry passes. One of hundreds of women arrested in Johannesburg protesting these Pass Laws, she spent six weeks in jail. In 1964, Walter was arrested and sentenced to life imprisonment; during the twenty-five years he was imprisoned, Sisulu raised their five children while continuing her political activities. Often called "Mother of the Nation," in 1994, she was elected to South Africa's first democratically elected parliament. She retired from political life in 1999.

"Women are the people who are going to relieve us from all this oppression and depression. It is the women who are on the street committees educating the people to stand up and protect each other."

12 SEPTEMBER

Mahalia Jackson

(1911–1972)

Singer and civil rights activist Mahalia Jackson was born to a poor New Orleans family. She grew up singing in gospel choirs and pledged never to sing secular music – though she sometimes upset ministers by setting traditional gospel to simple rhythms. After unsuccessful early recordings, in 1948, Jackson recorded "Move on Up a Little Higher." An instant hit, it sold millions, making her an international star. A European tour, record deal and annual sell-out concerts at Carnegie Hall followed. In 1954, *DownBeat* magazine called Jackson the "world's greatest gospel singer." Seven years later, she sang at John F. Kennedy's inaugural ball.

Like many other people of color in the arts, Jackson put her celebrity to the service of civil rights, at great personal risk. An early ally of Martin Luther King, she sang at many of his rallies, including the 1963 March to Washington where King made his famous "I Have a Dream" speech. Five years later, Jackson sang at the assassinated leader's funeral. Fellow singer and civil rights activist Harry Belafonte once described Jackson as "the single most powerful black woman in the United States."

Known as "the Queen of Gospel," Jackson was an inspiration to singers like Mavis Staples and Aretha Franklin. "Blues are the songs of despair," she said. "Gospel songs are the songs of hope."

13 SEPTEMBER

Elizabeth McCombs

(1873–1935)

In 1893, New Zealand women were the first in the world to win the right to vote. Thirty-five years later, Elizabeth McCombs ran as the Labour Party's first female candidate under the slogan: "Vote the first Woman to the New Zealand Parliament." She wasn't elected, but when her husband, James, died, she fought to stand for his seat. Where he had won by thirty-two votes, on this day in 1933, she won by a majority of 2,600 and became New Zealand's first female MP.

In 1921, Elizabeth had been the second woman elected to Christchurch City Council. During her fourteen-year tenure, one of her major achievements was the creation of a crèche and public toilets for women, the lack of which had kept them from venturing far from home (see How far can you go?).

The lone female voice in Parliament, in her first speech McCombs said: "Women are never satisfied unless they have their own way. It happens in this case that the woman's way is the right way."

She fought for equal pay and equal unemployment support for women and for recruiting women as police officers. A long-term sufferer from asthma, McCombs died less than two years after being elected.

Anni Albers

(1899–1994)

Anni Albers was one of the earliest female students at the German avant-garde Bauhaus art school. She was a member of the weaving workshop – one of the few options available to women – although she would have preferred to paint. "I thought [weaving] was rather sissy . . . Just these threads."

However, in 1933, when the Nazis came to power, Albers and her husband, Bauhaus master Josef Albers, emigrated to the US, where she continued to develop her weaving practice. Through her experimental approach, including the use of materials such as wood, raffia, grass and cellophane, she created the field of "textile art." On this day in 1949, Albers became the first weaver to have a solo exhibition at New York's Museum of Modern Art. In articles such as "On Designing" (1959) and "On Weaving" (1965), she set her modern weaving methods against the craft's long and global history.

On trips to Mexico, Chile and Peru, she collected many ancient textiles whose patterns had a huge influence on her work.

In 1965, Albers was commissioned by New York's Jewish Museum to create a Holocaust memorial. Although she was baptized a Protestant and referred to herself as Jewish only "in the Hitler sense," the work she produced – *Six Prayers* (1966–67) – shows a deep engagement with Jewish tradition and ritual.

"I thought [weaving] was rather sissy . . . Just these threads."

Tammy Wynette

(1942–1998)

In September 1968, Tammy Wynette released "Stand By Your Man," the biggest-selling country music single of all time. The song – also the title of Wynette's memoir and her third number one hit of 1968 – coincided with feminism's second wave, and many feminists were enraged by what they took to be the song's "pro-man" message.

Wynette, married to her third of five husbands when she wrote it, explained that her lyrics were a way of saying "I love you – without reservations." "I spent fifteen minutes writing it," Wynette said, "and a lifetime defending it." She was not happy when First Lady Hillary Clinton referenced the song in 1992 in the midst of the scandal about her husband's affairs, saying: "You know, I'm not sitting here, some little woman standing by my man like Tammy Wynette." Clinton later apologized.

Born Virginia Wynette Pugh, and renamed "Tammy" by a record producer, Wynette, who started out earning money for music lessons by picking cotton on her grandfather's Alabama farm, won two Grammys and eight Billboard awards. She was posthumously inducted into the Country Music Association Hall of Fame in 1998.

Properzia de' Rossi
(1490–1530)

The sixteenth-century Italian sculptor Properzia de' Rossi lived and worked in Bologna, a city known for its relatively high number of women artists and intellectuals. But female artists were still rare and sculpture was considered a man's discipline.

Unlike most of her female contemporaries, de' Rossi was not born into an artistic family, so it must have been difficult for her to access training in sculpture. But she succeeded: first studying at the University of Bologna and then with master engraver Marc Antonio Raimondi.

De' Rossi first became known for carving fruit stones, the only artist famous for the discipline at that time; the cherry stone onto which she carved sixty saints' heads can be seen in the Uffizi Gallery in Florence. Later, she sculpted portrait busts and, after winning a competition to create a sculpture for the Basilica di San Petronio in

Bologna in the 1520s, her talent was recognized and she began to receive more church commissions than her male rivals. De' Rossi is the only woman of 142 artists to whom Giorgio Vasari devotes a whole chapter in his *Lives of the Most Eminent Painters, Sculptors, Architects* (1550).

Hildegard of Bingen

(1098–1179)

On this day in 1179, a giant of medieval culture died. Hildegard of Bingen was a prolific writer on science and medicine, a renowned composer and a Christian visionary who ruled over religious houses. Her sacred songs and poems are still regularly performed.

Hildegard had visions as a child and entered a monastery before she was fourteen. She became a great monastic leader, founding several communities in Germany. She conducted preaching tours, was consulted by European religious thinkers and wrote three major books on her theology and visions.

An authority on botany and medicine, she drew on classical and contemporary texts as well as her experience in a monastic hospital and its herb gardens. Listing healing substances, Hildegard advised on diagnosis and treatment in people and animals; she made the first reference to hops in beer. Her writings – including 400 letters to popes, emperors and scholars, 70 musical pieces and a morality play, *Ordo Virtutum* – probably comprise the largest surviving body of work by a medieval author.

When she died, witnesses claimed that two streams of light appeared in the sky above the room. In 2012, she was declared a saint. Hildegard is one of only four female Doctors of the Catholic Church – scholars who have made a significant contribution to its theology.

"I heard a voice from Heaven saying to me, 'Cry out, therefore, and write thus!'"

18 SEPTEMBER

Belva Lockwood (1830–1917) and Victoria Woodhull (1838–1927)

On this day in 1884, forty years before American women won the vote, Belva Ann Lockwood (pictured) gave a speech as the first woman to run a full US presidential campaign: "I cannot vote, but I can be voted for." She received 4,100 votes in the election – impressive, since women couldn't vote and many newspapers opposed her. The *Atlanta Constitution* called her "old lady Lockwood," warning of the dangers of "petticoat rule." One of several women admitted to law school only after a struggle with trustees – and awarded her diploma only after appealing to US President Grant – Lockwood was the first woman admitted to the Bar of the Supreme Court and the first to argue a Supreme Court case.

However, Lockwood wasn't the first woman to run for president: in 1870, publisher and free love advocate Victoria Woodhull had run a partial campaign as the Equal Rights Party candidate.

Woodhull used money she and her sister had made as the first female Wall Street stockbrokers and the first women to run a weekly national newspaper. Her candidacy was never taken seriously: called "Mrs. Satan," her name was removed from many ballot papers because she and her sister were in jail on election day, arrested for publishing "an obscene newspaper"; they were later cleared. Woodhull received no votes.

Madam C.J. Walker

(1867–1919)

Madam C.J. Walker was the first black millionaire, an African-American entrepreneur who made a fortune by selling hair products to women of color. Born Sarah Breedlove, daughter of formerly enslaved parents, by six she was an orphan; by fourteen a wife; by twenty a widow with a toddler. Suffering hair loss, she developed a hair care system involving lotions and iron combs. Her second husband, journalist C.J. Walker, helped with branding and promotion.

Walker's products catered to a market ignored by white beauty culture. She advertised in the black press, gave demonstrations and employed thousands of women as door-to-door sales staff. Walker reveled in her visibility as a rich woman of color, building lavish homes and driving a Model T car at a time when few white men could afford one.

She used her fortune to benefit those who had created it; people of color. Her country home was designed by a black architect and her Manhattan townhouse became a Harlem Renaissance salon. Walker donated to charity, gave political lectures, created scholarships and used bonuses to encourage employees towards charitable work. The charter of her company stipulated that only a woman could become its president.

Kitty Wilkinson

(1786–1860)

Disease spread swiftly amongst the poor in Britain's crowded industrial cities, in part because doing laundry required hot water, fuel and drying space. So, during the cholera epidemic of 1832, Kitty Wilkinson turned her Liverpool home into a "wash-house," spreading the word about the importance of cleanliness. On this day in 2012, a statue of this "saint of the slums" was unveiled.

Wilkinson had moved to Liverpool from Ireland in 1786; her father and sister had drowned on the journey so, aged eleven, she began work in a cotton mill. Later, with her second husband, she established a school for orphans. When cholera broke out, Wilkinson encouraged people to wash bedding at her house, demonstrating how to disinfect using chloride. After a lengthy campaign, Britain's first public bath- and wash-house opened in Liverpool in 1842; four years later, Wilkinson was named superintendent of public baths.

The only woman among the twelve statues in Liverpool's St George's Hall, her legacy is also preserved by a new non-commercial community wash-house and social space, Kitty's Laundrette, which opened in Liverpool in May 2019, "in honour of Kitty Wilkinson, an Irish immigrant to Liverpool, the pioneer of the wash-house movement in the UK."

21 SEPTEMBER

Lou Andreas-Salomé

(1861–1937)

Lou Andreas-Salomé was a Russian author, philosopher and early psychoanalyst. A prolific writer, she explored new ways for women to be sexually and socially free. Like many *fin-de-siècle* intellectuals, Salomé moved around Europe to study and work. In Zurich, she studied theology; in Rome, she mixed with philosophers including Nietzsche; in Berlin, she married Carl Friedrich Andreas. Their marriage was celibate and Salomé openly had relationships with other men. She wrote on female sexuality in her 1910 book *Die Erotik* and was the only woman in Sigmund Freud's Vienna Psychoanalytic Circle. She practiced as a psychoanalyst in Göttingen, Germany – the first female therapist of this kind.

However, like many women in this book, Salomé is usually documented in terms of her male colleagues. She is described as a "muse," "inspiration" or "mistress"

of men to whom she was in fact a partner or peer. Late in life, Salomé complained: "I have really done nothing but work all my life, work . . . why?" Though men of the early 1900s might have struggled to see her as a professional equal, historians in subsequent decades should have known better (see We are not a muse).

22 SEPTEMBER

Hannah Shapiro

(c.1893–unknown)

On this day in 1910, a seventeen-year-old textile worker called Hannah Shapiro led a walkout of women workers at Chicago garment manufacturer Hart, Schaffner & Marx. It became one of the most important industrial actions in the US.

Thousands of women worked in the clothing trade; many were immigrants like Shapiro, a Ukrainian Jew. Most worked long hours in terrible conditions with low pay. Shapiro walked out because she was incensed by a sudden cut in the piece rate for making trouser pockets. She and her co-workers in Shop 5 were soon joined by those in other company shops. Within the week, 2,000 workers were out. When the United Garment Workers' Union lent their support, around 45,000 workers downed tools; it had become a general strike. This was one in a domino-chain of stoppages, including the famous New York shirtwaist strike of 1909. Many of them were organized by women such as Clara Lemlich, Agnes Nestor and Bessie Abramovitch.

The textile workers were represented by star lawyer of the left, Clarence Darrow. The company at the heart of the dispute agreed to workers' representation on a committee but continued to forbid union membership. Interviewed in 1976 about her part in the protest, Shapiro confirmed that she had initiated the walk-out, saying, "I'm a strong girl; I never regretted it."

Virginia Apgar
(1909–1974)

On this day in 1952, American anesthesiologist Virginia Apgar presented her revolutionary five-point method for assessing a newborn's health to the twenty-seventh Annual Congress of Anesthetists. The Apgar Score has now been used worldwide for nearly seventy years, drastically reducing infant deaths. "Nobody, but nobody, is going to stop breathing on me," said Apgar. Studying medicine when many medical schools didn't admit women, Apgar wanted to become a surgeon. But her mentor suggested anesthesiology instead, not then a recognized specialty. Apgar decided to focus on a neglected topic: anesthesia's effect on mothers and babies. When asked by a student how to evaluate a newborn's health, the list she jotted down became the basis of the Apgar Score. Babies are tested one minute and five minutes after birth according to five factors: appearance, pulse, grimace, activity and respiration. This allows doctors to rapidly spot problems and has saved countless lives.

Apgar was appointed director of Columbia University's anesthesia department and, in 1949, the first full female professor at Columbia University College of Physicians and Surgeons. However, she couldn't socialize with her colleagues after work because they met in men-only social clubs. She traveled widely, giving talks on premature birth and birth defects, and published many papers and a book, *Is My Baby Alright?* (1973). In 1994, the US Postal Service included her in its "Great Americans" postage stamp series.

"Nobody, but nobody, is going to stop breathing on me."

Rita Levi-Montalcini

(1909–2012)

Born into a Jewish family in Turin, Rita Levi-Montalcini was drawn to science in her twenties, deciding to study medicine after her beloved governess died of cancer. Receiving her degree in 1936, she worked as assistant to her professor, a neuroscientist. After the Italian government passed anti-Semitic laws in 1938, she was no longer allowed at the university, so she set up a laboratory at home. When Turin was bombed by Allied forces in 1940, Levi-Montalcini and her family fled to Florence, where they lived under assumed identities.

In September 1946, Levi-Montalcini was invited to Washington University for a one-semester fellowship; she stayed for thirty years, becoming a professor. In 1986, together with biochemist Stanley Cohen, she was awarded the Nobel Prize for research that began in her wartime home laboratory: the discovery of nerve growth factor, a protein that helps stimulate nerve cell growth. Nerve growth factor plays a vital role in current research into Alzheimer's disease, cancer, Parkinson's disease and muscular dystrophy. In 1975, Levi-Montalcini was the first woman to join the Vatican's Pontifical Academy of Sciences; when she turned 100, she became the oldest living Nobel laureate. "Young women can now look toward a future molded by their own hands."

Louisa May Alcott

(1832–1888)

In September 1868, Louisa May Alcott published her novel, *Little Women*. The story of the four March sisters and their mother, Marmee, has become an American classic. Alcott only wrote the novel because of the persistence of a publisher who wanted "a book for girls." A tomboy, the only girls she knew were her sisters, and Alcott wasn't sure she could write a popular book when her childhood had been so unusual. Her parents were Transcendental philosophers and hosts for the Underground Railroad, helping African-Americans escape from slavery. Finally persuaded, Alcott wrote the book in two months, then collapsed with fatigue.

There was very little money and often not much to eat at home, so she was determined to make her writing pay. Writing racy gothic fiction under the pseudonym A.M. Barnard, Alcott claimed that these were "necessity stories," done for the money, but admitted privately she enjoyed this "lurid style." However, she was also keen to write about reality. Her novel *Work: A Story of Experience* (1873) portrayed a young woman finding her feet in the world of employment and as an activist. Alcott herself was a passionate suffragist and one of the first twenty women in Concord, Massachusetts, to vote. "No bolt fell on our audacious heads," was her comment on the event.

26 SEPTEMBER

Plectrude

(unknown–718 CE)

In the early eighth century, Plectrude, Duchess of the Franks, was a key political figure in a turbulent Europe. Government at this time was a question of pedigree as well as aptitude. A few capable women with both of these qualifications were able to rule, either indirectly or in their own name. In an age of descriptive names like Louis the Stammerer and Charles the Bald, Plectrude was married to Pepin the Fat, duke of the Franks. A wealthy and influential woman, her signature is attached to all the ordinances of her husband's reign, an uncommon detail which suggests that she took an active role in government.

In 714, Plectrude's husband died. His named heir was their grandson, Theudoald, who was still a child. Plectrude assumed control as regent and imprisoned the rival claimant, Charles Martel. Martel, however, had powerful allies; the duchess was met with rebellion and force, and ultimately defeated. Martel assumed power and ruled over a united Francia for over twenty years. Plectrude retired to a convent and died there, with a promptness which was very convenient for Martel.

In an age of descriptive names like Louis the Stammerer and Charles the Bald, Plectrude was married to Pepin the Fat.

27 SEPTEMBER

Alice Chaucer

(c.1404–1475)

Alice Chaucer is usually spoken of as either the granddaughter of the poet Geoffrey Chaucer or the wife of three wealthy and influential men, but she was an interesting and powerful individual in her own right. In 1437, she established almshouses for retired workers in her Oxfordshire village and founded a grammar school to encourage boys from her estates to go to Oxford University. Both institutions still exist – the school is the UK's oldest primary school.

When her third husband was executed in 1450, Chaucer was left in a vulnerable situation and had to act quickly to ensure ownership of their property passed to her and her son. By the end of her life, through inheritance and acquisitions, she owned estates in twenty-two English counties.

A patron of literature and visual arts, Chaucer built an extensive library, which included <u>Christine de Pisan</u>'s *Book of the City of Ladies;* she was an example of the "valiant ladies and women of authority" to whom the book is dedicated.

She commissioned tapestries of the life of St. Anne, mother of the Virgin Mary, an important figure for women in the Middle Ages. For her own tomb, she commissioned a "memento mori" sculpture of herself as a corpse, the only known instance of such a cadaver sculpture of a woman.

She founded a grammar school to encourage boys from her estates to go to Oxford University.

Elizabeth Garrett Anderson
(1836–1917)

On this day in 1865, Elizabeth Garrett Anderson became the first woman to qualify as a doctor in Britain. Inspired by meeting Dr. Elizabeth Blackwell, an Englishwoman who had become a doctor in the US, Garrett Anderson could find no medical school that would accept her. She enrolled as a nursing student at Middlesex Hospital and attended classes in medicine until she was banned after male students complained. She eventually took and passed the Society of Apothecaries examination.

In 1872, Garrett Anderson set up the New Hospital for Women (later the Elizabeth Garrett Anderson Hospital), with Blackwell as professor of gynecology. The hospital had an all-female staff until the 1980s. Garrett Anderson was also co-founder, along with Blackwell and Sophia Jex-Blake, of the London School of Medicine for Women.

Garrett Anderson's example and her campaigning for roles for women in medicine were key in bringing about the Medical Act 1876, which prohibited the exclusion of women from universities and medical schools.

After her retirement, in 1908, Garrett Anderson became the first female mayor in England: in Aldeburgh, Suffolk. She was also a passionate campaigner for women's suffrage, like her daughter, Louisa Garrett Anderson, and her sister, Millicent Fawcett.

Lillian Moller Gilbreth

(1878–1972)

Lillian Moller Gilbreth was the first industrial or organizational psychologist, an ergonomics pioneer labeled "a genius in the art of living." Lillian was less interested in productivity than in making employees' lives better. She and her husband, Frank, invented the concept of motion studies, making "micromotion films" to study workplace efficiency and assess "happiness minutes": the amount of time each day a worker was satisfied with their job. In 1917, they were the first to examine how workplaces might be modified for disabled employees. However, although they co-authored many books, Lillian, who had a psychology doctorate, wasn't always credited; publishers feared a female author would undermine the book's credibility.

After Frank's death in 1924, Lillian moved into other fields, including cooking and housework. She interviewed women to determine ideal heights for kitchen appliances, inventing the foot-pedal-operated rubbish bin, shelves inside fridge doors and an improved electric can opener. In 1929, she unveiled her Kitchen Practical at a Women's Exposition, an L-shape design based on motion and ergonomics studies. Many kitchens today are organized along these lines.

Lillian was also known for having eleven children, two of whom wrote bestsellers about their unusual family life; *Cheaper by the Dozen* was made into a film.

The first woman elected to the US National Academy of Engineering, in 1996 Lillian was awarded the Hoover Medal for "great, unselfish, non-technical services by engineers to humanity."

30 SEPTEMBER

Poly Styrene
(1957–2011)

On this day in 1977, punk band X-Ray Spex released their single "Oh Bondage Up Yours!", launching Somali-British singer Poly Styrene as an unlikely icon of UK popular culture. Born Marianne Elliott-Said in Kent, she ran away from home at fifteen and formed X-Ray Spex four years later. She became a leading figure in the punk movement, writing the songs and making the band's artwork. Melodic she was not – "A bagful of cats was more harmonic," said one reviewer.

Punk was discordant, amateurish and profoundly shocking to mainstream culture. Its impact went far beyond music, challenging attitudes to class, race and gender, consumerism and politics. X-Ray Spex joined the ranks of bands like Blondie, the Slits and the Pretenders, all fronted by sexually confident women with loud voices, untidy hair, ripped clothes and foul mouths. Poly Styrene was a mixed-race, working-class woman with braces on her teeth and Day-Glo clothing. She rejected traditional ideas of ladylike behavior and sex appeal, asserting that if anyone tried to turn her into a sex symbol she would shave her head. The vision she offered was anarchic, unsettling and liberating, paving the way for later "riot grrrl" groups like Bikini Kill and Pussy Riot.

OCTOBER

"It would have been
more comfortable
to remain silent . . .
I felt that I had to
tell the truth."
– Anita Hill

Wives, or great women

"Behind every great man there's a great woman," is often understood to mean that without the woman supporting him, the man wouldn't have become great. Although this was (and is) often the case, many women across history have managed not to let marriage and expectations of "wifely" behavior stand in the way of their own achievements; marriage has sometimes even enabled women to flourish alongside their husbands.

Too many interesting women "disappeared" from history when they married and had children. Serbian physicist Mileva Marić Einstein discussed his work with her more famous husband Albert when they were students together and throughout their marriage; it's unknown how much she contributed to the theory of relativity attributed solely to him. Some became less well-known than their husbands, even though they were at least as famous during their lifetimes.

After nineteenth-century German pianist and composer Clara Wieck married Robert Schumann, they kept a joint artistic diary. Although much of her time was taken up with their eight children, she was the main breadwinner. After Robert's early death, Clara started touring again.

Some see the convention of a married woman taking her husband's surname as suggesting that upon marriage, a woman becomes merely an add-on to her husband. But when Lucy Ridsdale became Mrs. Lucy Baldwin in 1892, and after her husband, Stanley, became British prime minister, she was still very much herself. She held meetings of her cricket club in Downing Street; she used her position of influence to help women with the trauma of childbirth.

For some women, legally prevented from having a career, their choice of husband determined not only their companion and home but also their workplace; her husband might represent a career opportunity, so long as a woman could do this "non-domestic' work at home and fit it in around responsibilities such as childcare. For example, seventeenth-century British printer Eleanor James was hidden behind her husband for much of her working life – he was the "master printer" and business owner – but thanks to her extraordinary writing, she became more historically important than him. Other women have worked with their husbands as equal partners: Marie Curie with Pierre, Annie Russell Maunder with Edward, Lillian Gilbreth with Frank. So when we hear "she was the wife of" let's think: "I wonder what she did and how she managed to do it?"

1 OCTOBER

Maria Mitchell

(1818–1889)

On this day in 1847, Maria Mitchell, who often slipped away from parties to use her telescope, became the first American to officially discover a comet. Comet 1847-VI, "Miss Mitchell's Comet," won her a gold medal from the King of Denmark.

Mitchell – the first woman elected to the US Academy of Arts and Sciences – believed women were ideally suited to astronomy: "The eye that directs a needle in the delicate meshes of embroidery will equally well bisect a star with the spider web of the micrometer."

When Vassar College appointed her America's first female astronomy professor and director of their observatory, Mitchell complained that her salary was less than male professors: "We cannot accept anything as granted, beyond the first mathematical formulae. Question everything else." She traveled to many European observatories, becoming great friends with British mathematician <u>Mary Somerville</u>.

A promoter of female scientists, Mitchell gave a speech in 1876 on "The Need for Women in Science," invited feminists to talk to her class and led an all-female expedition to see a solar eclipse. Three of her students were included in the first "Academic Men of Science' [sic] list in 1906. Said one: "A chance meeting with Miss Mitchell . . . gave one always an electric shock. At the slightest contact, a spark flashed."

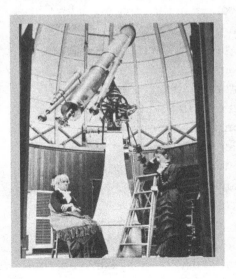

2 OCTOBER

Aemilia (Bassano) Lanyer
(1569–1645)

On this day in 1610, Aemilia Lanyer's book of poetry, *Salve Deus Rex Judaeorum* ("Hail, God, King of the Jews"), was entered into the Stationers" Register in London; it was published a year later.

Lanyer, considered to be the first professional female poet in the English language, used religious poetry to express an early "feminist" awareness. Her title poem puts the responsibility for the crucifixion at the door of powerful men, while the women in the story plead for Christ and mourn his suffering. In "Eve's Apology in Defense of Women," Lanyer rewrites the Old Testament story, claiming that Eve's sin was no greater than Adam's, and stemmed only from her innocence and her desire for knowledge. Lanyer builds on this claim to demand contemporary women's freedom from patriarchy.

In 2018, *Emilia* [sic], a play about the personal and professional difficulties faced by Lanyer because of her sex, opened at the Globe theatre in London with an all-female cast.

> "Then let us [women] have our liberty again, And challenge to yourselves [men] no sovereignty. You came not in the world without our pain, Make that a bar against your cruelty."

3 OCTOBER

Eve Ensler

(1953–)

On this day in 1996, Eve Ensler's play, *The Vagina Monologues*, opened in New York. Ensler, whose father abused her, assembled the play from interviews with 200 women of different ages, races and sexualities on the topics of sex, relationships, body image and violence. The *New York Times* wrote that, "No recent hour of theater has had a greater impact worldwide."

Each year a new monologue is added to the play – originally intended "to celebrate the vagina" – on a specific issue. In 1998, Ensler shifted her focus towards ending violence against women, announcing the first annual "V-Day," held on 14 February: the "V" stands for victory, valentine and vagina. Funds raised have, for example, helped Agnes Pareyio – known as "the Vagina Warrior" for her fight against female genital mutilation in Kenya– to establish a safe house for girls fleeing from FGM.

In 2013, Ensler launched One Billion Rising, calling for women to "strike, rise and dance" on V-Day. "We have broken taboos, spoken the word 'vagina' in fifty languages in one hundred and forty countries, called up stories and truths about violence against women . . . But we have not fulfilled our mission to end violence against women and girls."

"I was worried. I was worried about vaginas. I was worried about what we think about vaginas, and even more worried that we don't think about them."

4 OCTOBER

Henrietta Lacks

(1920–1951)

In January 1951, Henrietta Lacks, a thirty-one-year-old African-American woman with five children, arrived at the Johns Hopkins Hospital in Baltimore, Maryland, with vaginal bleeding. A malignant tumor was discovered on her cervix. Despite radium treatments, the cancer couldn't be stopped; Lacks died on this day in 1951.

Before her death, without her knowledge or consent, Lacks's cancer cells had been harvested by hospital researcher Dr. George Gey. While samples from other cancer patients rapidly died, Lacks's cells were found to have a remarkable property, doubling every twenty to twenty-four hours. Gey created a "cell line," isolating and multiplying one specific cell, calling it "HeLa" after Lacks. After HeLa cells were used to develop the polio vaccine, demand for them grew worldwide. To date, over 10,000 patents involving HeLa cells have been registered. HeLa cells have revolutionized modern medicine, forming the basis of research into not only cancer but leukemia, influenza, hemophilia, herpes, Parkinson's disease and many other diseases.

Lacks's family, who only learned about what happened to their mother and grandmother twenty years after her death, have never received payment from the discoveries. Following a BBC documentary and the publication of Rebecca Skloot's book, *The Immortal Life of Henrietta Lacks*, they signed an agreement in 2013 with the National Institutes of Health to control access to the HeLa genome.

HeLa cells have revolutionized modern medicine.

5 OCTOBER

Tu Youyou

(1930–)

On this day in 2015, Tu Youyou became the first Chinese woman to win a Nobel Prize – in physiology and medicine – for the malaria drug artemisinin, which has saved millions of lives.

After graduating in pharmacology, Youyou worked as a researcher at the Academy of Chinese Traditional Medicine. In 1967, Communist leader Mao Zedong set up a secret research unit to find a cure for malaria which, spread by mosquitoes, was killing Chinese soldiers fighting Americans in Vietnam. Two years later, after over 240,000 compounds had already been tested, Youyou was appointed head of the unit and sent her team looking to ancient books for clues. Finding a reference to sweet wormwood, used to treat malaria around 400 AD, they isolated one active compound, artemisinin, but it didn't work. Re-reading the original text, Youyou altered the drug recipe, heating it

without allowing it to reach boiling point. After the drug showed promise in mice and monkeys, she tested it on herself before clinical trials in humans.

"No doubt, traditional Chinese medicine provides a rich resource. Nevertheless, it requires our thoughtful consideration to explore and improve," YouYou said in her Nobel Prize speech.

6 OCTOBER

Germaine Greer

(1939-)

"I refuse to be a female impersonator," Australian academic Germaine Greer wrote in her bestselling book, *The Female Eunuch*, published in October 1970. Using "eunuch" to refer to women who "castrate" themselves in order to be more feminine, she wrote: "It takes a great deal of courage and independence to decide to design your own image instead of the one that society rewards, but it gets easier as you go along." The first print run sold out on the first day; it hasn't been out of print since.

The Female Eunuch became an important text of feminism's second wave – in the 1960s and 1970s – for its emphasis not on women's equality with men, but on self-determination. Criticizing the suffragettes – "genteel middle-class ladies clamouring for reform" – Greer called instead for revolution. "The old process must be broken, not made new," she says at the end of the book.

Greer has since written over twenty books, and caused controversy with her opinions on topics from transgender people and sexual harassment to rape. Thirty years after *The Female Eunuch*, Greer published a sequel, *The Whole Woman*, critiquing the supposed gains of the women's movement: "On every side, we see women troubled, exhausted, mutilated, lonely, guilty, mocked by the headlined success of the few."

Toni Morrison

(1931–2019)

African-American author Toni Morrison grew up in a house in Ohio filled with books. "My mother joined the Book of the Month Club. That was like resistance." On this day in 1993, she became the first black woman – and only the eighth woman – awarded the Nobel Prize for Literature.

The first in her family to go to college, in Washington DC Morrison became aware of "skin privileges"; she could only use the bathroom in one department store and the buses had "white only" signs. She wrote her debut novel, *The Bluest Eye*, while working as an editor at Random House. "After all these years of reading books, editing books, working in libraries, I thought, 'Wait a minute, there's no book in there about me!' So if I wanted to read it, I would probably have to write it."

The novels, essays and plays that followed – including *Beloved*, inspired by the story of Margaret Garner, an enslaved woman who killed her own daughter – range widely, taking the themes of slavery, violence, history and memory, and weaving in magic, music and myth. Morrison chose to focus on the black community, saying: "[W]ithin the community, there are no major white players. Once I thought: 'What is life like if they weren't there?' Which is the way we lived it, the way I lived it."

8 OCTOBER

Marjorie Pollard

(1899–1982)

Although records show women's cricket matches in Britain dating back to July 1745, when "eleven maids of Bramley and eleven maids of Hambledon, all dressed in white" gathered to play on Gosden Common near Guildford, for almost 200 years women's cricket had no official footing. In October 1926, Marjorie Pollard changed this, joining with several other women – all leading hockey players – to set up the Women's Cricket Association (WCA). The WCA organized their first public match at Beckenham in July 1929: London and District v Rest of England. Pollard played for the latter team.

An all-round athlete, Pollard's other sports included lawn tennis, golf, track athletics and hockey. In 1921, she was selected to play hockey for England and went on to win forty-one caps, becoming one of the team's most prolific goal-scorers. Pollard had begun her adult life as a teacher and journalist;

she used her media experience to promote women's sport, editing the magazines *Hockey Field* for thirty-four years and *Women's Cricket* for nineteen years. She also wrote in the national press and broadcast on BBC radio – "a foremost figure in the fight for the establishment and recognition of women's team games," according to cricketing bible *Wisden*.

Nellie Bly

(1864–1922)

On this day in 1887, reporter Nellie Bly (real name Elizabeth Cochran) published an exposé of conditions in Blackwell's Island Asylum in New York, making her name as an investigative journalist.

At the age of eighteen, Bly had written a response to an article in the *Pittsburgh Dispatch* which dismissed working women as "a monstrosity." She argued her case so well that the paper hired her. Moving to scandal sheet *New York World*, she was not only a celebrity correspondent but also went undercover, most famously at Blackwell's Island Asylum. Once inside, Bly behaved normally and found that many equally sane women were incarcerated. Her sensational story exposed neglect and physical abuse of inmates, leading to mental health care reforms. Bly also published exposés of jails and sweatshops, reported on poverty in Mexico and interviewed prominent women, including suffragist Susan B. Anthony.

In 1889, in a publicity stunt that made her a star, Bly was pitted against fellow reporter Elizabeth Bisland, both attempting the fictional record set by Phileas Fogg in Jules Verne's *Around the World in Eighty Days*. Bly won, establishing a record of seventy-two days.

She left journalism after marriage, but returned in 1920 to report on topics including the suffrage movement.

10 OCTOBER
Emmeline Pankhurst
(1858–1928)

On this day in 1903, Emmeline Pankhurst and friends founded the Women's Social and Political Union (WSPU). One of the best-known names in the history of women's emancipation, Pankhurst was autocratic and uncompromising, alienating many supporters but keeping her cause in the public eye.

Pankhurst joined or founded various parties to campaign for the women's vote before establishing the WSPU – an all-women, single-issue pressure group. Initially non-violent, as Pankhurst and the WSPU became frustrated by a lack of progress, they became increasingly militant. They smashed windows, assaulted police officers and suffered demoralizing cycles of arrest and hunger strike (see Marion Wallace Dunlop). Finally, they turned to small-scale arson and property damage. Many members left, but publicity grew exponentially. Only at the outbreak of the First World War did Pankhurst, an unquestioning patriot, suspend the WSPU campaign. She urged women to work in the war effort, and men to fight.

In 1918, the vote was extended to all men over twenty-one and most women over thirty. This was presented as a "reward" for women who had demonstrated their worth by war work. Pankhurst died in June 1928, weeks before the vote was extended to all women over twenty-one.

314

11 OCTOBER

Anita Hill

(1956–)

On this day in 1991, Anita Hill, a thirty-five-year-old African-American law professor, testified to a US Senate committee that she had been sexually harassed by Judge Clarence Thomas. The stakes were high: Thomas was a nominee for the Supreme Court and, if elected, he would be only the second black judge there. The hearing became a landmark case of victim shaming, which still has echoes today.

Hill attested that Judge Thomas repeatedly asked her out and talked in detail about pornography and his sexual prowess. She was questioned aggressively by an all-white, all-male panel: "Are you a scorned woman? . . . Do you have a martyr complex?" A second woman, Angela Wright, traveled to Washington to corroborate Hill's evidence, but was not heard due to "time constraints."

Judge Thomas denied Hill's accusations, claiming they played into stereotypes of black men, and presented the case as an example of institutional racism against himself – not institutional sexism against Hill. Seen on national television, Hill's dignified testimony and the dismissive reactions of powerful white men later provoked many women to run for office. However, the Senate voted to confirm Thomas as a member of the Supreme Court by a margin of fifty-two to forty-eight; the narrowest in the twentieth century.

Toshiko Kishida

(1863–1901)

On this day in 1883, Japanese feminist Toshiko Kishida made her "Daughters Kept in Boxes" speech, advocating for education and better social structures for girls. Kishida, already a celebrity reformer, was jailed for eight days for giving a political lecture – an activity forbidden to women.

A prodigy in the study of classical literature, she had been the first "commoner" to serve the empress, but she found the court out of touch and misogynist. In 1882, she left and joined a tour of progressive speakers. Part of a growing social reform movement, Kishida addressed large audiences and was often harassed by police.

"Daughters in Boxes" criticized the usual upbringing of Japanese girls. They were physically, emotionally and intellectually boxed in, said Kishida. She argued that women needed better education to perform traditional roles and to keep up with a changing world. Her slogan – "*ryōsai kenbo*" – no longer seems radical: it means "good wife, wise mother."

Even in the West, where the women's suffrage movement was gathering force, Kishida's ideas would have been challenging; in imperial Japan, marriage and education were particularly restrictive for women. Ironically, Kishida withdrew from speaking after her own marriage in 1884 and instead wrote under the pen name Shōen.

"You men shout 'reform' and 'revolution' when-ever you open your mouths. Why is it only in regard to the question of equal rights that you still yearn for the customs of old?"

13 OCTOBER

Agrippina the Younger
(15–59 CE)

On this day in 54 CE, Agrippina the Younger, the most powerful woman in the Roman world, allegedly poisoned her husband, the Emperor Claudius, with mushrooms. Born into the top of the Roman political class at a time of conspiracy and skulduggery, in 39 CE Agrippina had been exiled for her part in an unsuccessful plot to kill her brother, the Emperor Caligula. Ten years later, she married Claudius.

Agrippina allegedly poisoned the emperor to prevent him disinheriting her son, Nero. Nero was Agrippina's child from a previous marriage, and Claudius had named this stepson his heir in preference to his own son, Britannicus. When Nero succeeded to the throne, he not only had his rival killed, but also detached himself from Agrippina's influence and sent her into exile.

Agrippina's reputation is probably one of the worst in history. Roman historians assert that she slept with her son and brother; poisoned not only Claudius but her previous husband; had a woman killed because Claudius complimented her; drove political rivals to suicide and forced one man to kill himself because she wanted his gardens. It's hard to distinguish true from false accusations. Roman historians seeking to discredit a woman invariably accused her of sexual impropriety, poison or undue influence on male relations. The same flamboyant storytelling applies to accounts of Agrippina's death. By some accounts, she escaped three poisonings and an attempted drowning. She finally died by the sword – on Nero's orders.

14 OCTOBER

Anna Atkins

(1799–1871)

Anna Atkins, whose mother died shortly after she was born, grew up very close to her father. He encouraged her education (see <u>Passing it on</u>) and his connections in London's scientific circles enabled her to take part in the male-dominated scientific world of the nineteenth century. She became a skilled illustrator, making more than 200 drawings for her father's 1823 translation of Lamarck's *Genera of Shells*.

Atkins was introduced to photography at a Royal Society meeting in February 1839, at which William Henry Fox Talbot demonstrated "photogenic drawing" – prints of objects on light-sensitive paper. Using the cyanotype process to make plates of her collection of native seaweeds, in October 1843, Atkins published *Photographs of British Algae: Cyanotype Impressions*. It was the first book illustrated with photographic images; previously, botanical images in books were either engravings or woodcuts. Over the next ten years, Atkins printed and bound copies of her book to give to friends and scientific institutions: the text was photographs of her handwriting; the thousands of plates were printed on hand-coated paper; the books were hand-stitched.

Atkins's vivid blue cyanotypes have proved to be much longer-lasting than other early photographs. In recent years, her work has attracted renewed attention; an exhibition of her cyanotypes opened at the New York Public Library in November 2018.

It was the first book illustrated with photographic images.

Coco Chanel

(1883–1971)

In October 1926, Vogue featured a simple black silk dress with a clean, uncomplicated shape by Gabrielle "Coco" Chanel; it became her signature design. The "Little Black Dress" was a symptom of social change that went far beyond fashion. *Vogue* rightly predicted that it would become "a sort of uniform for all women of taste," calling it "Chanel's Ford." Like Henry Ford's early cars, which came in "any color you like, so long as it's black," the dress was at once luxurious, practical and affordable.

Chanel's life began in poverty. Raised in an orphanage, she sang in cafés and possibly worked as an escort. In 1913, a long-term lover financed a shop where Chanel began to sell her clothes. She introduced her fragrance, Chanel No. 5, in 1921; by the end of the decade, together with her clothing empire, it had made her fortune.

Chanel understood that women's needs were changing and that fashion design must change too. Emancipated women had more opportunities to leave the home; they had new physical freedoms in sport, dancing, driving or simply walking unchaperoned. These women wanted modest, stylish and versatile clothing, not the unforgiving and hard-to-maintain corsetry of their mothers. "Luxury must be comfortable – otherwise, it is not luxury."

Wu Zetian

(624–705 CE)

On this day in 690, Empress Wu Zetian was crowned as the only female emperor in Chinese history.

Brought to court as a teenage concubine, Wu married the Emperor Gaozong and effectively ruled in his name. His first wife and mistress supposedly had their hands and feet cut off on her orders before being drowned in a vat of wine. After her husband's death, she installed first one son then another on the throne, but later removed both and took power herself. One minister denounced her: "It is suitable that you lead the quiet life of a widow . . . otherwise I fear further disasters will befall us." He was exiled.

Wu reset the dynastic clock, declaring the beginning of her Zhou dynasty, and set up a network of spies and secret police. She also reformed education, taxation and the army, raised agricultural production to a record level and extended the empire by military force, conquering Korea in 668. By removing layers of officialdom, she made access to government easier. These changes were all based on a single principle: that government jobs should go to competent, well-trained men, rather than those with the right bloodline. In her seventies, say sources of the time, Wu took two young lovers and became addicted to aphrodisiacs. In 704, she was overthrown and died a year later.

Mekatilili Wa Menza

(c.1840–c.1924)

On this day in 1913, anti-colonial activist Mnyazi or Mekatilili Wa Menza was arrested in eastern Kenya and exiled to a distant province for leading the Giriama tribe's uprising against British rule. British colonizers had recently pressed Giriama men into work on plantations or to fight in inter-colonial skirmishes; they had requisitioned land for new farmsteads and railways to "improve" the subsistence economy and culture of the indigenous people. Shrines had been destroyed and unpopular taxes and laws imposed. In August 1913, when a British representative defended these policies at a meeting, Wa Menza replied in strong terms and allegedly struck him.

In Giriama culture, women traditionally had little public influence, but Wa Menza, a widow probably in her sixties, became a figurehead for resistance. She gave speeches at gatherings with her ally, spiritual leader Wanje wa Mwadorikola. They encouraged followers to swear a rebel oath and Wa Menza performed the *kifudu* funeral dance, which became an anthem for resistance. After her exile to a distant province, Wa Menza walked 600 miles back to continue her campaign. The British retaliated by destroying Kaya Fungo, the spiritual capital of the Giriama. Wa Menza was again exiled; again she escaped, becoming leader of a new Giriama women's council. She died in the 1920s, forty years before Kenya finally became independent.

Wa Menza, a widow probably in her sixties, became a figurehead for resistance.

The Famous Five

Nellie McClung (1873-1951); Louise McKinney (1868-1931); Henrietta Muir Edwards (1849-1931); Emily Murphy (1868-1933); Irene Parlby (1868-1965)

On this day in 1929, women were declared "persons" under Canadian law due to the persistence of "The Famous Five" – feminists and campaigners Nellie McClung, Louise McKinney, Henrietta Muir Edwards, Emily Murphy and Irene Parlby.

By 1918, all Canadian women had the right to vote but they were still excluded from many public offices, including the Senate. In 1927, the five challenged this by asking the Supreme Court of Canada: "Does the word 'persons' in Section 24 of the British North America Act, 1867 [which stated that only 'qualified persons' could be appointed to the Canadian Senate] include female persons?"

In early 1928, the Supreme Court gave its answer: No. The women persuaded the Canadian government to appeal to the Judicial Committee of the Privy Council in London – at that time Canada's highest court. On 18 October 1929, the Committee Chair, Maurice Hankey, ruled that: "The exclusion of women from all public offices is a relic of days more barbarous than ours. And to those who ask whether the word 'person' should include females, the obvious answer is: why should it not?" The Famous Five had won their battle.

> "Get the thing done and let them howl."
> – Nellie McClung

Irena Sendler

(1910–2008)

After the Nazis invaded Poland in 1939, Jews were forced into ghettos. The Warsaw Ghetto was sealed in November 1940. When social worker Irena Sendler – who had an access permit to check for typhus – realized the horror of the Jews' situation, she devised a scheme to rescue children, saying to her colleagues: "Listen. We have to declare war on Hitler."

Her network of helpers transported some children in coffins, suitcases and sacks; others escaped through underground sewers. Sendler and her co-workers hid lists that recorded the children's locations and their original (Jewish) and new (Christian) names with the aim of reuniting them with their families after the war. In October 1943, Sendler's house was raided by the Gestapo and she was arrested. Despite being tortured, she refused to betray her colleagues. She was sentenced to death but an underground activist bargained for her release before her execution.

On this day in 1965, Sendler was recognized by Yad Vashem, the World Holocaust Remembrance Center in Jerusalem, as "Righteous Among the Nations" for saving the lives of 2,500 children. In her old age, Sendler was cared for in a Warsaw nursing home by Elzbieta Ficowska, who had been smuggled out of the Warsaw Ghetto by Sendler at six months old in a carpenter's workbox.

Maria Theresa of Austria

(1717–1780)

On this day in 1740, twenty-three-year-old Maria Theresa Habsburg began her forty-year reign over the Austro-Hungarian Empire. Her realm, which encompassed present-day Germany, Austria, Belgium, Hungary and Croatia, was immediately invaded by neighboring powers, led by Frederick of Prussia. Their hopes – that a new ruler (and a woman) would be docile – were confounded.

Maria Theresa waged war with Frederick for years, levying military support from within the empire and making a surprise alliance with the traditional enemy, France. The struggle to rule central Europe would continue for decades.

Like her near-contemporary Catherine the Great, Maria Theresa recognized that European society was changing. Her reforms reduced the aristocracy's power without actually empowering the peasant class. She appointed capable politicians, centralized the state, ordered educational, legal and tax reforms, overhauled the army and allowed modest protections for the peasantry. The empress was no liberal, however. Maria Theresa was a zealous Catholic and vicious anti-Semite who taxed Jews heavily and expelled them from Prague in 1744. She established a "chastity court" to police morals.

Maria Theresa inherited an unsettled and bankrupt state: she left her empire largely intact, with its wealth enhanced. During her long and difficult reign, she also gave birth to sixteen children. She died in 1780, before the upheavals which would unseat her daughter, Marie Antoinette of France.

Their hopes – that a new ruler (and a woman) would be docile – were confounded.

21 OCTOBER

Mariya Oktyabrskaya

(1905–1944)

After her marriage to a Soviet army officer, Mariya Oktyabrskaya embraced military life. She joined the Council of Military Wives, trained as a military nurse and learned to use various weapons: "An officer's wife is not only a proud woman, but also a responsible title." She didn't know this responsibility would take her into battle.

In 1943, Oktyabrskaya discovered that her husband had been killed during Hitler's attack on the Soviet Union. Determined to avenge his death, Oktyabrskaya sold her possessions to buy a tank for the army – on condition that she would drive it. After a five-month course, she was assigned to the 26th Guards Tank Brigade and given a T34 tank; she painted Боевая подруга ("fighting girlfriend") on its turret. On this day in 1943, Oktyabrskaya fought her first battle, displaying great technical skill and bravery. Her tank was the first to break through enemy positions, destroying artillery and machine gun nests. When it was hit, she jumped out and repaired it. She wrote to her sister: "I've had my baptism by fire. I beat the bastards."

In January 1944, Oktyabrskaya was hit by shrapnel while fixing her tank. She never regained consciousness and died two months later. In August of that year she was made a Hero of the Soviet Union, the highest honour for bravery during combat.

"I've had my baptism by fire. I beat the bastards."

22 OCTOBER

Ellen Johnson Sirleaf (1938–); Leymah Gbowee (1972–); Tawakkol Karman (1979–)

In October 2011, Liberian President Ellen Johnson Sirleaf, Liberian activist Leymah Gbowee and Yemeni journalist Tawakkol Karman were jointly awarded the Nobel Peace Prize for their non-violent struggle for women's safety and women's rights.

Johnson Sirleaf had accepted a position in the newly formed Liberian government in 1980 but fled to the US after criticizing the new leaders, who had executed most of the previous cabinet. In 1997, she resigned as director of the UN Development Programme's Africa Bureau and returned to Liberia, where she ran for president, coming second. In 2005, she stood again, for the Unity Party, and won, becoming Africa's first elected female head of state. During her presidency, she introduced reforms, including free compulsory education. In 2009, she apologized for having supported Charles Taylor, now a convicted war criminal.

Leymah Gbowee – who organized Women of Liberia Mass Action for Peace in 2002 – played a vital role in Johnson Sirleaf's victory, mobilizing women to vote. She is co-chair of the Nobel Women's Initiative and the International Campaign to Stop Rape & Gender Violence in Conflict.

Yemeni journalist Tawakkol Karman is the first Arab woman to win the Nobel Peace Prize. The founder of Women Journalists Without Chains, she was imprisoned and persecuted for protesting against Yemen's dictatorship and demanding democracy and freedom of speech. During the Arab Spring in 2011, she promoted reconciliation between Shia and Sunni Muslims and between Islam and other religions.

23 OCTOBER

Jeannette Piccard

(1895–1981)

"I was nervous right after the take-off," Chicago-born chemist Jeannette Piccard told a reporter on this day in 1934. She had just become the first woman to reach the stratosphere, in the Century of Progress balloon, accompanied by her husband and their pet tortoise.

"The wind bumped the gondola around . . . but before long we began to ascend rapidly and when we got into the upper air it was very calm." Piccard, who had a master's degree in organic chemistry and was the first American licensed female balloon pilot, took the balloon up to an altitude of 57,979 feet over Lake Erie, on the border of the USA and Canada. In order to study cosmic radiation, the Piccards took with them 168 Geiger counters and other scientific instruments. They landed safely seven hours later in Ohio.

Piccard later received a doctorate in education and, after her husband's death in 1963, worked as a consultant at NASA, giving talks about the space program. Some call her the first woman in space, if "space" is taken to begin at a height of 45,000 to 50,000 feet. In 1963, Russian astronaut Valentina Tereshkova journeyed further to become the first woman to orbit the Earth.

24 OCTOBER

Annie Edson Taylor

(1838–1921)

"Nobody ought ever to do that again," said Annie Edson Taylor on this day in 1901, when she became the first person to survive going over Niagara Falls in a barrel. (Although she claimed to be in her forties, it was actually her sixty-third birthday.)

Taylor wrote in her 1902 memoir, *Over the Falls*, that she'd come up with the idea in order to make money; her income as a charm school instructor had dried up and she wanted to help friends in financial difficulties. She designed the barrel, padded with a mattress, and paid a local beer keg company to construct it before successfully testing it on her cat. Then, on 24 October, the barrel – which had air pumped into it before Taylor's friends sealed her inside – was towed to the middle of the Niagara River and released. Twenty minutes later, after going over the edge of the Falls, Taylor reached the other shore.

While Taylor did make some money from promotional events, talks and sales of memorabilia, she ran into trouble when her second manager stole the barrel and recruited a much younger woman to go on tour and impersonate her. Taylor spent much of her funds hiring private detectives to get the barrel back, but never succeeded. She died in poverty; her grave is in Niagara Falls Cemetery.

25 OCTOBER

Clara Peeters
(1594–after 1657)

On this day in 2016, Madrid's Prado museum, which opened in 1819, held its first solo exhibition by a woman: Clara Peeters. A renowned Flemish painter of the early seventeenth century, Peeters was one of the first to produce meticulous still-life paintings known as "breakfast" or "banquet" pieces. Almost photo-realistic in their detail and showing heaped cheeses, pies or fish in glass or gilt serving vessels, these were conversation pieces in the dining halls of wealthy patrons.

Peeters was trained as a professional artist, but no work is known by her after 1621; she probably stopped paid work when she married. During her short career, her theme and techniques influenced other artists in the "circle of Peeters."

In several compositions, Peeters places a distinctive "bride knife" with two figures on the handle. The blade occasionally carries a hallmark from Antwerp – probably her home town and a famed center of still-life painting. In some pictures, the knife handle bears Peeters's signature. In others, if you look closely, you will see that coffee pots or other shiny surfaces show the small, barely noticeable reflection of Clara Peeters's face.

During her short career, her theme and techniques influenced other artists in the "circle of Peeters."

26 OCTOBER

Alexandra Kollontai

(1872–1952)

On this day in 1917, Marxist revolutionary Alexandra Kollontai became People's Commissar for Social Welfare, the first woman to hold a Russian cabinet position.

Raised in Russia and Finland, Kollontai's activism had begun in 1896 when she helped organize a strike of female St. Petersburg textile factory workers. In 1908, she was exiled after calling for the Finnish people to rise up against the Russian Tsar and, in 1914, was arrested and imprisoned for agitating against the war in Germany and Austria. Russian women won the vote in March 1917; in October of that year Kollontai returned to Russia to take part in the revolution.

After Lenin appointed her to his cabinet, Kollontai focused on equal rights for women. She was instrumental in the legalization of abortion, divorce and maternity benefits. She founded the *Zhenotdel* or "women's department" of the Communist Party to fight illiteracy and inform women about new marriage, education and work laws, despite hostility from male Bolshevik leaders, who insisted it be located in a corner of the building so the women's "jabbering" didn't disturb them. Kollontai was sidelined in 1921 after supporting a left-wing Communist Party faction and gave up fighting for women's rights, supporting the Stalinist regime and its purges, deportations and executions.

Eleanor/Elinor James

(1644/5–1719)

On this day in 1662, seventeen-year-old Eleanor Banckes married Thomas James, journeyman printer, at St Olave's Church in London. It was an important date, not only in her personal but also in her professional life: the marriage enabled her to become a printer and an activist (see Wives, or great women). Thomas became a freeman of the Stationers' Company in that year and later set himself up as a master, with his own printing house. When he died in 1710, Eleanor took over the business, but her career had begun many years before: in around 1715 she wrote, "I have been in the element of Printing above forty years."

And she wasn't just printing other people's words. Between 1681 and 1716, Eleanor wrote, printed and distributed over ninety broadsides and pamphlets on politics, religion and business – with titles such as *Mrs. James's Advice* – addressed to church and city leaders and various monarchs.

While Thomas was competent and well-read, bookseller John Dunton said he was "better known for being husband to that She-State Politician Mrs. Elianor [sic] James."

In 1689, Eleanor was arrested and sent to Newgate Prison for printing a broadsheet that accused William III of ruling illegitimately. She remained unrepentant and, on her release, continued to print and share her opinions.

Eleanor wrote, printed and distributed over ninety broadsides and pamphlets on politics, religion and business.

28 OCTOBER

Margaret E. Knight

(1838–1914)

Margaret E. Knight was twelve years old when she came up with her first invention. Working in a cotton mill in Manchester, New Hampshire, to help her widowed mother, she noticed how the steel-tipped shuttles would fly off the looms at dangerously high speeds, so she created something to restrain them. Not understanding the patent system, she made no money from her life-saving device, despite its widespread adoption.

In 1867, Knight started work at the Columbia Paper Bag Company and, once again, spotted problems that required a solution. She developed a machine for folding and glueing bags with a flat base, making them easier to pack. This time she was savvier about the patent process. But when she tried to register her patent, Charles Annan, who worked in the company's machine shop, claimed the idea was his. When he declared in court in 1871 that no woman could have designed such a complex machine, Knight produced her hand-drawn blueprints and won the case. On this day in 1879, Knight was granted a patent for her updated design for the machine that makes the flat-bottomed paper bags now ubiquitous in supermarkets across the US. Knight would patent over twenty other inventions, including a combustion engine and a window frame with a sash.

Margaret E. Knight was twelve years old when she came up with her first invention.

332

29 OCTOBER

Stephanie "Steve" Shirley
(1933–)

At the age of five, Stephanie Shirley, born Vera Buchtal, arrived in the UK with her sister as part of the *Kindertransport*, which rescued mostly Jewish children from the Nazis. Growing up with foster parents, Shirley discovered a talent for mathematics and computing.

In 1962, after leaving a job where her suggestions were ignored "but when a man made the same point five minutes later it would be, 'Oh yes, we must do that,'" she set up Freelance Programmers, a software company, from home. Employing almost exclusively women, the company was radical for being "family friendly," with flexible hours and the possibility of home-working. Shirley began signing letters "Steve" when she realized her name was a problem in the male-dominated IT industry; from this moment the business took off. Her team programmed Concorde's black box flight recorder; in 1993, Shirley took the company public,

making her and seventy of her staff millionaires.

While running her business, Shirley was also caring for her autistic son. Since his death she has donated around £135 million to autism research, becoming the UK's first Ambassador for Philanthropy.

On this day in 2012, Shirley published her memoir, *Let It Go*. In a 2015 TED talk, she said: "I decided to make mine a life that was worth saving. And then I just got on with it."

333

Frances Glessner Lee

(1878–1962)

Frances Glessner Lee's childhood love for the stories of Sherlock Holmes and Dr. Watson would lead, fifty years later, to her revolutionizing forensic science. Forbidden to study medicine by her parents, after their deaths, Glessner Lee donated $250,000 to Harvard to establish a Department of Legal Medicine and set up the department's library with her collection of crime- and criminal-justice-related manuscripts and photos.

In October 1943, Glessner Lee was appointed New Hampshire State Police's first female captain and educational director. It was while developing a forensic evidence training course that she came up with her greatest innovation: dollhouse-sized dioramas of crime scenes she called the "Nutshell Studies of Unexplained Death." Based on true crimes, the scenes – all dwellings of poor or marginalized people – were imagined by Lee and intricately detailed, with working doors, windows and lights, enabling the "Nutshells" to be used to train police in gathering forensic evidence. For each scene – which bore titles like "Dark Bathroom" and "Unpapered Bedroom" – Glessner Lee carved clothes pegs out of matchsticks, rolled tiny cigarettes and knitted jumpers with pins. The meticulous care given to each model (her carpenter said it took as long as building a real house) demonstrates her empathy for people with lives so different from her own.

Now called "the mother of modern CSI," Glessner Lee insisted that each death requires equal attention. "Convict the guilty, clear the innocent and find the truth in a nutshell."

"Convict the guilty, clear the innocent and find the truth in a nutshell."

31 OCTOBER

Mary Swanzy

(1882–1978)

In October 2018, the first retrospective of an "unsung hero" of Irish art, Mary Swanzy, opened at the Irish Museum of Modern Art in Dublin, forty years after her death.

After her first solo exhibition in 1905, aged twenty-three, Swanzy had moved to Paris to study art at exactly the time the twentieth century's major modern art movements began to flourish. Moving in the same circles as Gertrude Stein – the American writer and champion of artists including Pablo Picasso – Swanzy took inspiration from the first exhibitions of the Cubists, the Futurists and Surrealists. After volunteering as an aid worker in Czechoslovakia during the First World War, in 1920 she journeyed further, to Hawaii and Samoa.

The enormous and varied body of work she produced throughout her seventy-year career was unparalleled in Irish art; her best-known paintings are in Cubist and Futurist styles.

Swanzy exhibited regularly alongside artists who are now familiar names, including Marc Chagall, Picasso and Georges Braque – so why was she "unsung?" Her apparent shyness and distrust of galleries may have played a part. But the fact that she was a woman cannot be overlooked.

"If I had been born Henry instead of Mary my life would have been very different."

NOVEMBER

"[A]n error that ascribes to a man what was actually the work of a woman has more lives than a cat."
– Hertha Ayrton

Class acts

There are many kinds of prejudice; some people are affected by more than one. All of the women here did something memorable in a culture where men had more opportunity, but many of them also contended with prejudice against their race, religion or sexuality. One of the major factors affecting a woman's potential, beyond her sex, has been class – which often cannot be easily separated from issues of race.

Money and social prestige give a woman access to education, coaching or work. Victorian gentlewomen wanting adventure and a "respectable" occupation could become missionaries, campaigners, antiquarians; middle-class women like Gertrude Bell built a career out of travel and networking. Even in the distant past, women like Egeria or Hildegard of Bingen could study or make long journeys, if it were seen as part of a religious calling. At a certain social level, even "forbidden" sexualities could be openly acknowledged. Women like Anne Lister or

Radclyffe Hall could live relatively openly as lesbians, despite social disapprobation. But working-class women were always subject to a wider inequality. Not only did they do the domestic work for which wealthier women had servants, but they were (and are) disproportionately affected by debt, taxation and poor health.

In sport or music, sheer talent can help such women to a place in the record – Poly Styrene, Cesaria Evora, Sister Rosetta Tharpe and Alice Coachman are proof of this. These are all women of color: race and class are intimately linked in the West, where institutional racism often keeps talented people in an underclass. The haircare empire of Madam C.J. Walker, the first black millionaire, began when – orphaned, widowed and a single parent in segregated America – her own hair fell out through stress. Hattie McDaniel, Oscar-winning actor, started as a child busker to supplement her mother's wages as a maid. These women succeeded even within a white mainstream, but most women of color could not.

Other working women came to fame by trying to improve industrial conditions. Hannah Shapiro led sixteen women out of a sweatshop and began a general strike; Big Lil Bilocca, worried for her husband's wellbeing, started a campaign that quickly improved safety for trawler fishermen. But too many women of genius and capability were lost to the world because their daily tasks took up all their time and energy. Childcare, housework and shopping are still largely the work of women. More than this, however, working-class women have found it impossible to study, work or create without money and social approval. Fortune favors the brave – but the well-off still have a head start, and they can afford childcare.

1 NOVEMBER

Hertha Ayrton

(1854–1923)

After studying English and mathematics at Cambridge University, Hertha Ayrton met her husband, William, an electrical engineer, when taking his evening class on electricity. Working together, one of the problems they tackled was the hissing of the widely used electric arc lamps. Hertha discovered a method to reduce the noise and also make the lamps safer; in 1899, she presented her discovery to the Institution of Electrical Engineers (IEE), the first woman to do so. She was also the first woman to present to the Royal Society, though she was denied membership because she was married. Nevertheless, on this day in 1906, Ayrton became the first woman awarded the Royal Society's Hughes Medal for Physics, for her work on electric arcs and ripples in sand and water.

Ayrton registered twenty-six patents – including a fan for clearing gas from trenches used by the British Army during the First World War, which she later modified for mines and sewers. She was also a women's rights activist; Emmeline Pankhurst and other suffragettes often stayed with Ayrton while recovering from hunger strikes. Another guest was physicist Marie Curie, the first woman to win a Nobel Prize. When Curie's discovery of radium was misattributed to her husband, Ayrton wrote:

"[A]n error that ascribes to a man what was actually the work of a woman has more lives than a cat."

2 NOVEMBER

Emma Lazarus

(1849–1887)

Poet Emma Lazarus – whose ancestors were among the first Jews to settle in America – was helping Jewish immigrants at New York's Wards Island when she was commissioned to write a poem to raise funds for a "Liberty Enlightening the World" statue. The sonnet, "The New Colossus," that she wrote on this day in 1883, speaks in the voice of Liberty herself, and contains the now-famous lines: "Give me your tired, your poor/ Your huddled masses." Seventeen years after her death, Lazarus's friend Georgina Schuyler rediscovered the poem and spent two years campaigning for her lines to be engraved on a plaque on the pedestal of the Statue of Liberty, which stands in New York Harbor.

Lazarus's first collection, *Poems and Translations Written Between the Ages of Fourteen to Sixteen*, was published in 1866; she also translated medieval Hebrew poetry, wrote a play about the persecution of Jews and spoke out about European anti-Semitism, which had brought a wave of Jewish immigration to America. Her biographer, Esther Schor, wrote: "She was a woman so far ahead of her time that we are still scrambling to catch up with her – a feminist, Zionist and internationally famous Jewish American writer before these categories even existed."

3 NOVEMBER

Caresse Crosby

(1891–1970)

Born into a wealthy American family, Mary "Polly" Phelps Jacob, was dressing for a debutante ball when she decided her whalebone corset ruined the line of her dress. She made herself an undergarment by sewing two silk handkerchiefs together with ribbon; when she wore it to the party, her friends wanted one too. On this day in 1914, Jacobs was granted a patent for the first modern bra, that "may be worn even by persons engaged in violent exercise like tennis," and set up the Fashion Form Brassiere Company. Her bras were not as supportive as today's models, but their lack of wires was an advantage in the First World War, when the War Industries Board commandeered metal from corset ribbing to construct battleships.

Selling her patent to the Warner Brothers Corset Company for $1,500 (it apparently earned them $15 million) in 1922, and now calling herself "Caresse," she moved to Paris with her second husband, Harry Crosby, and her whippet, Clytoris. The Crosbys began publishing – not only their own poems, but also work by Anaïs Nin, Dorothy Parker and Ezra Pound.

After her husband's suicide pact with his mistress, Crosby returned to America in the mid-1930s. Her activities became more political and, in the 1950s, she founded two organizations, Women Against War and Citizens of the World.

She moved to Paris with her second husband, Harry Crosby, and her whippet, Clytoris.

Jane Goodall

(1934–)

Jane Goodall's ambitions were shaped by the Dr. Doolittle and Tarzan books she loved as a child and encouraged by her mother, who "never laughed at my dream of Africa, even though everyone else did because we didn't have any money, because Africa was the 'dark continent' and because I was a girl."

Without a research background, Goodall secured a job observing chimpanzees in Tanganyika (now Tanzania); her mother went with her, in line with British colonial rules. Goodall lived close to the chimps for a long time to win their trust. In November 1960, she became the first person to record chimps making tools: she saw a male bend a twig, strip its leaves, and poke it into a termite nest to dig out food. Her discovery shattered accepted wisdom that only humans made tools. Goodall observed that the chimps were like humans in many ways: they showed physical affection and formed mother-child bonds; they were manipulative, capable of territorial violence and even genocide. Humans' uniqueness, she concluded, lies in our ability to use language and to imagine things that aren't there.

Throughout her career, Goodall has campaigned for conservation, founding the Jane Goodall Institute to "advance the power of individuals to improve the environment for all living things."

5 NOVEMBER

Thea Rasche

(1899–1971)

The first Women's Air Derby race, held in California in 1929, was mockingly called the "Powder Puff Derby"; in response, in early November 1929, American aviator <u>Amelia Earhart</u> and ninety-eight other female pilots set up the Ninety-Nines, a mutual support group for women in aviation. Thea Rasche, the first female German pilot with an aerobatics license, was the Ninety-Nines' sole non-American founder member.

In 1926, Rasche had been the only woman among thirty-three aviators at the Berlin Air Show and the first woman to win first prize for skill flying in the Industrial Race. She traveled to the US in July 1927 to learn more about long-distance flying – and, wrote the *New York Times*, "to show the United States that daring stunts in the air are not the province of men alone."

Nicknamed "the Flying Fräulein," she acquired a reputation for stunts, including flying under the Brooklyn Bridge. She was also (apparently) the first woman to join the "ancient and secret order" of the Quiet Birdmen, set up by First World War pilots.

Returning to Germany, Rasche worked as a journalist. Although she joined the Nazi Party, and later the National Socialist Flying Corps, after the war a "denazification' tribunal ruled she hadn't been a Nazi and that, in fact, her books had been banned because they "glorified the Anglo-American sporting spirit."

Marija Gimbutas

(1921–1994)

In 1974, archaeologist Marija Gimbutas published *The Goddesses and Gods of Old Europe*. The book reimagined the earliest European societies as communities in which women had important spiritual roles, sparking arguments which continue to this day.

During the Second World War, Gimbutas had escaped Lithuania, fleeing German and Soviet invaders, carrying nothing but her one-year-old daughter and a thesis on prehistoric burial rites. By the 1970s, she was a well-respected archaeologist. In a time when all social norms and authorities were being challenged, her unorthodox theories drew on linguistics and myth, artifacts like the Venus of Willendorf and the work of authorities including Jacquetta Hawkes.

Gimbutas suggested that early people in south-eastern Europe were peaceful goddess-worshippers whose religious leaders were women, and that new peoples arriving from the east in the fifth millennium BCE brought a violent society dominated by men. This new culture, Gimbutas believed, led ultimately to industrialization, environmental collapse and the combative politics we know today.

Some scholars felt that Gimbutas's "mother goddess" society was based in great part on wishful thinking with little evidence. It appealed to those whom a 1989 *LA Times* article called "feminists with a spiritual orientation" and it is not widely believed now. Nonetheless, Gimbutas's creative and controversial view of antiquity reminds us that the past is always being reinvented.

The Daring Ladies: Abigail Aldrich Rockefeller (1874–1948); Lillie P. Bliss (1864–1931); Mary Quinn Sullivan (1877–1939)

In May 1929, Abby Rockefeller invited friends and fellow modern art collectors Lillie P. Bliss and Mary Quinn Sullivan to lunch to discuss doing something about the stifling conservatism of the New York art establishment. The Metropolitan Museum of Art wouldn't touch anything created after the mid-nineteenth century; according to *TIME*, contemporary artists viewed it as merely "a trysting place for shop girls and their beaux."

The women decided to establish a space in New York for showing modern art but had no hope of financial support from Rockefeller's wealthy husband, John D. Rockefeller, Jr., who disliked it with a passion. So the "Daring Ladies" sought sponsorship from corporations, dignitaries and the public and rented rooms on Fifth Avenue. On this day in 1929, New York's Museum of Modern Art (MoMA) opened to the public. Its first exhibition, "Cézanne,

Gauguin, Seurat, Van Gogh," ran until 7 December, attracting 47,293 visitors.

The museum moved three times in its first ten years but this didn't prevent it from hosting many major exhibitions. In the 1930s, MoMA was one of the few places to exhibit a wide array of European avant-garde art, a cultural bulwark against the fascist denunciation of so-called "degenerate art." In 1939, MoMA moved to its current location on 53rd Street, on land donated by John D. Rockefeller, Jr.

The women decided to establish a space in New York for showing modern art.

Kate Marsden

(1859–1931)

In November 1890, British nurse Kate Marsden made a trip to Russia to receive an award for her medical work during the Russo-Turkish war. During her audience with the Russian empress, Marsden persuaded her to finance a daring, lengthy – and ultimately fruitless – 11,000 mile expedition.

Having seen the effects of leprosy during the war, Marsden was obsessed with possible treatments for the disease. Claims were made for a herb grown in Siberia, which might be a cure. Marsden set off on her epic journey in February 1891, traveling by train, horseback, boat and sledge, sometimes wrapped in so many furs and blankets that three men had to lift her onto her sledge. She finally returned to Moscow in December, without the legendary herb.

Marsden published a book about the expedition, *On Sledge and Horseback to the Outcast Siberian Lepers*, but her reputation thereafter was dogged by financial and personal scandal when she was accused (and cleared) of fraud in her charity work. More shocking for the Victorian public, Marsden confirmed she had had lesbian relationships.

In 1895, Marsden founded the St. Francis Leprosy Guild, followed by a leper hospital in Sosnovka, Siberia. As the scandals faded from memory, in 1916 Marsden was granted honorary life fellowship of the Royal Geographical Society. She inspired the creation of Bexhill Museum in East Sussex, and is fondly remembered in Siberia, where a statue of her was dedicated in 2014.

Lucille Ball

(1911–1989)

In 1948, American actress Lucille Ball was asked to develop her radio show, *My Favorite Husband*, for television. She agreed on condition that she star with her real-life husband, Cuban bandleader Desi Arnaz. The TV executives were reluctant to have "mixed-race" co-stars, but eventually agreed and the hit comedy *I Love Lucy* was born.

The character of Lucy – a housewife resisting domesticity and dependence – was radical but Ball got away with it because Lucy's wit and clowning made her seem harmless. Ball also influenced how the show was made: *I Love Lucy* was recorded in front of a live studio audience with three cameras, instead of being broadcast live with one – a pioneering set-up which would become the standard for television sitcoms.

In 1960, Ball and Arnaz divorced, and Ball bought out his holdings in their Hollywood production company, Desilu. On this day in 1962, Ball became the company's president, the first female CEO of a major television and movie studio. Desilu produced classic 1960s shows like *The Untouchables*, *Mission: Impossible* and *Star Trek*; it was Ball herself who fought for *Star Trek* after other executives dismissed the pilot as "too cerebral." She financed a second pilot, which was accepted, beginning a franchise that has lasted more than fifty years.

10 NOVEMBER

"Ninon" (Anne) de l'Enclos
(1620–1705)

On this day in 1620, Anne de l'Enclos, nicknamed "Ninon," was born in Paris. Determined to remain independent, in her late teens she slept with a count to "ruin" herself for marriage. Her mother dispatched her to a convent, but she left after her mother's death a year later and became a courtesan and writer with many rich lovers. She was sent to a convent again – this time on the orders of Anne of Austria, Queen of France, because of her writing and lifestyle. Christina, the former queen of Sweden, visited her and, charmed by l'Enclos, secured her release.

Undeterred by the threat of confinement, l'Enclos stuck by her own version of morality. In 1659, she claimed in her book *La coquette vengée* ("The Flirt Avenged") that it was possible to lead a good life without religion. She saw romantic, physical love as the greatest pleasure, insisting that women are just as entitled to it as men, and became famous for controversial witticisms, such as: "Much more genius is needed to make love than to command armies." L'Enclos hosted literary salons and became a patron of writers such as Molière. When she died, she left money for her notary's nine-year-old son to buy books. That boy became the philosopher Voltaire.

11 NOVEMBER

Moina Michael (1869–1944) and Anna Guérin (1878–1961)

On Remembrance Day, we honor two women, both known as "The Poppy Lady."

Moina Belle Michael was an American professor who did war work at the Young Men's Christian Association (YMCA). On 9 November 1918, just after the end of the First World War, she was moved by Canadian John McCrae's war poem, "In Flanders Fields" – "We shall not sleep, though poppies grow / In Flanders fields" – and pledged to wear a red poppy for remembrance. Following her lead, the YMCA created a logo of a red poppy entwined with a torch for its Flanders Fields memorial campaign. Back at her university, Michael sold silk poppies to raise funds for the disabled servicemen she taught.

Anna Guérin, a member of the French Young Women's Christian Association, was at the American Legion National Convention in 1920 when it adopted Michael's poppy as a symbol of remembrance. Back home, she began selling poppies to raise funds for French war victims, in particular orphans. Traveling the world to spread the message, she met with Field Marshal Douglas Haig, president of the British Legion; in 1921, the first British Legion Poppy Day Appeal was held, with hundreds of thousands of poppies sold. A year later, the Poppy Factory opened in London, followed in 1926 by Lady Haig's Poppy Factory in Edinburgh. Staffed by veterans, both still produce around 50 million poppies a year.

12 NOVEMBER
Rosika Schwimmer
(1877–1948)

In November 1918, Rosika Schwimmer, already a world-famous advocate for peace and women's causes, was appointed Hungary's ambassador to Switzerland.

In 1897, Schwimmer had founded a National Association of Women Office Workers – the first of many organizations she set up, which became key in winning suffrage for Hungarian women in 1920. A determined pacifist, Schwimmer campaigned for an end to the First World War as soon as it began. In 1915, she co-founded the Woman's Peace Party, lobbied US President Woodrow Wilson to mediate in Europe and was a key instigator of pacifist industrialist Henry Ford's Peace Ship mission. The mission failed, having been ridiculed as the "Ship of Fools."

After the war, Schwimmer was appointed to the national council of a newly independent Hungary, and then to the Swiss Embassy, but a change of government drove her out of Europe. She settled in Chicago in 1921, conspicuous in inter-war America as a radical European Jewish woman. Publicly attacked, she was denied citizenship for refusing to swear to bear arms in the defense of America; she remained stateless. Schwimmer received the World Peace Prize in 1937. In 1948, she was nominated for the Nobel Peace Prize; she died that year.

13 NOVEMBER

Helena Normanton

(1882–1957)

In her book, *Everyday Law for Women*, Helena Normanton describes how, at twelve years old, she went with her widowed mother to a solicitor's office. When her mother became confused, the solicitor said, "I am sure your little girl quite understands what I have told you," calling her "quite a little lawyer!" After her application to become a barrister was rejected in 1918, Normanton appealed to the British House of Lords. Before her case could be heard, the Sex Disqualification (Removal) Bill was passed; she applied again and became the first female law student. In November 1922, she became England's first practicing female barrister. (Ivy Williams was called to the Bar six months earlier but never practiced.)

Normanton campaigned for women's rights, writing pamphlets about equal pay; in an essay, "Magna Carta and Women," published on its 700th anniversary, she claimed that denying women the vote contravened the historic legal document. She was the first woman to obtain a divorce for a client, to lead the prosecution in a murder trial and to conduct a case in the US for a woman's right to keep her name. Normanton herself caused controversy by keeping hers after marrying in 1921; she later became the first married British woman to hold a passport under her maiden name.

Ruby Bridges

(1954–)

On this day in 1960, six-year-old Ruby Bridges became the first African-American child to integrate into a white Southern school. Although the US Supreme Court case *Brown v Board of Education* had ruled six years earlier that separate schools were unconstitutional, state governments had been slow to enforce the ruling.

One of just six children who passed the test – said to have been made deliberately hard – to be able to attend, Bridges would be the only African-American student at the William Frantz School in New Orleans. Due to concerns about civil unrest, on her first day she was accompanied by her mother and four federal US Marshals. Met by yelling crowds, Bridges spent that day in the principal's office until one teacher, Barbara Henry, agreed to take her. Bridges was taught alone for a year. Many parents removed their children from the school in protest at her presence.

The Marshals carried on escorting Bridges to school and she ate only food brought from home after a local woman threatened to poison her.

In 1999, Bridges founded the Ruby Bridges Foundation to promote tolerance, respect and appreciation of differences; two years later she received the Presidential Citizens' Medal. "It's about brothers and sisters and taking care of each other. That's the moral obligation."

15 NOVEMBER

Constance Spry
(1886–1960)

On this day in 1929, florist Constance Spry unveiled her first window display in a London perfumery, shocking the establishment by using hedgerow flowers. Long interested in plants and gardening, it wasn't until the age of forty-one that Spry opened her first shop, Flower Decoration. Her unique approach – often inspired by the Dutch Old Masters and combining cultivated flowers with plants like kale and pussy willow, putting them in objects such as jam jars – brought her celebrity. In 1937, she arranged flowers for the Duke of Windsor's wedding to Wallis Simpson.

In 1942, Spry published *Come into the Garden, Cook*, encouraging the British to help the war effort by growing their own food. She set up a domestic science school with her friend, chef and writer Rosemary Hume, with whom she created the coronation chicken recipe for Queen Elizabeth II's coronation in 1953. Hume and Spry later published the bestselling *Constance Spry Cookery Book*.

"Do what you please, follow your own star," wrote Spry, who wasn't actually married to the man she called her second husband and was in a relationship with painter Hannah Gluckstein. "Be original if you want to be and don't if you don't want to be."

16 NOVEMBER

Radclyffe Hall

(1880–1943)

On this day in 1928, judgement was passed in an obscenity trial in London, held to decide whether Radclyffe Hall's novel, *The Well of Loneliness*, was obscene and should be removed from circulation.

A published poet, Hall's lesbianism had been dismissed as an artistic eccentricity until the publication of this book. It had no explicit sexual content and lesbianism was not illegal, but same-sex attraction was at the center of its plot. The *Sunday Express* called for the book to be withdrawn and cultural figures were impelled to declare either "for" or "against" publication; writers including T.S. Eliot, George Bernard Shaw and Virginia Woolf were summonsed to defend the novel. Woolf was willing to do so, while noting archly that "Most of our friends are trying to evade the witness box."

Hall's declared purpose was to write from the point of view of "a misunderstood and misjudged minority." The judge ruled that the book was inclined to "corrupt," precisely because of that viewpoint: "There is not a single word from beginning to end of this book which suggests that anyone with these tendencies is in the least blameworthy," he said. The verdict of obscenity was both an injustice and a source of never-ending publicity for the book. It was published in America the next year.

Elizabeth I

(1533–1603)

On this day in 1558, Elizabeth I acceded to the throne of England. She ruled for forty-four years, testament to her extraordinary ability to prevail in a hostile environment. The survivor of political intrigue, smallpox, imprisonment and threatened execution, there is also evidence that she was a child victim of grooming and sexual harassment by Thomas Seymour, her stepmother's husband.

Although she spoke and read at least seven languages, including Latin, Greek, Hebrew and Italian, and translated works by Boethius, Horace, Plutarch and Tacitus, she had to battle the belief that the "imbecility" of women made them unfit to rule. A patron of the arts, during her reign literature flowered, theatre companies were invited to perform for her and six new theatres were built in London.

Elizabeth's reign was a period of stability and domestic peace, bringing about economic prosperity. Her leadership was a key factor in England's victory over the Spanish Armada in 1588. In a speech to the troops, she said: "I know I have the body but of a weak and feeble woman; but I have the heart and stomach of a king, and of a king of England too . . . I myself will be your general, judge, and rewarder of every one of your virtues in the field."

Karimeh Abbud

(1893 or 1896–1940)

On this day in 1913, Karimeh Abbud received a camera as a birthday present. From photographing family members and the landscapes around her home in Palestine, she progressed to portraits of women and children and weddings, becoming the first Palestinian woman to work as professional photographer.

Her success was such that in the 1930s she had four studios – in Nazareth, Jerusalem, Haifa and Bethlehem – driving herself between them in her own car, extremely unusual for a Palestinian woman at that time. She also traveled into local villages; her photographs, rare documents of everyday life in Palestine, include scenes from the private lives of women that were inaccessible to male photographers. Often using a side-light, her subjects appeared relaxed and natural.

Abbud stamped her photos with "Karimeh Abbud / Lady-Photographer / Photographer of the Sun." She also photographed public spaces and places with Christian significance, such as the village (Kafr Kanna/"Cana") where biblical stories describe Jesus Christ turning water into wine and the site (Mary's Well) where the Angel Gabriel appeared to Mary.

Abbud's photographs – 4,500 of which survive in private collections – are testament to the vibrancy of Palestinian life and culture in the first half of the twentieth century and to landscapes which, in some cases, no longer exist.

"Lady-Photographer / Photographer of the Sun."

19 NOVEMBER

Ellen Swallow Richards

(1842–1911)

In November 1876, America's first professional female chemist, Ellen Swallow Richards, opened the Women's Laboratory at the Massachusetts Institute of Technology (MIT). During her career, around 500 women studied chemistry with her in person and thousands more by correspondence.

Known as "Ellencyclopedia" by her family, Richards's own achievements covered a wide range of expertise, from air and water quality, food and consumer sciences to sanitary engineering and industrial chemistry. The first female environmental engineer, she conducted the first consumer-product tests and pioneered water purity tables.

Worried about wasting time, she would knit on the way up to her room at Vassar College, where she took almost every science class. After graduation, Richards persuaded Boston's new Institute of Technology to take her as a "special student of chemistry" – their first female student. She didn't pay fees so, she later discovered, they could disclaim her if anyone objected. After her Women's Laboratory opened, she sent lessons to thousands of women, along with microscopes and specimens. Richards never felt she had achieved enough, telling a friend: "I wish I were triplets." Always an educator, she ended letters with: "Keep thinking."

20 NOVEMBER

Susanna Centlivre

(c.1667–1723)

On this day in 1705, a play called *The Basset Table* opened at the Theatre Royal, Drury Lane, London. It was written by Susanna Centlivre, one of the eighteenth century's most popular playwrights. Following Aphra Behn's example, she was one of a few women to make a living in creative writing.

Having lost two husbands in duels, according to her own account, Centlivre began writing to support herself. At first, she was both playwright and player, occasionally taking "breeches roles," where female actors appeared in trousers. After her first play, *The Perjur'd Husband*, in 1700, Centlivre wrote around one play a year until her death in 1723.

Her most successful play, *The Busy Body*, was not an immediate hit with actors. With comedies such as *A Bold Stroke for a Wife* and *The Wonder! A Woman Keeps a Secret*, Centlivre both played to gender stereotypes and mocked them; *The Basset Table* includes a gambling widow and a female scientist. In later years, Centlivre became increasingly political, supporting the Whig party, and irritating satirist Alexander Pope sufficiently to be included in his *Dunciad*. Her plays were continuously in production for two centuries. *The Busy Body* was revived at the Southwark Playhouse as recently as 2012.

Rosalind Franklin

(1920–1958)

When English chemist and crystallographer Rosalind Franklin arrived at King's College, London, in 1951 to investigate DNA – deoxyribonucleic acid, the "building block of life" – Maurice Wilkins, researching the same field, assumed she was his assistant, not his colleague. Their relationship never recovered from this mistake.

On this day in 1951, Franklin showed him an X-ray image of DNA, known later as Photo 51, at a lecture, demonstrating that she was probably the first to see DNA's helix-like structure. Although scientists worldwide were racing to publish definitive proof of what DNA looked like, a cautious Franklin wanted to gather more data. However, without her permission, Wilkins shared Franklin's work with biologists James Watson and Francis Crick, and in 1953 they published their "double helix" theory of DNA structure in the journal *Nature* without acknowledging her.

Shortly afterwards, Franklin, fed up with King's College's sexist atmosphere – the main dining room was only open to men – transferred to another laboratory, focusing on plant viruses. She published twenty-one papers, including insights about a different crucial nucleic acid, RNA. Watson, Crick and Wilkins won the Nobel Prize in 1962 for their work. Franklin had died four years earlier, at the age of thirty-seven. Her vital contribution would only come to light years later, another example of the "Matilda effect" of female scientists being overlooked.

They published their "double helix" theory without acknowledging her.

Stephanie Kwolek

(1923–2014)

American chemist Stephanie Kwolek's interest in science had been sparked by nature walks with her father. She joined chemical company DuPont in the 1940s, researching new synthetic polymers strong enough to replace steel in car tires. After fifteen years, she found a promising candidate, persisting in the face of colleagues' skepticism to discover that, when it was "cold-spun," her polymer became unusually stiff. It turned out to be five times stronger than steel – and fire resistant. It's now known as Kevlar.

The patent for Kevlar, granted to Kwolek on this day in 1966, is owned by her employers, DuPont, who have reaped enormous rewards from the $500 million spent developing it: the first Kevlar bullet-proof vest was unveiled in 1975 and the fiber, which can be spun into ropes or fabric sheets, is used in everything from smartphones, spacecraft, bridge reinforcements, safety equipment and cut-resistant gloves to musical instruments, body armor, armored cars and hurricane safe rooms. Kwolek, who headed polymer research at DuPont until she retired in 1986, was awarded the National Medal of Technology.

It turned out to be five times stronger than steel – and fire resistant.

Im Yunjidang

(1721–1793)

Today we celebrate Im Yunjidang, the first female Confucian philosopher in Korea. In the eighteenth century, she defended a woman's right to become a Confucian sage and argued that, "Though I am a woman, there is no difference between man and woman in terms of human nature."

Yunjidang was a member of the Korean nobility and lived in a society which operated according to the doctrine of the sixth century BCE Chinese philosopher Confucius. Women, especially upper-class women, lived in separate housing from men and were subject to curfews.

In the thirty-five pieces of her work that survive, Yunjidang gives her views on the neo-Confucian theories of reason and energy, the Four Beginnings and the Seven Emotions, explaining her belief that energy has supremacy over reason. Due to her society's constraints on women, her work was not published until after her death.

> "Though I am a woman, there is no difference between man and woman in terms of human nature."

24 NOVEMBER

Marlene Dietrich

(1901–1992)

In November 1930, German-American actor Marlene Dietrich caused a sensation in the film *Morocco* by wearing a man's tailcoat and kissing a woman. The performance earned her a Best Actress Oscar nomination. Dietrich, whose career began in silent movies, moved to Hollywood from Germany after her breakthrough role in *The Blue Angel* (1930). By 1933, she was Paramount Studios' highest paid actor. She created her trouser suit look, the "Dietrich silhouette," together with her mentor, *Blue Angel* director, Josef von Sternberg. "I dress for the image. Not for myself, not for the public, not for fashion, not for men."

Dietrich had been part of Berlin's gay scene in the 1920s, but she and others in Hollywood's underground "Sewing Circle" group of lesbian and bisexual actresses had to be discreet due to "morals clauses" in their contracts. After becoming a US citizen in 1939, Dietrich publicly denounced Nazism and helped create a fund to assist the escape of Jews and dissidents from Germany. In 1937, she donated her salary for *Knight Without Armor* to help refugees. She sold more war bonds – which financed military operations – than any other star, as well as entertaining the troops in Algeria, Britain, France and Italy. In 1945, she was awarded the US Presidential Medal of Freedom.

25 NOVEMBER

Patria Mirabal (1924–1960); Minerva Mirabal (1926–1960); María Teresa Mirabal (1935–1960)

Sisters Patria, Minerva and María Teresa Mirabal were co-founders of a resistance group in the Dominican Republic called the Movement of the Fourteenth of June, whose aim was to topple brutal dictator Rafael Trujillo, who was responsible for over 50,000 deaths. Known as *Las Mariposas* ("butterflies"), the sisters distributed pamphlets and planned protests.

In 1960, hundreds of the Movement's members – including Minerva, María Teresa and their husbands – were arrested in a move intended to deter protest. However, Trujillo's plan backfired when the powerful Catholic Church condemned the arrests; all the women were released. On this day in 1960, driving home from visiting their jailed husbands, the Mirabal sisters were stopped by Trujillo's secret police, who beat them and their driver to death, then pushed their jeep over a cliff to make it look like an accident.

The outrage over *Las Mariposas'* deaths was a major factor leading to Trujillo's assassination less than six months later.

The sisters became national heroes, the subject of Dominican-American writer Julia Alvarez's novel, *In the Time of the Butterflies*, which was made into a film. The Mirabals, she says, are "a reminder that we [Latinas] have our revolutionary heroines, our Che Guevaras, too." In 1999, the United Nations General Assembly designated 25 November, the anniversary of the sisters' deaths, as International Day for the Elimination of Violence Against Women.

Annie Oakley
(1860–1926)

In November 1875, a fifteen-year-old girl won a shooting contest in Cincinnati, hitting twenty-five targets in a row. Within ten years, she was a superstar sharpshooter, part of the growing folklore of the Wild West. Her given name was Phoebe Anne Moses; her stage name was Annie Oakley. Her rival, Frank Butler, became her husband and they toured America as professional sharpshooters.

Oakley's stunts were breathtaking, shooting upside down or sideways, she split playing cards in two, hit moving targets and shot an apple off her dog's head; once she shot a cigarette out of Prince Wilhelm of Prussia's mouth. From 1885, she traveled the world with Buffalo Bill's Wild West show, representing frontier life – already a curiosity to many urban Americans.

Orphaned as a child, Annie learned to shoot to get food; as a teenager, she earned money supplying game to hotels. Like many women in this book, poverty spurred her outside "proper" boundaries for women and into the spotlight. Oakley's was a happier life than that of fellow frontierswoman Calamity Jane. Her showbusiness career included endorsements for a gun cartridge company, and by 1922 she was planning a film of her life when she was injured in a car crash. She died in 1926; her first shooting rival, and husband of fifty years, died three weeks later.

Fe Villanueva del Mundo

(1911–2011)

On this day in 1957, her forty-sixth birthday, pediatrician Fe del Mundo opened the Children's Memorial Hospital in Quezon City, the Philippines' first pediatric hospital. She had personally funded and organized its construction.

Del Mundo, one of eight children, decided to study medicine after the death of her sister, Elisa, who had wanted to be a doctor, and graduated from the University of the Philippines College of Medicine in 1933. In 1936, she received a scholarship to study at Harvard University Medical School, although women weren't officially accepted; it's said that the admissions staff hadn't realized from her name that she was female.

Returning to the Philippines, in the 1950s, del Mundo sold her home and many of her belongings and secured a loan for her hospital. Nine years after opening, an Institute of Maternal and Child Health – the first of its kind in Asia

– was added. Always interested in isolated communities, as a student intern del Mundo had invented an incubator for babies born in areas without electricity; later she organized teams to advise mothers in rural communities on breastfeeding and child care. Del Mundo received many awards, including the Elizabeth Blackwell Award as a Woman Doctor of World Renown. In 1980, she became the first female National Scientist of the Philippines.

It's said that the admissions staff hadn't realized from her name that she was female.

Lucy Baldwin

(1869–1945)

Lucy Ridsdale was a member of England's first women's cricket club, the White Heather Club, founded in Yorkshire in 1887. She met her future husband, Stanley Baldwin – elected prime minister three times between 1923 and 1937 – on the cricket field. But it was not as a sporting pioneer that Lucy Baldwin would change women's lives.

In 1929, using her prominent position (see Wives, or great women), Lucy founded an Analgesics Appeal Fund to provide pain relief in childbirth for all women, regardless of means, to reduce maternal mortality. "When a woman is going to have a child it is like going into battle," she said in a speech. "She never knows . . . whether she will come out of it alive or not." She spoke from experience, having given birth to seven children.

In February 1930, Lucy Baldwin was the main signatory on a letter to the British Medical Journal: "We believe that if anaesthetics were given the mother would be in a far stronger state of health to combat any possible after-effects than she would be if she had previously passed through hours of suffering. The shock to the nervous system also would be lessened." In 1959, the British Oxygen company named their gas-and-air anesthetic machine "The Lucy Baldwin Apparatus" in tribute to her; it was in use until 1980.

Helen B. Taussig

(1898–1986)

In 1930, Helen B. Taussig became head of the Children's Heart Clinic at Johns Hopkins University in Baltimore, US, despite her dyslexia and the limited opportunities for women. Suffering worsening deafness, she developed a method of "listening" to her young patients' hearts with her fingertips instead of using a stethoscope.

Taussig's pioneering work on cyanosis or "blue baby syndrome" led to an operation to correct the congenital heart defect that causes it, which was performed for the first time on this day in 1944. Although the procedure had been perfected on laboratory animals by African-American technician Vivien T. Thomas, as a non-surgeon he wasn't allowed to perform it, but advised the surgeon, Dr. Alfred Blalock, with Taussig also present. The operation, now called the Blalock–Thomas–Taussig shunt, has prolonged thousands of lives and was a key step in the development of open-heart surgery for adults after the Second World War. Taussig's *Congenital Malformations of the Heart* (1947) was the first textbook for pediatric cardiology.

In 1962, Taussig traveled to Europe to investigate malformations in newborns thought to be caused by thalidomide. Her campaign to stop the pending approval of the drug for use in America was successful; thalidomide was never licensed in the US.

30 NOVEMBER

Leokadiya Kashperova
(1872–1940)

On this day in 1920, virtuoso pianist Leokadiya Kashperova gave her final solo recital, at the Moscow Conservatoire – a powerful all-Beethoven program. For many years, Kashperova was remembered only as "Stravinsky's teacher"; his descriptions of her as "antiquated" further diminished her reputation. In fact, Kashperova was a brilliant solo pianist and highly respected composer in many genres; her output included a symphony, a piano concerto and songs, most of which were performed during her lifetime.

In 1916, Kashperova married Sergei Andropov, a Bolshevik leader, and became a teacher at the Smolny Institute, a school founded by <u>Catherine the Great</u> to educate the daughters of the Russian nobility. When the Russian Revolution began on 8 March 1917, the school was used as Bolshevik headquarters; Lenin had his office there. Fearing for their lives due to their Tsarist connections, the couple fled Petrograd. This move marked the beginning of the end of Kashperova's career; she performed only a few times between 1918 and 1920.

However, many unpublished compositions have since been discovered which must have been written in secret. On 8 March 2018, Kashperova finally received recognition when her Symphony in B minor (1905) was performed in a BBC Radio 3 International Women's Day concert – on the 101st anniversary of the revolution that split her life in two.

DECEMBER

"Feminism . . .
is about making life more
fair for women everywhere.
It's not about a piece of the
existing pie . . . It's about
baking a new pie."
– Gloria Steinem

Work

The words "woman" and "work" have an odd relationship. The saying "a woman's work is never done" refers to domestic chores and family obligations, including childcare. Yet women who stay at home to look after children are still frequently asked, "Don't you work?", as though running a home came as easily to them as breathing. Traditional male jobs such as teaching and secretarial work became less valued, and less well paid, once they became "women's work."

There is also a belief that women in history "didn't work," as though before the twentieth century every woman lived in some version of a Jane Austen novel. In fact, we know that women have always done "non-domestic" work because of the extraordinary lengths to which men have gone to stop them. As Virginia Woolf remarked, "The history of men's opposition to women's emancipation is more interesting perhaps than the story of that emancipation itself."

For example, we know that there were female doctors 500 years ago because in 1511 an Act of Parliament in England was passed to ban them. As recently as 1895, the Royal College of Physicians voted against a motion to grant membership to women, stating that "allowing" women to study medicine was "an experiment which another generation may show to be a mistake." It's a story repeated across many fields. Women have always worked in science, if it could be done at home – hence the many astronomers in this book. But during the nineteenth century, as science became professionalized, women like fossil-hunter Mary Anning were prevented from joining the professional organizations that would have provided them with colleagues and validated their work.

If a woman managed to get a high-level job, she was often forced to give it up after marriage. Annie Russell Maunder could only stay at the Royal Observatory as a volunteer, "fortunate" to have a husband who not only worked alongside her but also credited her and co-founded a professional body open to male and female astronomers. In sport too, men have kept official organizations "male-only" – see the stories of Lily Parr and Elizabeth Wilkinson. After skater Madge Syers won a silver medal at the 1902 World Figure Skating Championships – until that point implicitly only for men – the International Skating Union swiftly officially banned women.

Thanks to the many women around the world who have combined "working" – whether in or outside the home, paid or unpaid – with activism, attitudes and structures have changed. But the gender pay gap is still alive and well and, until there is full parity, women will continue to fight to do the work they want to do and to be paid properly for it.

Veronica Guerin

(1958–1996)

A background in accountancy naturally led Irish journalist Veronica Guerin to delve not only into the activities of Ireland's organized crime gangs but also their financial dealings. Joining Ireland's largest newspaper, the *Sunday Independent*, in 1994, she became known for pursuing stories of fraud and drug trafficking. Since identifying criminals in print was illegal, Guerin invented pseudonyms such as The Penguin, The Coach and The Monk. She first came under attack herself that same year: shots were fired at her house after her article on a murdered drug lord was published. In January 1995, she opened her door to a man who shot her in the thigh.

In December 1995, Guerin received the International Press Freedom Award from the Committee to Protect Journalists for reporting on Irish drug and gang culture with little thought for her own safety. Six months later, on 26 June 1996, she was shot and killed while stopped at a traffic light – two days before she was to speak at a Freedom Forum conference titled "Dying to Tell a Story: Journalists at Risk." Guerin's murder shocked Ireland – and had an immediate effect. 150 arrests were made and the Proceeds of Crime Act 1996 and the Criminal Assets Bureau Act 1996 were passed, allowing the government to seize assets funded by crime.

2 DECEMBER

Emma Clarke

(1876–after 1903)

Born on this day in 1876 in Liverpool, Emma Clarke grew up playing football on the streets; she became the first black professional female footballer in Britain. She made her debut as a member of the South team, in "The North vs The South" match held in London on 23 March 1895 in front of 10,000 spectators. The *Manchester Guardian* reported that the women's "costumes came in for a good deal of attention . . . one or two added short skirts over their knicker-bockers. When the novelty has worn off, I do not think women's football will attract the crowds."

Clarke joined Nettie Honeyball's British Ladies' Football Club and played for them for a year before joining Mrs. Graham's XI – set up in 1881 by suffragette Helen Graham Matthews – on a tour of Scotland. Team members were paid expenses plus around a shilling a week: a decent wage for the time. Women's football teams didn't just play each other. In 1897, Clarke was a member of "The New Woman and Ten of Her Lady Friends" in a match against "Eleven Gentlemen." The women won 3–1. Clarke's career continued until at least 1903, but no further records of her have been found, even of the date of her death.

She made her debut as a member of the South team, in "The North vs The South" match held in London on 23 March 1895 in front of 10,000 spectators.

Friedl Dicker

(1898-1944)

A founding student at Germany's Bauhaus art school, Friedl Dicker later taught art in the most appalling of circumstances – a concentration camp.

After graduating, Dicker worked with her Bauhaus colleagues; she and Franz Singer designed the interior of the Montessori kindergarten for one of "Red" Vienna's social housing blocks (see Naomi Mitchison). After moving to Prague with her husband, Pavel Brandeis, she taught art to refugee children. After the Nazis occupied Czechoslovakia, Dicker turned down two opportunities to leave Europe because her husband wasn't included.

In December 1942, Dicker and Brandeis, both Jewish, were deported to the Theresienstadt ghetto and concentration camp. Having used most of her meager luggage allowance for art materials, Dicker taught in the camp's secret school, sharing with fellow inmates her belief that art lessons gave children some mental freedom and individuality.

In October 1944, Dicker requested to be deported to the Auschwitz concentration camp, where her husband had already been sent; he survived, but she was murdered in a gas chamber. After the war, two suitcases containing over 5,000 children's drawings were found, hidden by Dicker in an attic at Theresienstadt. Many of these extraordinary artworks are now displayed in Prague's Jewish Museum. Edith Kramer, founder of the art therapy movement, calls Dicker "the grandmother of art therapy." Kramer, who worked with her in Prague, sees Dicker living on in the field she pioneered: "There are many forms of survival."

4 DECEMBER

Ms. magazine (1971–) and Gloria Steinem (1934–)

In December 1971, *Ms.* magazine's first issue was published as an insert in *New York* magazine. The magazine sold out 300,000 copies in eight days and *Ms.*"'s editors received thousands of subscription requests. The magazine was born after a hundred women staged an eleven-hour sit-in in the (male) editor's office of *Ladies' Home Journal* in March 1970, demanding they hire a female editor-in-chief. *Ms.* was intended as a counterpoint to women's magazines which were "limited to advice about finding a husband, saving marriages, raising babies, or using the right cosmetics."

One of its founders, writer and activist Gloria Steinem, has been called the "world's most famous feminist." After coming to national attention with her 1963 article "I Was a Playboy Bunny" about going undercover at Hugh Hefner's Playboy Club, her focus shifted to politics. Co-founder of the National Women's Political Caucus in 1971,

she has spent decades traveling widely to campaign on women's issues. "Feminism . . . is about making life more fair for women everywhere. It's not about a piece of the existing pie . . . It's about baking a new pie." Despite (male) critics giving it a shelf-life of six months and hostility from within the feminist movement, *Ms.* – which calls itself "more than a magazine . . . a movement" – is still going strong, as is Steinem, now in her eighties.

Eloísa Díaz Insunza

(1866–1950)

In December 1886, Eloísa Díaz Insunza graduated from the school of medicine at the University of Chile – she was its first female medical student and the first woman to become a doctor of medicine in South America. She had enrolled in 1880, shortly after a new law enabled women to study at the university. Life for a female student wasn't easy: university rules stipulated that Díaz could only attend classes if accompanied by her mother. Nevertheless, she completed the course. Her final thesis was titled, "Brief observations on the apparition of puberty in Chilean women and their pathological predispositions about sex."

Díaz worked as both a doctor and a teacher. In 1898, she was appointed director of Santiago's School Medical Service. A philanthropic social reformer, she founded kindergartens and healthcare centers for the poor

and organized school camps. She extended this work after 1911 as director of the School Medical Service of Chile, introducing school breakfasts and mass vaccination of students. She also initiated and oversaw campaigns to fight alcoholism, rickets and tuberculosis.

6 DECEMBER

Kitty O'Neil

(1946–2018)

On this day in 1976, American Kitty O'Neil became the fastest woman alive, reaching 512.710 mph in her Motivator three-wheeled rocket car. Deaf since contracting measles, mumps and chickenpox as a child, O'Neil had hoped to become a diver. But spinal meningitis before the 1964 Olympic trials put an end to that dream. After facing cancer twice, and told she didn't have the strength for athletics, she began racing – cars, motorcycles, boats and high-speed waterskiing. "My mother pushed me to read lips, but she didn't push me in sports – I did that myself. Because I was deaf I had a very positive mental attitude. You have to show people you can do anything."

Within six months of becoming a stuntwoman, O'Neil developed a reputation for risk-taking. She set the record for the longest fall for a woman and the highest attempted fall on fire, wearing a protective suit. The first woman accepted into Hollywood's Stunts Unlimited, she worked on films including *The Bionic Woman* (1976) and *Blues Brothers* (1980). In 1979, Stockard Channing played her in *Silent Victory: The Kitty O'Neil Story*, with O'Neil as her stunt double, and Mattel brought out a Kitty O'Neil Barbie doll. She retired in 1982 having set twenty-two land and water speed records. "I'm not afraid of anything," she said.

Mary Somerville

(1780–1872)

Forbidden to study math by her father, Scottish mathematician Mary Somerville taught herself in secret using the books in her family's library. After her first husband's death, she used her small inheritance for books and tutoring; her second husband was more supportive of her ambition.

When Somerville was asked to write an English version of Laplace's *Mécanique Céleste* ("Celestial Mechanics"), she took on the task with gusto, not only translating and condensing the work but explaining the equations, which weren't understood by many British mathematicians at the time.

In December 1831, the publication of *Mechanism of the Heavens* brought Somerville instant fame throughout the scientific world. Her second book, *On the Connexion of the Physical Sciences* (1834), was devoted to interdisciplinary thinking, including what we would now call astronomy, physics, meteorology and geology. A short note in the third edition – that problems calculating Uranus's position might indicate an undiscovered planet – led to the discovery of Neptune.

The difficulty in describing Somerville – an accomplished polymath who happened to be female – led scientific historian William Whewell to coin a new word, "scientist," not only to avoid "man of science" but also to convey her knowledge of many disciplines.

In 1835, the Royal Astronomical Society elected Somerville and astronomer Caroline Herschel as its first honorary female members. Somerville College in Oxford is named after her.

Mavis Batey

(1921–2013)

Mavis Batey was nineteen in 1940 when she arrived at Bletchley Park, Britain's codebreaking center during the Second World War. The first words she was greeted with were: "Hello, we're breaking machines. Have you got a pencil? Here, have a go," upon which she was handed "a pile of utter gibberish." Batey soon became an expert in "gibberish," deciphering Italian plans to ambush a Royal Navy convoy.

Her greatest achievement came on this day in 1941, cracking a message that enabled the team to understand how the German Secret Service's Enigma coding machine was wired. Reading their messages, the British Secret Service saw that the Germans believed the false information being fed to them by captured Allied spies. Based on this misinformation, Hitler, convinced the Allies were landing at Calais in June 1944, sent forces there instead of Normandy, where the Allies actually landed on D-Day, which marked the beginning of the liberation of France.

Batey's work was classified; her role only came to light when a book on Bletchley Park was published in the 1970s. She described the work she and others did as "marvellous."

> "This was a crossword puzzle where men's lives were at stake. So if you knew . . . men's lives could literally be saved."

Qiu Jin
(1875–1907)

In 1906, revolutionary and poet Qiu Jin, often called "China's <u>Joan of Arc,</u>" published "A Respectful Proclamation to China's 200 Million Women Comrades." She demanded the personal liberation of women – an end to foot binding and arranged marriages – and political and social reform.

As a child, Jin had read the Confucian classics, history, poetry, and novels, and had studied martial arts. In 1896, after she and her husband moved to Beijing, Jin met like-minded women for the first time. She became interested in politics, unbound her feet and experimented with cross-dressing and sword-fighting. Eight years later, she sold her jewelry, left her family and, dressed as a man, sailed to Japan, where she enrolled in Shimoda Utako's Women's Practical School. It was here that her revolutionary activities began.

When she returned to China, she established the *Chinese Women's Journal* and ran the Datong School, a front for training revolutionaries to topple the Qing government, which had been ruling China for almost 300 years. Warned to flee after the school's founder was assassinated, Jin refused. In 1907, at the age of thirty-one, she was captured, taken back to her home village and publicly beheaded.

10 DECEMBER

Marie Curie

(1867–1934)

On this day in 1911, Polish-French scientist Marie Curie, the first woman to win any Nobel Prize, became the first – and to date only – person awarded two Nobels in different scientific fields: physics and chemistry.

The university in Warsaw didn't accept women, so in 1891 Marie Skłodowska and her sister moved to Paris, where Marie studied mathematics and physics. Here she met French physicist Pierre Curie, who would become her husband and collaborator. Intrigued by the recent discovery of X-rays, Marie realized that the element uranium also emitted rays and, in 1898, coined the term "radioactivity." She and Pierre discovered two new radioactive elements: polonium and radium. In November 1903, Marie, Pierre and Henri Becquerel shared the Nobel Prize in Physics for their work on radiation – although Pierre had to persuade the Nobel committee, reluctant to include a woman, that Marie had done the original research.

After Pierre's death, Marie became the Sorbonne's first female physics professor. When the First World War began, Curie sent mobile X-ray machines to doctors at the front. By 1920, she was experiencing health problems, possibly related to radiation. A year after she died, her daughter, Irène Joliot-Curie, became the second woman to win a Nobel Prize in chemistry.

11 DECEMBER

Mary Anning

(1799–1847)

Even before she made her extraordinary fossil finds, Mary Anning was a mythical figure in Lyme Regis, in southern England: at a year old, she'd survived a lightning strike – locals thought this explained her extraordinary intellect and energy. Anning's family hunted fossils to supplement their income; as children, she and her brother spotted a skeleton, one of the first findings of an Ichthyosaurus. Anning soon became famous for her finds, including the first British example of a fossilized flying reptile. In December 1823, she found the fossilized skeleton of a nine-feet-long animal with a small head. At a Geological Society meeting in London, the specimen was named as a virtually complete example of the little-known Plesiosaurus.

During her lifetime, Anning was called "the Geological Lioness," "Princess of Palaeontology," and "St Georgina of Lyme Regis." But,

despite her renown, as a provincial working-class woman she wasn't invited into the London-based, upper-class, male scientific community. Members of the Geological Society bought her fossils and published papers about them – sometimes omitting to credit her – while refusing her membership. Anning opened a shop – Anning's Fossil Depot – and made a living from her finds. Lyme Regis Museum is built on the site of the depot; its Mary Anning Wing opened in 2017.

As a provincial working-class woman she wasn't invited into the London-based, upper-class, male scientific community.

12 DECEMBER

Salma AlRashid

(unknown)

On this day in 2015, 130,000 Saudi Arabians were able to vote in an election for the first time. Women had always been denied a voice in Saudi politics, but were now allowed to vote in local elections. The first to register was Salma AlRashid, a prominent Saudi women's rights activist who heads the Al Nahda Philanthropic Society for Women.

This was only the third election held in the nation. Women were also able to stand as candidates for the first time: 978 registered to do so, even though they had to be represented by a man in public or speak from behind a panel. Saudi Arabia is "a bleak and deadly region" for women, according to journalist Diane Francis. In a 2016 survey of gender equality by the World Economic Forum, the nation was ranked 141 out of 144 countries. Women are discriminated against in health, education and politics. Activists campaigning against restrictive laws were jailed and apparently tortured in 2018. The sexes are segregated in public spaces – including polling stations.

There have been some changes. Women have been allowed to drive since 2017 and, since 2019, can travel without the signature of a male "guardian." "There is still a lot of work to do," said AlRashid. But after casting her vote, she said, "It felt really good."

"There is still a lot of work to do."

Miina Sillanpää

(1866–1952)

Miina Sillanpää started work in a Finnish cotton factory at the age of twelve. Later employed as a maid, she began campaigning on behalf of working-class women, founding the Servants' Association in 1898. "Maids are not as timid as before," she said in a speech. "They dare to call for improvements to their slavish conditions." In 1907, a year after Finland became the first European country to give women the vote, Sillanpää stood as a Social Democratic Party candidate and won. She would remain in Parliament for over thirty years – Finland's second longest-serving female MP.

On this day in 1926, Sillanpää was appointed Minister of Social Affairs, Finland's first female minister. Called "the mother of Finland's welfare state," she focused on social policy and the status of women, working to improve the legal status of wives through the Marriage and Health Insurance Acts. In 1907, together with Finland's other female MPs, she had helped establish homes and shelters for unmarried mothers and their children.

Tarja Kaarina Halonen, who in 2000 became Finland's first female president, said Sillanpää's strength was "looking at the world with fresh eyes and then thinking how to change it." As Sillanpää herself said: "Even in the toughest situations, one should say 'I will try.'"

14 DECEMBER

Wilma Mankiller

(1945–2010)

Born in Oklahoma to a Cherokee father and a Dutch-Irish mother, Wilma Mankiller's family was moved to San Francisco under the Bureau of Indian Affairs' Relocation Program when she was a child. Twenty years later, the 1969 Native American occupation of the former prison at Alcatraz in San Francisco Bay inspired her to become involved in civil rights. After divorcing her husband, who opposed her activism, she returned to Oklahoma in 1976 with her daughters.

Despite injury in a car crash and a neuromuscular disease, Mankiller involved herself in community work, organizing projects on a Cherokee reservation for clean water and better housing. In 1983, she became deputy chief of the Cherokee Nation, taking over when the chief resigned. However, when she ran for election herself, there was opposition to the idea of a woman chief. Nevertheless, on this day in 1985, she became principal chief of the Cherokee Nation, the first woman to lead a major Native American tribe. She later won a second term with 83 per cent of the vote.

In 1990, Mankiller signed a self-determination agreement with the federal government, giving the Cherokee Nation control of funding, programs and services. Awarded the Presidential Medal of Freedom in 1998, she told a film-maker:

"I hope that when I leave it will just be said: I did what I could."

Hattie McDaniel

(1893–1952)

Actor Hattie McDaniel was the first African-American to win an Oscar, for her role in *Gone with the Wind*, released in the US on this day in 1939.

As a child, McDaniel could make more from busking than her mother earned as a maid. She became a vaudeville actor, renowned singer, set up a theatre company and was one of the first black women on radio – while working as a maid herself. Making a film career in the few roles available to her, McDaniel worked with stars including Marlene Dietrich and Clark Gable, yet the black press dismissed her for only playing a nurse or cook. McDaniel retorted, "I'd rather make $700 a week playing a maid than earn $7 a day being a maid."

The script for *Gone with the Wind* included the N-word. McDaniel refused to utter it and it was removed. At the Oscar ceremony, she received a standing ovation – then walked through hundreds of white guests to the one table set at the back, for her party. The Ku Klux Klan burned a cross on her lawn, and even her funeral, attended by 5,000 people, was sullied by racism: her chosen cemetery refused to accept a black body. In 2010, the actor Mo'Nique accepted her own Oscar, wearing the same outfit as McDaniel had: "I would like to thank Hattie McDaniel for enduring all that she had to, so that I would not have to."

16 DECEMBER

Jyoti Singh Pandey

(1989–2012)

What happened on this day in December 2012 caused shock waves across India. That evening, at 9.30pm, a twenty-three-year-old student called Jyoti Singh Pandey got on a bus in Delhi with a male friend. As the bus traveled on, Pandey was raped and tortured by all five of the other male passengers and the driver. She and her friend were badly beaten and thrown out.

As her ordeal became known, other women in Delhi began to demonstrate in the streets. For them, the atrocity was part of a wider culture where sex crimes are not taken seriously. The protestors were themselves attacked by police, who beat many of them with iron-tipped batons. The prime minister's son called the protestors "completely disconnected from reality . . . they go to discotheques."

Pandey wrote: "I want to survive" on a piece of paper for doctors treating her. She did not survive; her injuries were too great. She died two weeks after the attack. In the following days, her parents formed the Nirbhaya Jyoti Trust to raise money for women's safety measures. In response to the public outcry, anti-stalking laws and other measures were introduced. However, a government task force set up to deal with violence against women was soon disbanded. Pandey's mother complained in 2017 that money from the trust had been diverted to road building campaigns. Pandey's father said, "If you ask me if there has been any change in the system, I would say no with a capital N."

"I want to survive"

17 DECEMBER

Edith Smith

(1880–1924)

While 4,000 women took part in voluntary patrols during the First World War, on this day in 1915, Edith Smith became the first sworn in as a British constable with the same powers as male officers. The UK Home Office protested on the grounds that women weren't "proper persons" under the law – a stance that Theresa May apologized for as Home Secretary a hundred years later.

Smith worked alone in her Lincolnshire town; her first annual report recorded that she concentrated on the regulation of "frivolous girls" attracted to the town by the servicemen in two nearby army camps. She described how her "black list" banned those engaging in "unseemly conduct" from cinemas and theatres; some "fallen" women apparently left town because "the policewoman was such a nuisance." Smith also approached couples in public to warn them about sexually transmitted diseases and passed information on to husbands about their wives' movements when the husbands were away, angering many feminists at the time.

Smith retired in January 1918. It would take another fifty years for the first black female police officer, Sislin Fay Allen, to be hired, and a further fifty until a woman, Cressida Dick, was appointed to the Metropolitan Police's highest office, commissioner, in 2017.

18 DECEMBER

Anne Germaine de Staël
(1766–1817)

Anne Germaine de Staël-Holstein's life was as colorful as her turbans. A woman of letters, she had many lovers, saved many people from the guillotine and conducted a long-running feud with Napoleon, who thought women should stick to knitting. She was exiled by him twice: after her first novel, *Delphine*, was published in December 1802, because the book examined the limits set on women's freedoms, and again after the publication in 1807 of *Corinne*, which listed all the works of art Napoleon had plundered from Italy.

De Staël saw Napoleon as a threat to social progress: his military victories distracted people from fighting for greater freedoms; he corrupted idealistic leaders by offering them wealth or promotion. "Bonaparte is not only a man, but a system . . . One must therefore examine him as a great problem, whose solution matters for the thought of all ages." Her home in Switzerland became a salon for Napoleon's exiled opponents; the novelist Stendhal called it "the general headquarters of European thought."

"Ought not every woman, like every man, to follow the bent of her own talents?"

389

19 DECEMBER

Anna Comnena

(1083–1153)

Around 1148, Byzantine princess Anna Comnena wrote the *Alexiad*. It is a life of her father, the emperor Alexius I, a lively, readable narrative that makes her the first known woman historian. Alexius had ruled the Byzantine Empire, centered on Constantinople (now Istanbul). When his throne passed to Comnena's brother John, she rebelled and was exiled.

She became a scholar and patron of learning. The *Alexiad* – begun by Comnena's husband and finished by her after his death – records the region's history at a turbulent time. It is a unique source of information about, for instance, the First Crusade, which looked very different from Constantinople than it did from Normandy or Rome. Comnena celebrates her grandmother Anna Dalassena, co-ruler with Alexius: "He ran alongside her as she drove the imperial chariot . . . She could organise and administer so well that she was capable of governing not only the Empire but every kingdom under the sun."

Historians have cast doubt on Anna's authorship, attributing the whole text to her husband (see We are not a muse). One suggests there are not enough hints of the author's gender. The author's introduction, "I, Anna, daughter of the Emperor Alexius and the Empress Irene," and the phrase "I was the lawful wife of the Caesar Nicephorus," are apparently not sufficient. Anna gives this advice to future historians:

"The historian . . . must shirk neither remonstrance with his friends, nor praise of his enemies."

Selma Lagerlöf

(1858–1940)

Best known for her children's books about the adventures of Nils Holgersson, Selma Lagerlöf also wrote novels, stories, plays and memoirs. In December 1909, she won the Nobel Prize for Literature, the first woman and the first Swede to do so. Twelve hundred women attended a celebratory banquet at the Grand Hotel Royal in Stockholm; Swedish suffragist Lydia Wahlström delivered the main speech entitled "Every Woman's Gratitude," thanking Lagerlöf on behalf of all the women she supported. Women were central to Lagerlöf's life, as friends, patrons, assistants. She spoke publicly in support of women as a political class in her suffrage speeches; as a member of the Swedish Academy she advocated for female Nobel laureates and nominees.

Lagerlöf was a mentor to German-Jewish writer Nelly Sachs, giving her guidance in correspondence written over thirty-five years. In 1940, Lagerlöf secured safe passage for Sachs and her mother out of Nazi Germany but died without knowing that they had reached Stockholm on the last plane out of Berlin. In December 1966, Nelly Sachs herself won the Nobel Prize for Literature. In her acceptance speech she paid tribute to Lagerlöf, "the great novelist," for bringing her to Sweden and thereby saving her life.

21 DECEMBER

Mary-Claire King

(1946–)

American geneticist Mary-Claire King had already made a major impact on the international science world with her PhD, which changed the accepted view of evolution by showing that the protein-coding DNA sequences of humans and chimpanzees are 99 per cent identical. Then, on this day in 1990, King published a paper identifying the breast cancer gene BRCA1 on chromosome 17, demonstrating that breast cancer may be hereditary. It had taken seventeen years for King's team to locate BRCA1.

In 1984, the *Abuelas* ("Grandmothers") of Plaza de Mayo in Argentina asked the publishers of *Science* to recommend a geneticist to help in their search for the bodies of their children – murdered by Argentina's military dictatorship – and their grandchildren, some of whom may have survived. The *Abuelas* had realized that it was possible to identify a child on the basis of its grandparents' genes, even if its parents were missing, presumed dead. "I went in June 1984 for what I thought would be one symbolic trip of solidarity," said King. "It became a thirty-year collaboration." She used dental genetics to identify fifty-nine children who had been separated or stolen from their families. Her technique is now widely used to identify missing people.

22 DECEMBER

Nana Asma'u

(1793–1864)

Nana Asma'u was a Muslim philosopher in the Sokoto caliphate, known today as northern Nigeria. Her father, a Caliph and advocate of a woman's right to an education, gave his daughter the same education as her brothers. Asma'u became a *hafitha* – one who memorized the Quran – and a respected spiritual and political leader.

Concerned about occult beliefs among women in rural areas, she set up a revolutionary education system, *Yan-Taru*: "the coming together," or "sisterhood." The curriculum consisted of educational poems written by Asma'u in the local spoken language to be learned by heart, so no initial reading ability was required. Later, poems became a basis for more advanced learning and could be recited by the village women to their husbands to assert their rights.

Asma'u recruited teams of traveling teachers, each formed of one woman past childbearing age and one unmarried girl. These teachers were provided with a hat similar to those worn by occult priestesses – a symbol of recognized authority – but were wrapped with a red turban, signaling a new order. Asma'u also wrote poems about female teachers and students, establishing a written tradition of respect for women's rights and education and for their role as leaders. There are still *Yan-Taru* groups in parts of Nigeria today, and in the United States.

Asma'u became a hafitha – one who memorized the Quran.

23 DECEMBER

Billie Jean King

(1943–)

On this day in 1972, tennis player Billie Jean King was the first woman named *Sports Illustrated*'s Sportsperson of the Year. Winner of thirty-nine Grand Slams – including singles and doubles tournaments – King's talent and activism have combined to make her one of the most notable athletes in world sport.

In 1973, King threatened to boycott the US Open unless male and female champions were given the same prize money. As a direct result, the Open was the first major tennis tournament to offer equal prizes (the last being Wimbledon, in 2007). In the same year, the famous "Battle of the Sexes" televised match pitted twenty-nine-year-old King against fifty-five-year-old Bobby Riggs. Watched by over 90 million TV viewers, King won the match (and $100,000) in three straight sets. This high-profile stunt, and King's skill, were crucial in raising the value of women's sport.

Outed as a lesbian in 1981, King lost all her sponsorships but became a champion of LGBT rights and continued playing. She retired in 1984. In 2006, the home of the US Open was renamed the Billie Jean King National Tennis Center. Already included in the US National Women's Hall of Fame, in 2009 King was awarded the Presidential Medal of Freedom for her work in gender equality and gay rights.

Lotte Reiniger

(1899–1981)

In December 1918, *The Pied Piper of Hamelin* was released, the first film for which German film-maker and animator Lotte Reiniger created the animation. The director was having trouble with live rats so asked Reiniger to animate wooden ones. It was a triumph.

Joining a Berlin experimental animation studio, Reiniger made six short films, using techniques she could do at home: "Take your best dining table, cut a hole into it, put a glass plate over it, and over the glass plate some transparent paper." Reiniger's original style involved making black silhouettes, often with colors in the background, which came from a childhood fascination for telling stories with paper cut-outs. Photographing scenes in a friend's garage, she invented a technique which, by placing silhouettes on different planes and photographing them from above, gave the illusion of depth and may have been the inspiration for Disney's multiplane camera.

After fleeing the Nazis in the 1930s, Reiniger settled in London, where she made animated films and adverts for the Post Office and gave puppet performances. Reiniger made more than forty films, including the first animated feature film, *The Adventures of Prince Achmed*, in 1926, eleven years before Disney's first animation, *Snow White and the Seven Dwarfs*.

25 DECEMBER

Jodie Whittaker

(1982–)

The title character of *Doctor Who*, the British science fiction TV show that debuted on the BBC in November 1963, is a Time Lord, an alien with two hearts who travels through time and space with human companions, fighting injustice and solving interplanetary disputes. The Doctor has the ability to regenerate – appear in a new physical form – allowing a series of actors to take on the role. For fifty-four years, this form had been male. But, on this day in 2017, the Doctor regenerated and, for the first time, was played by a woman, Jodie Whittaker.

This caused both delight and controversy. Said Whittaker: "It's not that shocking, a woman playing an alien – that's not the weird bit!" Some fans – and even one previous *Doctor Who* actor – complained the show had been "ruined" due to "political correctness"; others posted videos of themselves reacting to the news, including one young girl screaming, "The new Doctor is a girl!" Whittaker was thrilled with the girl's response: "Her reaction was so honest and reflects how the Doctor will be important for so many girls – they don't have to be the sidekick to their heroes any more. It's important for male fans, too, especially the younger ones," she said. "It's telling them that there's nothing wrong with looking up to a woman."

26 DECEMBER

The Dick, Kerr Ladies Team (1917–1965); Lily Parr (1905–1978)

On this day in 1920, a women's football match at Goodison Park in Liverpool drew over 53,000 spectators, with 10,000 more turned away. St Helen's Ladies were playing the Dick, Kerr Ladies, one of the most famous teams in England, which had been formed in 1917 at the Dick, Kerr & Co munitions factory in Preston. The game raised £3,115 for charity; the players were paid expenses and recompensed for loss of work time. One of the Dick, Kerr's star players was Lily Parr, who "takes corner kicks better than most men, and scores many goals from extra-ordinary angles with a left foot cross drive, which nearly breaks the net."

Women's football had started in England in the 1880s and grew in popularity during the First World War. In 1921, the male-run English Football Association Council banned women from playing on FA grounds, declaring: "The game of football is quite unsuitable for females and ought not to be encouraged." Many women's teams continued to play on land that didn't belong to clubs – the Dick, Kerr Ladies team continued until 1965 – but the ban was only lifted fifty years later. The Football Association finally apologized in 2008, when Lily Parr became the first woman in the Hall of Fame at the National Football Museum in Manchester; a statue of her was erected in the museum in 2019.

> "Takes corner kicks better than most men, and scores many goals from extra-ordinary angles."

Benazir Bhutto

(1953–2007)

In 1977, during a military coup, Benazir Bhutto's father was removed as Pakistan's prime minister and later executed. "I told him on my oath in his death cell, I would carry on his work," Bhutto said. Imprisoned herself, and exiled in 1984, she returned when martial law in Pakistan was lifted. She was elected prime minister for the Pakistan People's Party in 1988, the first woman to head a democratic government in a Muslim majority nation.

Although Bhutto implemented some improvements to women's rights, she was constrained by the military and religious mullahs during her two terms in office. Her lavish lifestyle while much of the country lived in poverty, paired with increasing inflation, led to corruption allegations and, after a bribery scandal, the president dismissed her government in 1996.

Bhutto moved to Dubai. When she returned to Pakistan in October 2007, she began campaigning for another term as prime minister. But on this day in 2007, she was killed at an election rally by a fifteen-year-old suicide bomber recruited by the Pakistan Taliban. Bhutto said that her father had told her at their last meeting that she must sacrifice everything for her country. "This is a mission I shall live or die for," she said.

28 DECEMBER

Josephine Cochran

(1839–1913)

Illinois socialite Josephine Cochran gave frequent dinner parties and was constantly concerned for the safety of her fine china when it was washed up by her servants. When her husband died suddenly, leaving her in debt, Cochran, the mechanically minded daughter and granddaughter of engineers, decided to solve the washing-up problem. On this day in 1886, she received a patent for the first mechanical dishwasher. The only invention by a woman at the 1893 World's Columbian Exposition in Chicago, it was awarded a prize for "best mechanical construction, durability and adaptation to its line of work." While not the only dish-washing invention, it was the best; others required users to pour boiling water over the dishes. Cochran's was also the first to spray water under pressure.

Cochran established a company to market the machine, and although it was expensive – around $350 – she received orders from as far afield as Mexico and Alaska.

She died in 1913, apparently from nervous exhaustion. "If I knew all I know today when I began to put the dishwasher on the market, I never would have had the courage to start. But then, I would have missed a very wonderful experience." Her company later became part of KitchenAid, who produced the first KitchenAid dishwasher based on her design in 1949.

29 DECEMBER

Emma Snodgrass (c.1835–unknown) and Harriet French (unknown)

On this day in 1852, Emma Snodgrass and Harriet French were arrested in Boston, US, for wearing trousers, because the garments were "men's clothing." A month earlier, the *New York Daily Times* reported that Snodgrass had been caught "donning the breeches," calling herself George Green and securing a job as a clerk. The police returned her to her father, a police officer: "What her motive may be for thus obstinately rejecting the habiliments of her own sex, is not known."

Snodgrass had been arrested with her friend "Charley" (Harriet French), who smoked cigars and chewed tobacco: "Snodgrass was finally sent to New York [back to her father] in charge of an officer, and her friend was packed off to the House of Industry for two months." One newspaper theorized that French's punishment was greater because she didn't have money, "the difference between breeches without money, and breeches with."

Further sightings of Emma Snodgrass in trousers were reported in Richmond, Albany, Louisville, Buffalo, and Cleveland. In March 1856, the *New York Daily Times* published an item about "an unfeminine freak" who was arrested and charged as a vagrant: Harriet "Charley" French. She was sentenced to two months' imprisonment on Blackwell's Island. The reporter asked why she dressed in that way. "Can get more wages," she said. (See What are you wearing?)

> **Snodgrass had been caught "donning the breeches," calling herself George Green and securing a job as a clerk.**

400

30 DECEMBER

Věra Chytilová
(1929–2014)

Czech New Wave director Věra Chytilová's film *Sedmikrásky* ('Daisies'), released on this day in 1966, was banned by the Czech authorities for "depicting the wanton" and "spoiling the fruit of the work of our toiling farmers": one scene shows the two main characters spearing food with their stilettos. Nevertheless, *Daisies*, which won Grand Prix at the Bergamo Film Festival, brought Chytilová international recognition and became her best-known film.

The first woman to study directing at Prague's Film Academy, Chytilová would direct a total of thirty films, working through 1960s liberalism, the Soviet Union's invasion of Czechslovakia in 1968 and the post-Communist era. Dark, satirical, experimental and subversive, her films often explore the experiences of women. She's also known for "pseudo-documentaries" – scripted films with actors based on sociological research, such as *Pytel blech* ("A Bagful of Fleas," 1962), about a group of female textile workers.

After the 1968 invasion, liberal film-makers were banned; Chytilová was only permitted to make TV commercials. After seven years, the ban was lifted, though her films were subject to government censorship. When her film *The Apple Game* opened in 1978, there were queues around the block.

31 DECEMBER

Venus of Willendorf
(made c.25,000–30,000 BCE)

The Venus of Willendorf, an eleven-centimeter-tall statuette of oolitic limestone colored with red ochre, was found in Austria in 1908. It was named "Venus" because of the contemporary belief that such figurines – of which around 140 have been found in Europe and Asia – were fashioned by male artists and connected to a worship or fetishization of female fertility. However, recent research suggests that the Venuses may have been created by women as self-portraits; when we look down at our own bodies we see them from the "lozenge perspective" which, for women, exaggerates the breasts and diminishes the feet. This theory challenges the default assumptions that women in history were objects to be looked at, rather than the ones doing the looking.

We chose the Venus of Willendorf as our @OnThisDayShe mascot to represent the "Unknown Woman." We want to ensure that we remember the women who were not seen in history because their achievements, whatever they may have been, were attributed to men. As this Venus seems to represent a pregnant woman, she also reminds us of those whose lives would have been so different if they had been men, if the expectations and obligations placed upon them had been different. Most of these women will remain unknown to us. On this day, we remember them.

What next?

In writing this book, we became both curious and furious. Whether you are male or female, we hope that you feel the same as you read it. History is not over, and women have not won their battles yet. Perhaps, like us, you feel moved to make the world a more equal place. There are many ways to do that; here are some ideas to start you off.

- Become a Wikipedia editor. Wikipedia is an amazing resource, but women are massively under-represented in both its content (around 17 per cent) and its editors (fewer than 16 per cent). If you know of women who should have entries and don't, register as an editor. You can look at @WikiWomeninRed on Twitter to signpost the women who need new entries, or simply check the language of existing entries to make sure that it isn't full of bias.
- Follow the many social media accounts which concentrate on women in history, or in specialist fields. On Twitter these

include @TrowelBlazers, @WomensArt1, @Thehistorychix, @FindingAda, @WomenWhoMadeMe, and the hashtag #WomenInSTEM. Good podcasts include History Chicks and What's Her Name.

- Make women more visible in your town. Lobby the council to name new streets after women; often they are perfectly willing but simply haven't thought of it. Visit your local studies library and ask for help in finding the stories of women who made an impact in your area – activists, suffragettes, health reformers, scientists, musicians. Recommend them as street names, as statues, as blue plaques.
- If you're a teacher or student, you are well placed to ensure that women are included in formal learning. Lobby for the inclusion of women in the syllabus and in the fabric of your institution. If you're a teacher, call your math sets Hypatia and Lovelace as well as Pythagoras and Newton. If your lecture hall or sports field is about to be named for a great sportsperson or musician, consider the great women as well as the men.
- Whatever your job, you may be able to encourage a more equal approach. If you're a town planner, think about women's names for municipal buildings; if you're a librarian or bookseller, make sure that women are fully represented on the shelves.

We had only 200 words to tell the story of each of the women in our book. We always knew that it was impossible, but in an internet age these short biographies can be a gateway to further research. Read more about the women who interest you; each entry here is only a flavor of their full and fascinating lives. Use our book as a prompt to pursue your own interests. Write poems, films or history books about them; draw or quilt or sing them into visibility. Whatever it is that you want to do, there is a woman here who did it too, so draw strength from her. Let these women inspire you to activism, making the world a better place.

The price of freedom is eternal vigilance; there are new victories every day but also a backlash against women's rights. In this context, we want to end with hope. End the book, that is: the @OnThisDayShe project will go on as long as we have energy for it. We're not afraid of running out of women to write about. Perhaps you will become one of them.

Picture Permissions

All photos supplied by Alamy excepting the following instances:

Getty Images

p8, p44, p61, p123, p146, p152, p159, p162, p167, p194, p241, p248, p255, p257, p268, p295, p352, p366, p367, p377

Mirrorpix
p43 ©Mirrorpix/Reach Licensing.

Shutterstock
p62

Index

Bell, Gertrude   8 Sep
Bentz, Melitta   8 Jul
Bess of Hardwick   14 Feb
Beyoncé   7 Feb
Bhutto, Benazir   27 Dec
Biawacheeitchish   1 Aug
Biffen, Sarah   19 Jul
Bigelow, Kathryn   7 Mar
Bilocca, Lillian "Big Lil"   6 Feb
Blackwell, Elizabeth   28 Sep
Blankers-Koen, Fanny   9 Aug
Blatt, Josephine   15 Apr
Blake, Lillie   4 Jul
Bliss, Lizzie P.   7 Nov
Bly, Nellie   9 Oct
Boothroyd, Betty   27 Apr
Boudica   13 Jun
Boursier, Louise Bourgeois   13 May
Brazier, Eugenie   23 Jul
Bridgeford, Erricka   4 Aug
Bridges, Ruby   14 Nov
Brûlon, Marie-Angélique   15 Aug
Bjurstedt-Mallory, Molla   23 Aug
Burr Blodgett, Katharine   16 Mar
Burney, Linda   31 Aug

C

Calamity Jane   15 Jul
Cama, Bhikaji   22 Aug
Carson, Rachel   23 Jun
Catherine the Great   9 Jul
Caton-Thompson, Gertrude   20 Apr
Centlivre, Susanna   20 Nov
Chanel, Coco   15 Oct
du Châtelet, Émilie   18 Apr

Chaucer, Alice   27 Sep
Cheesman, Lucy   29 Aug
Chytilová, Věra   30 Dec
Christine de Pisan   31 Jul
Queen Christina of Sweden   4 Jun
Clarke, Emma   2 Dec
Cleopatra   12 Aug
Clinton, Hillary   28 Jul
Coachman, Alice   7 Aug
Cochran, Josephine   28 Dec
Collins, Eileen   3 Feb
Colvin, Claudette   2 Mar
Comăneci, Nadia   18 Jul
Comnena, Anna   19 Dec
Cook, Ida and Louise   5 Mar
Corday, Charlotte   13 Jul
Cotton, Mary Ann   24 Mar
du Coudray, Angélique   13 May
Couzins, Phoebe   4 Jul
Cristiani, Lise   10 Jul
Crosby, Caresse   3 Nov
Curie, Marie   10 Dec

D

Dalen, Frieda   29 Jan
Darling, Grace   7 Sep
Daring Ladies   7 Nov
Delaney, Shelagh   27 May
del Mundo, Fe   27 Nov
Desai, Jayaben   25 Aug
Devi, Phoolan   26 Jul
Diaz Insunza, Eloésa   5 Dec
Dicker, Friedl   3 Dec
Dietrich, Marlene   24 Nov
Wallace Dunlop, Marion   5 Jul

Thatcher, Margaret   4 May
Thomas, Helen   5 Aug
Tillion, Germaine   30 May
Toshiko, Kishida   12 Oct
Townsend, Lucy   8 Apr
Tristan, Flora   28 Jan
Truth, Sojourner   29 May
Tubman, Harriet   2 Jun
Twiggy   5 Feb

V

Varda, Agnès   4 Jan
Venus of Willendorf   31 Dec
A Viking Warrior   17 Feb
Villepreux-Power, Jeanne   31 Jan

W

Wa Menza, Mekatilili   17 Oct
Walker, Ann   30 Mar
Walker, Madam C.J.   19 Sep
Wanderwell, Aloha   25 Jan
Wells Barnett, Ida B.   19 Mar
West, Gladys   1 Jun
Westerdijk, Johanna   10 Feb
Whakaotirangi   1 Apr
Wheatley, Phillis   1 Sep
Bourke White, Margaret   9 Feb
Whittaker, Jodie   25 Dec
Whorwood, Jane   20 Mar
Wilkinson, Elizabeth   21 Jun
Wilkinson, Kitty   20 Sep
Williams, Ivy   10 May
Wills, Lucy   20 Jun
Wilson, Joanna   26 Jan
Wollstonecraft, Mary   4 Feb

Woodhull, Victoria   18 Sep
Bullock Workman, Fanny   7 Jun
Worthy, Kym   10 Mar
Shiung Wu, Chien   10 Jan
Wynette, Tammy   15 Sep

X

Y

Yourcenar, Marguerite   13 Jan
Youyou, Tu   5 Oct
Yunjidang, Im   23 Nov

Z

Didrikson Zaharias, "Babe"   24 Aug
Zazel   2 Apr
Zeb-un-Nissa   15 Feb
Zelter, Angie   26 Jan
Zenobia, Septimia   9 Jan
Zetian, Wu   16 Oct
Zhenyi, Wang   12 Jan

About the authors

JO BELL is a poet and writer based in Cheshire. Her first career was as an archaeologist, specializing in industrial remains, and recording sites in Turkey first surveyed by Gertrude Bell.

TANIA HERSHMAN is a poet and writer based in Manchester. A former science journalist, she is the author of three short story collections, three books of poetry and a hybrid book, and co-author of *Writing Short Stories: A Writers' & Artists' Companion*.

AILSA HOLLAND is a poet, artist and writer based in Macclesfield. Formerly a literary historian, she is the author of a poetry pamphlet and the founder of Moormaid Press. In May 2019 she gave a TEDx talk about @OnThisDayShe.

Acknowledgements

We would all like to thank our agent, Kate Johnson at MacKenzie Wolf, for helping us to make this happen. Thanks too to Ellie Carr at Bonnier Books and her team for their enthusiasm, for getting it and letting us get on with it. We owe many thanks to the thousands of people who have followed @OnThisDayShe, who have liked, retweeted, made suggestions of women to include and simply told us they loved the account. We also want to thank all our friends who have listened patiently while we tell our fascinating but endless stories about women from history.

While researching this book we read widely and deeply and are hugely grateful for all our sources. For a full bibliography, please visit www.onthisdayshe.com.

Ailsa: Many thanks to Jude d'Souza and Lynne Jones for asking me to do a TEDx talk in Macclesfield about the @OnThisDayShe project. Thanks to Robbi, Lili and Ben for being.

Jo: Thanks to Phil for working so hard to make space and time for me to work on this book. Thanks too to Jane Commane of Nine Arches Press, the Society of Authors and the other writers on the Hartsop Retreat who did the same, and gave such encouraging feedback.

Tania: Thanks to Sylvie, the best writing companion. Thanks to all the fellow writers on the Barmoor retreat who gave such excellent feedback on the early drafts of some entries in the book.

We also want to thank each other. Throughout this project, we three women have shared our learning and enthusiasm – about women in history, about the construction of history and about ourselves. We have supported (and sometimes exasperated) each other and we owe each other hearty thanks.

CPSIA information can be obtained
at www.ICGtesting.com
Printed in the USA
LVHW110803270922
729326LV00001B/1

9 781538 164563